CW01372702

First published in 2022
by White Lion Publishing,
an imprint of The Quarto Group.
1 Triptych Place, 2nd Floor,
London, SE1 9SH,
United Kingdom
T (0)20 7700 6700
www.Quarto.com

Text © 2022 Ian Nathan
Design © 2022 Quarto Publishing plc

Ian Nathan has asserted his moral right to be identified as the Author of this Work in accordance with the Copyright Designs and Patents Act 1988.

All rights reserved. No part of this book may be reproduced or utilised in any form or by any means, electronic or mechanical, including photocopying, recording or by any information storage and retrieval system, without permission in writing from White Lion Publishing.

Every effort has been made to trace the copyright holders of material quoted in this book. If application is made in writing to the publisher, any omissions will be included in future editions.

A catalogue record for this book is available from the British Library.

ISBN 978-0-7112-7712-0
Ebook ISBN 978-0-7112-7713-7

10 9 8 7 6 5 4 3 2

Designed by Sue Pressley and Paul Turner, Stonecastle Graphics

Printed in China

This is an unofficial publication and has not been endorsed, sponsored or authorized by either any studios or Christopher Nolan. All trademarks, service marks and trade names used herein are the property of their respective owners and are used only to identify the products or services of these owners. The publisher and author are not associated with any product, service or vendor mentioned in this book and this book is not licensed or endorsed by the owner of any trademark, service mark or trade name appearing herein.

CHRISTOPHER NOLAN

THE ICONIC FILMMAKER AND HIS WORK

Ian Nathan

UNOFFICIAL AND UNAUTHORISED

WHITE LION PUBLISHING

CONTENTS

INTRODUCTION — 6

THE HYBRID KID — 10
The early days and *Following* (1998)

THROUGH THE LOOKING GLASS — 26
Memento (2000) & *Insomnia* (2002)

THE INTIMIDATION GAME — 42
Batman Begins (2005)

THE TRANSPORTED MEN — 58
The Prestige (2006)

WHY SO SERIOUS? — 72
The Dark Knight (2008)

HEAD SPINNING — 88
Inception (2010)

THE BIG GOODBYE — 106
The Dark Knight Rises (2012)

THE FIFTH DIMENSION — 122
Interstellar (2014)

ON THE BEACH — 138
Dunkirk (2017)

APOCALYPTIC THINKING — 154
Tenet (2020) *Oppenheimer* (2023)

SOURCES — 172

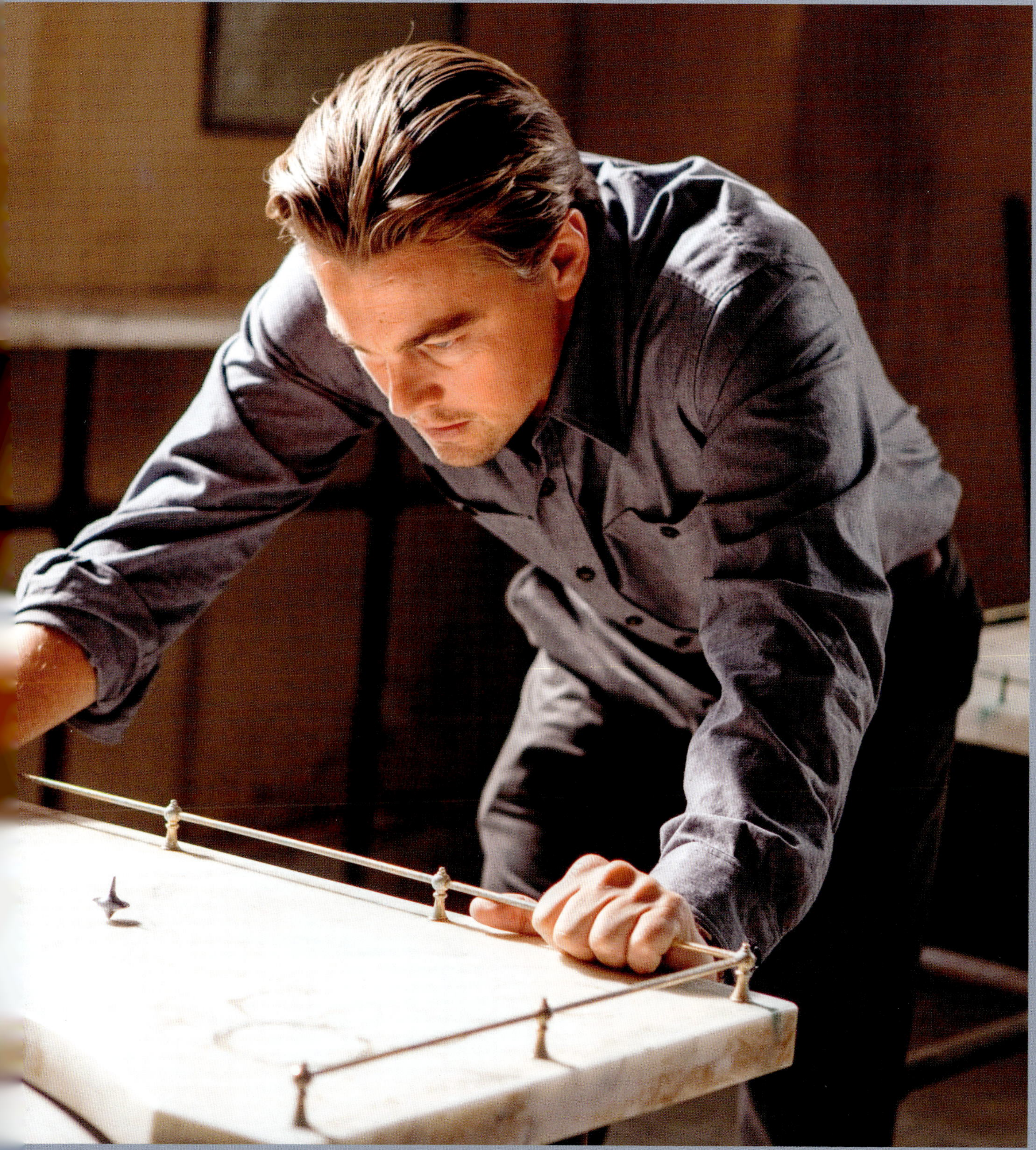

INTRODUCTION

'What is the most resilient parasite? Bacteria? A virus? An intestinal worm? An idea. Resilient … highly contagious. Once an idea has taken hold of the brain it's almost impossible to eradicate.'[1]

Cobb, Inception

Christopher Nolan doesn't make sense. And that is exactly how he likes it. In twenty-three years and through twelve films, he has defied the laws of Hollywood by creating startling, original genre pieces that have revelled in their own complexity, confounding every maxim by which the studios hope to appeal to the widest audience. And yet he does that too. Cinemas fill on the possibility of the next Nolan film. Whatever form it might take.

Nolan never stoops to conquer. He believes in his audience. That we are up to the epic journey he will set before us. He believes in the highest common denominator.

Put it another way, Nolan has done the impossible – pursued a personal, idiosyncratic, often brilliant, and consistent style *within* the studio system. Or in even simpler terms, he has never compromised. And never had to raise his voice, developing a calm, measured, above all dignified approach to dealing with Hollywood that runs contrary to a grand history of directors scratching and clawing their way to artistic expression. Then who would argue with him? He might be the only one who really knows what is really happening in his film.

Even assembling a basic description of the director sets a challenge before the prospective writer. He defies categories, even nationalities – he is half British, half American, and neither precisely. He spent his formative years shuttling between the antique rituals of boarding school in England and the freedoms of the family home in Chicago. Travelling between time zones in every sense. He crosses the streams of artist and scientist, entertainer and provocateur, lone wolf and one of the cool set. He has defined millennial Hollywood, yet stands apart from the crowd.

The great mystery of Nolan, compared with the other directors from the school of seriousness that arose in the nineties to great acclaim – calculating visionaries like Steven Soderbergh, David Fincher, Darren Aronofsky, Kathryn Bigelow, and the Wachowskis: those who could be classified as his peers – is his popularity.

Of course, the *Dark Knight* trilogy stands as the central achievement of his career thus far, taking a populist form like the comic-book movie and filling its boots with gravitas. Contrary to Hollywood's habitual excesses, Nolan wanted to know how superheroes and supervillains might spring out of the real world. He moved into the realms of the blockbuster without ever losing his identity. And in doing so, redefined an entire industry.

Press Nolan for the truth behind his riddles – the memory at the heart of *Memento*, the spinning top at the end of *Inception*, just what exactly is going on in *Tenet* – and his lips remain sealed. How he smiles, like Mona Lisa. Maintaining the enigma is all important. There is pleasure, he insists, in *not* knowing the answer. We must simply trust that he does. Yet here lies a delightful contradiction. Like so many of his characters we are driven to find the truth. Even as he implores us all to simply sit back and watch, we thrill to the challenge of deciphering his labyrinthine plots (which do often feature labyrinths). Graphs and diagrams, references to obscure tracts of philosophy and science, and extended tutorials proliferate on the internet from ardent Nolanologists. If the director puts years into his strategizing his screenplays, they take corresponding years to unpick what he has wrought.

▶ The unassuming icon – Christopher Nolan faces the cameras at the Cannes Film Festival in 2018.

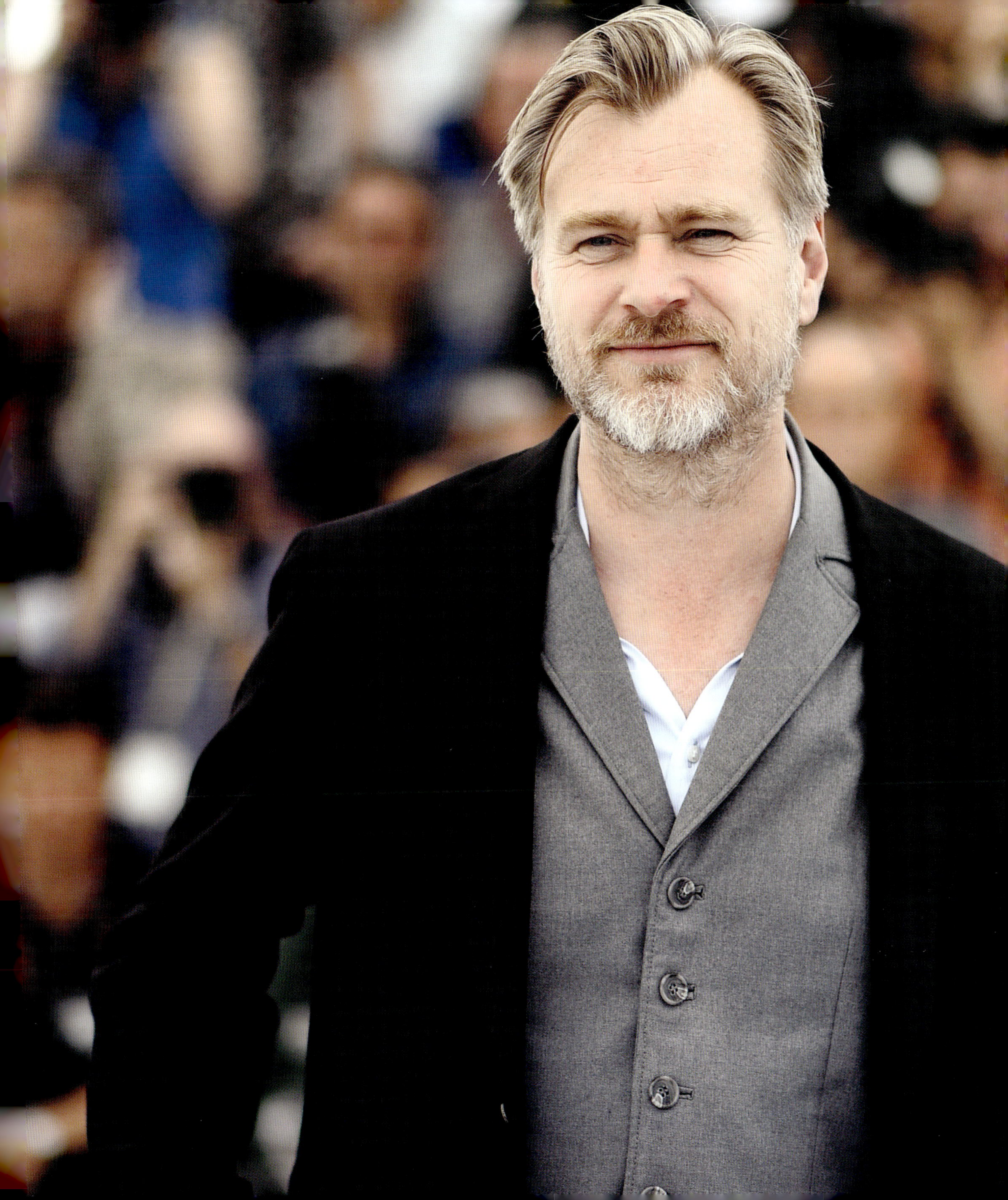

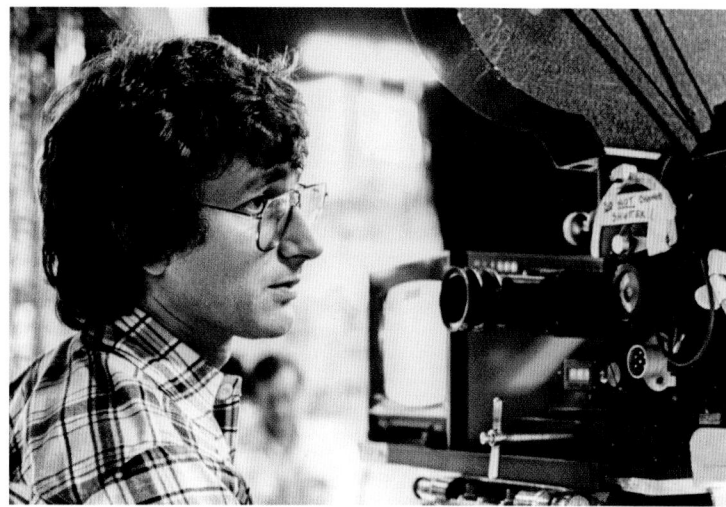

▲ Guiding lights: filmmaking legends Stanley Kubrick (above, on the set of *A Clockwork Orange*) and Steven Spielberg (above right, on the set of *Close Encounters of the Third Kind*) helped shape Christopher Nolan's entire view of cinema.

Nolan is truly a director of the digital age – with its layers unpeeling onto layers, its paranoid urges and knots of conspiracy, its urge to know more and more.

But it is also about how his films look and sound and ultimately *feel*. He sees film as an immersive experience, often shooting in his beloved IMAX so we cannot escape from the screen. Yet he is also a traditionalist. He holds onto the old ways: celluloid, cinema going, the practical effect over the digital solution. He builds extraordinary sets ready to spin reality on its head, allowing his valiant actors to touch the world of the story, taking his groundbreaking stunts to the streets.

Nolan wears his inspirations proudly. The directors who showed him the way: the revolutionary spirit of Fritz Lang, the intellectual rigour of Stanley Kubrick, the visual mastery of Ridley Scott, the soaring storytelling of Steven Spielberg, and the hypnotic modernism of Michael Mann all tug at his muse. And there are many more. Each film is made from a tapestry of film history. Genre fascinates him. He mixes the elements of film noir, science fiction, comic-book and period pieces into a new alloy – one we call Nolanesque. Impossible to define fully, it is unmistakable as soon as you see it. As soon as you feel it – and hear it. Sound is so vital to his holistic approach: music entwines with audio effect and image, creating a sense of both alarm and euphoria.

He also calls upon beloved novelists who saw the world differently, from Charles Dickens to Jorge Luis Borges, Raymond Chandler, Graham Swift, and Carl Sagan. He seeks out scientists like astrophysicist Kip Thorne to show him the nature of the universe. To fix his flights of fancy according to universal laws.

Over the following pages, film by film, I will contextualize Nolan's worlds – the inspirations, the ambitions, the ever-more-challenging shoots, and the success – and also go some way to getting to the secret heart of his stories. So I should issue a spoiler warning, though it is all but impossible to spoil the films – even describing what happens presents the writer-decoder with a unique challenge.

Fundamentally, his work is united in an exploration of perception and time, and drawn to the flame of subjectivity – what finally can we accept as real? Nolan is attempting to peer beneath the surface of this thing we call civilization to locate the secret machine that drives the world. And the closer you look, the more you realize that his films are on some level also about the nature of film – how the medium can be configured to express the existential angst of *Memento* and *Insomnia*, the dreamworld of *Inception*, or the swelling dread of *Dunkirk*. Alongside devoted collaborators like his wife and producer Emma Thomas, his screenwriting brother Jonah Nolan, cinematographers Wally Pfister and Hoyte van Hoytema, production designer Nathan Crowley, composer Hans Zimmer, and regular actors, exemplified by the near constant presence of Sir Michael Caine, he has shaken up what we understand as cinematic storytelling.

I have met Nolan. He is scrupulously polite, well spoken, finely dressed, with an aura of intelligence that is not something assumed or pretentious, but simply an expression of who he is. There was also something about him that was elsewhere, as if seeing calculations in the air, some great cinematic feat that has never been done. Some part of him is always in the cinema. The screen, he once said, is a 'jumping-off point for infinite possibilities.'[2] And there is never enough time …

▲ Exploring the world through the eye of a camera – Nolan lines up an IMAX shot for the opening opera sequence of *Tenet*.

INTRODUCTION   9

THE HYBRID KID

The early years to *Following* (1998)

Growing up between England and America, boarding school and golden summers, he became set on becoming a filmmaker. And for his first trick, he would tell the tale of a writer drawn into the charismatic company of a serial burglar, where all is not what it appears to be

The group would meet in a cluttered room beneath the Bloomsbury Theatre, a slab of 1968 brutalism sat on the quiet fringes of London's West End. The basement was tricky to find. You had to wend your way to the back of the building and head down an alley, before descending a narrow staircase and unlocking the red door that led to the future. Cramped and twisting corridors, labyrinths lurking beneath the surface, concrete mazes made of city blocks, would interlace the films to come. The mind leaps to the sewers of Gotham, or the endless, crumbling streets of Limbo on the lowest level of *Inception*, or the riddle of backstage passageways in *The Prestige*.

It was in the bowels of the Bloomsbury Theatre, owned and run by University College London, that Christopher Nolan, a nineteen-year-old student, with a crest of fine blonde hair and glacially blue eyes, had discovered the university's forgotten filmmaking equipment. Like Howard Carter breaking the seal on Tutankhamun's tomb, he saw 16mm cameras, tripods, dolly tracks, strips of film hanging from the ceiling, and a Steenbeck editing deck. Wonderful things, veiled in dust, waiting for him.

Spurred by his find, Nolan and Emma Thomas, fellow student and girlfriend, later wife and producer, instituted the UCL Film and Television Society. A crew of likeminded friends would gather in their sunless den on Wednesday afternoons, with Nolan presiding while sat in an old hospital wheelchair. Talk ranged from meaning to method. They would screen 35mm prints of new releases in the theatre above, the *Director's Cut* of Ridley Scott's visionary *Blade Runner*, Jean-Paul Rappeneau's arthouse epic *The Horseman on the Roof*, or *Wayne's World* – preceded by the old Pearl & Dean sting, a copy of which had been found among the curios below. Proceeds were siphoned back into their nascent summertime adventures in filmmaking. Between lectures, Nolan taught himself to edit by hand, running what film he could muster up back and forth through the Steenbeck, marvelling how the linear flow of time could be reshuffled into new forms. This was his film school. Among the antique gear, the most successful director of the modern era was coming into focus.

'I never studied filmmaking in any way,'[1] Nolan insisted to interviewers. He was seven years old when he first picked up a camera and began to fathom how it worked. 'I just carried on making films as I grew up, and over the years they got bigger, and hopefully better, and more elaborate.'[2]

▶ The fresh-faced Christopher Nolan in 2000, who – without formal filmmaking schooling but with a grand vision – is about to break into the mainstream.

FOLLOWING 11

'Chris was different,' said Matthew Tempest, the then-secretary of the UCL Film Society who went on to be a journalist. Even as a student, Nolan dressed differently, sporting linen suits and blue Oxford shirts. But it wasn't only his appearance, added Tempest, but 'his ambition and focus'[3] that made him stand out.

From the very start, he had his own wavelength.

We need to rewind the film. Back to 30 July 1970, when Christopher Edward Nolan was born in Westminster, London, second son of Christina and Brendan. Take note that Nolan was a child of two nations, a hybrid kid. His mother, a flight attendant turned English teacher, was from Evanston, Illinois, outside of Chicago – an American. His father, a creative director in the London advertising scene, was British to the tips of his brogues. He worked with Alan Parker, Hugh Hudson, and on two occasions with Ridley Scott: three British filmmakers who infiltrated the Hollywood of the eighties with sleek, designer movies. Three pivotal influences on the young filmmaker to come. In 1976, Nolan visited Pinewood Studios with his father, and he remembered seeing the pedal cars from Parker's kids-in-suits gangster-musical *Bugsy Malone*.

Raised in Highgate, London, Nolan and his two brothers would spend their summers in Evanston. Matthew was the eldest; his younger sibling Jonathan was known to all as Jonah, and would become a key collaborator. This double life, moving back and forth across the Atlantic, became the pattern of Nolan's youth. Moreover, both parents travelled extensively. The boys were constantly consulting atlases, as their father returned with tales from Africa or the Far East. Their mother got free tickets for her teenaged sons, who thought nothing of jumping on a jet to far-off locations. Time curved around their lives like the stream of air around a 747.

He was told that one day he would have to choose: English or American. That weighed on his mind – which was he? But the law changed, and he has retained a dual nationality, which is exactly what he is, a double helix of American and English. He now lives in Los Angeles, but his accent is pure public school. His diction is as precise as a pendulum – that brain always ticking – but soft and reasonable as a BBC presenter's. Identity can have many layers. Whichever direction he flies in, he is returning home.

At his father's behest, a notion of upholding family traditions, Nolan remained at boarding school in England, even as the family made a permanent home in Evanston. These were different planets. As friend and biographer Tom Shone recognized, 'He essentially spent his formative years commuting between a nineteenth-century English landscape and a twentieth-century American one.'[4]

Haileybury and Imperial Service College, which had once educated the sons of the Raj, covered 500 acres in Hertford Heath, Hertfordshire, including the second largest quadrangle in England. The dining hall sat beneath a vast dome, where seven hundred pupils gathered to eat and squabble, as old boys glowered from the walls. Granite memorials in the grounds commemorated those lost to conflicts as far back as the Boer War.

The Clock House loomed over the quad, striking every half-hour without fail, urging students to class. Nolan's daily regimen ran to prayers, Latin, Cadet training, and sudden breathless bursts of house rugby. The solemn layout of the dormitories, rows of cast-iron beds repeating into the distance, would slip out of his unconscious and into his films. The mind leaps now to the extractors from *Inception* experimenting with sleeping potions in Tangier, or the brutal fixtures of the *League of Shadows* forging Bruce Wayne into a superhero in *Batman Begins*.

Still, where other boys squirmed in the vice-like grip of old education, Nolan thrived. It was tough, of course. There was always an element of endurance. He recalled boarding-school life as an ideal training ground for

▼ The formidable architecture of Haileybury and Imperial Service College, the English boarding school which left a lasting impression on the youthful Nolan.

▲ Alan Parker on the set of *Midnight Express* in 1978 – one of the gang of highly visual British directors from the London advertising scene who were a huge influence on the Nolan aesthetic.

◣ Ridley Scott directing Harrison Ford on *Blade Runner* in 1981 – it is impossible to underestimate the importance of Scott's lyrical dystopia to Nolan. It was the film that showed him the way.

Hollywood, learning how to negotiate your own progress within a cloistered world. Playing the system from within. Knowing how far to push your luck. Being selected for the rugby First XV raised you up in Haileybury's social strata, just as box-office victories opened doors to the wood-panelled offices of Burbank.

With maths coming relatively easily to him, and being naturally artistic, he was encouraged by his mother to think about architecture as a career. In a sense, he took her advice. 'All architecture, and the best architecture in particular, has a narrative component to it,'[5] he said; and he builds films like skyscrapers, level upon level. When you think of Nolan's work, you immediately see cities gleaming by night. His storytelling will gravitate toward the modern, and even his period pieces channel the living immediacy of their present – what Shone called a 'traumatized rationality.'[6] Yet everything he does runs on classical clockwork: the influence of Dickens, Austen, Hardy, Goethe, Wilkie Collins, H.G. Wells, Arthur Conan Doyle, Edgar Allan Poe, and the gusto of the great composers. His foundations are traditional. What you might call old school. Indeed Nolan affects the air of a Victorian professor, his time machine cooling in the parlour next door.

Returning to America in his holidays brought sunshine and brotherhood. Evanston was the kind of spacious suburb mythologized by John Hughes movies: a dream of bright green lawns, driveways, and gently curving cul-de-sacs. The nearby woods through which they ran stretched out of sight. Time became elastic. The days endless. It was like arriving in Narnia. In America, he discovered movies, catching matinées at Edens Theater in Northbrook, its futurist exterior curved into a paraboloid. This is where he was baptized in *Star Wars*, the balmy delights of early Spielberg, and the rollicking, escapist pleasures of Roger Moore-era Bond. Sharing a film with an audience in the warm temple of the cinema, he would later claim, was a 'borderline mystical experience.'[7] It stirred a fanaticism for the theatre of film. There is no equivalent to that communal rush.

Nolan embraced both the stories and their telling. Borrowing his father's

FOLLOWING 13

▶ Christopher Nolan in New York in 2000. Location and architecture, particularly the modern, angular cityscape, would play a pivotal role in his filmmaking.

Super 8, he made his first forays into filmmaking. The camera had no facility for sound and each cartridge only ran to two-and-a-half minutes, so he conducted silent movies, roping in Jonah to play the parts and adding stop-motion scenes with his toys, replaying the space epics that had awed him on the big screen. They had an uncle employed by NASA, who brought Super 8 footage of Apollo missions on his visits, which Nolan would film off the television screen and splice into his own movies. It was important that they appeared real.

At school, he read books and comics, and listened to music on his Sony Walkman after lights-out, when the imagination could roam – but the only access to films came with the weekly war movies put on for the boys, such as the trumpet call of *The Bridge on the River Kwai*. Though Nolan was among a select group shown a pirated VHS of *Blade Runner* by a forward-thinking housemaster. It was like something illicit and magical. They had to watch it in segments, these isolated chapters of wonder and suspense. *Blade Runner* still stands as the true north of his career. When he first saw *Alien*, he recognized the similarities. A certain tone or mood or 'atmosphere'[8] was shared between two very different stories. Only later did he discover that they were the work of the same man – Ridley Scott. That knowledge decided things. He wanted to be the mood that connected films.

Growing older, between terms he would spend time in London, where he and Jonah frequented the cavernous Scala cinema in King's Cross, bolstering their film education, fixing their bearings. Here Nolan filled himself with the possibilities of *Manhunter*, *Blue Velvet*, *Full Metal Jacket*, and *Akira*.

'Movies become indistinguishable from our own memories,' he said. 'You file them away and they become very personal.'[9]

Fast forward the film to 1989. Going to university, said Nolan, was 'like joining the modern world.'[10] It was a period of self-creation, mixing with different classes, different cultures, different genders, his eyes opening to what the world could offer. On the advice of his old English master, he took English literature to expand his

14   CHRISTOPHER NOLAN

thinking on story – burrowing into the classics. The faculties of University College London encircled a concrete monolith looming over Bloomsbury, an area that was formerly the haunt of T.S. Eliot, anglicized postmodernist and poet laureate of human frailty, and unsurprisingly a big influence on Nolan. Those buildings would one day be used as part of the urban tapestry of Gotham and *Inception*.

Two contrasting literary gods would inspire the filmmaker-in-waiting to approach narrative in unconventional ways. Such is the hold they took on his imagination, all of Nolan's work rests in the Venn intersection of their names.

Argentinian poet-philosopher-fabulist Jorge Luis Borges' metaphysical tales woven from dreams and memory, libraries and labyrinths entered his life, in a fitting feedback loop, via the movies. We can also count Nicolas Roeg's reality-bending cinema as another electrical charge on Nolan's nascent muse, especially his wild debut

▲ The 1982 release poster for *Blade Runner*, which Nolan first saw – in instalments – on a VHS at school. He could already discern there was a distinctive style at work.

FOLLOWING   15

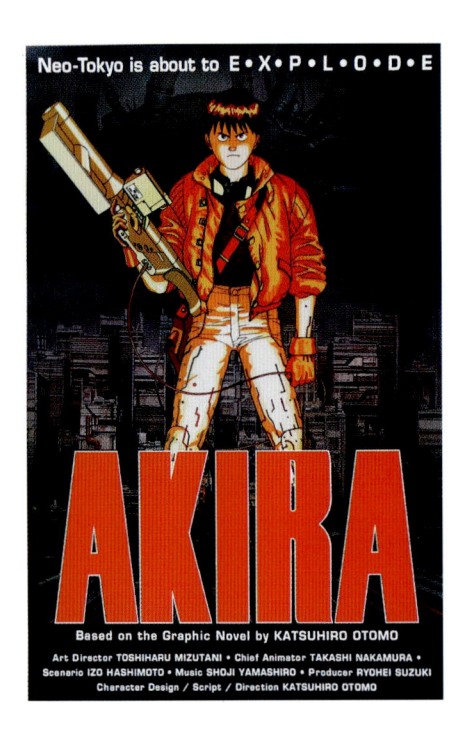

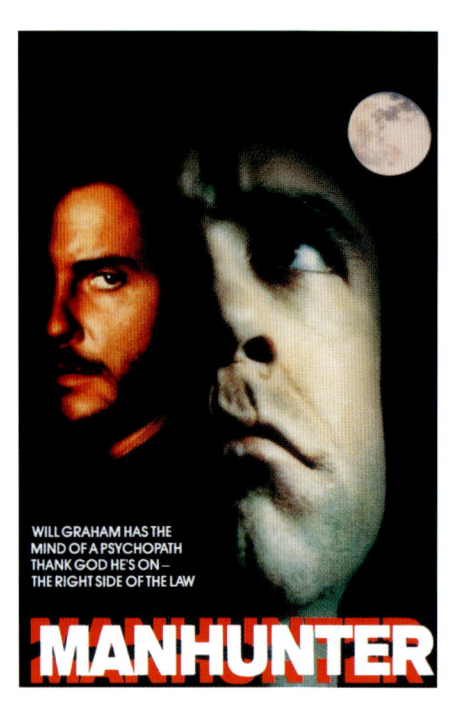

▲ Posters for three films, which in different ways would fuel Christopher Nolan's muse: the gripping anime dystopia of *Akira*; the trippy sixties cool of *Performance*; and the intensity and sleek style of *Manhunter*.

Performance. In which, the young Nolan noticed one of the London gangsters reading Borges' *Personal Anthology*. That chimed with an old student film, directed by Chester Dent, which he had unearthed among the treasures beneath the Bloomsbury Theatre. It was an unofficial adaptation of Borges' short story *Funes the Memorious*, about a man tormented by perfect recall.

Nolan immediately rushed out and bought everything by Borges he could lay his hands on, fact and fiction. Spinning classical mythology on its head, the avant-garde author and director are cut from similar cloth. Both deliver bizarre philosophical concepts via digestible stories.

Raymond Chandler, the pulp genius behind *The Big Sleep* and *Farewell My Lovely*, was another symbolic gift of the movies. Nolan had come across his credit as screenwriter on Hitchcock's *Strangers on a Train* – Chandler had spent his time at the coalface of Hollywood – before studying his devious L.A. thrillers in his second year at university. Their lives ran to uncanny parallels. Chandler had an Anglo-Irish mother and American father, with a childhood divided between Chicago and London. He later described himself as a 'man without a country.'[11] The godfather of noir, in witty, grimly poetic prose he told shadowy stories about finely tailored heroes of the night, cynical yet noble private eyes on the trail of crimes so twisted their ultimate solution remained out of reach. The world, as Chandler wrote it, was as riddled with corruption as Gotham.

Nolan loved the detail, the tactility, and Chandler's refusal to play by time-honoured rules of crime and punishment. 'The whole point is you're being lied to,'[12] he relished – it was all about perspective.

The gene pool of influences was growing deep. Graham Swift's 1983 novel *Waterland* was Nolan's first encounter with a story running along multiple timelines. He encountered the pictures of Dutch artist M.C. Escher in art class at school, and was mesmerized by his geometrically precise illusions, stairways that went nowhere, tessellations that swam beneath the eye. Once you were convinced of the effect there was no escape, you were trapped in the infinite loops of Escher's mind. Art and maths, science and fiction. Later he would be enraptured by the future-gazing architecture of Frank Lloyd Wright and Ludwig Mies van der Rohe, the German-American whose influence can be found across his home city of Chicago.

And there were matters of the heart. One night he followed the insistent throb of bass notes to a party in his student halls where he got talking to Emma Thomas for the first time, beginning the most important creative and personal partnership of his life.

Nolan described the 'profound impact'[13] she would have on his career, not only as a sounding board for his eccentric ideas, but as the guiding force that enables him to express them.

Having graduated from UCL, the path toward becoming a director was anything but straightforward. At least, at first. Having failed to get into the National Film and Television School and the Royal College of Art (which Scott had attended), he made his rent as a cameraman for the London-based industrial film company Electric Airwaves. Working on short, functional training films gave him a great grounding in shooting on the fly, with minimal lighting, and minimal access to some CEO itching to be elsewhere. All the while, he would return to the old Film Society nerve centre to continue his experiments (the university didn't appear to notice), intent on making a feature film.

'I remember stumbling in one afternoon to find Chris and a couple of others composing a special-effects shot,' recalled Tempest, 'which seemed to involve shooting through a large Pyrex baking bowl.'[14]

There had been an abortive first attempt at a feature entitled *Larry Mahoney*, about a student posing as other people, made up mainly as night shoots. The footage has never been seen. Shortly afterwards, two separate ideas entwined in his head to create *Following*.

Walking to work from his flat off the busy Tottenham Court Road, Nolan would be constantly amazed at the endless ebb and flow of crowds through

◀ The US Post Office Loop Station building in Chicago, as designed by architect Ludwig Mies van der Rohe in the International Style. The distinctive architecture of the city would have a huge influence on not only the Gotham City to come, but all of Nolan's filmography.

FOLLOWING 17

the West End, what he thought of as the 'throng.'[15] His daily rituals brought out the philosopher in him (it didn't take much), pondering how it was that no one would ever keep pace with a stranger. You either walked faster or slower. Crowds have their own social rules. In London you did not interact with strangers.

'The City for me has always functioned as a maze,' he explained. 'If you look at *Following*, it's all about loneliness in the middle of the crowd.'[16] He would find himself focusing on one person among many, and instantly they became an individual.

Then there was the burglary. Nolan by then was sharing a basement flat in Camden with Thomas. Looking back, he could reflect that the plywood front door was little more than a token gesture. And perhaps predictably, he returned from work one evening to find it had been kicked in and the flat was in disarray. The thieves got away with some CDs, a few personal items, nothing more. What they left behind was the launchpad for one of the most successful careers in modern Hollywood.

'The thing that stops people invading your life seemed to be about social protocols,'[17] reflected Nolan. More than the loss of your things, it was the violation of personal space that was so disturbing. It reduced your individuality, your privacy. The social bargain collapsed. Years hence, with *Inception*, he would extend the notion of personal invasion to a fantastical level, with thieves who could crash through the front door of your psyche.

The merger of these ideas about shattering social convention initially translated into a short film called *Larceny*, almost a trial run for *Following*, that was shot over a single weekend. The idea was then expanded into his debut feature film, made six years after he graduated.

▲ Raymond Chandler, maestro of crime fiction and godfather of film noir, is another key influence. His devious thrillers pioneered a dark, poetic fictional world where solutions were rarely forthcoming.

◀ The poster for Howard Hawks' *The Big Sleep*, adapted from Chandler's most celebrated novel. Nolan would devise his own versions of Bogart's private eye roving the midnight streets.

▶ Actors, friends and film noir archetypes – Lucy Russell as the blonde femme fatale and Jeremy Theobald as the patsy in Nolan's consciously derivative debut *Following*.

> " *Following's ingenious, now tell-tale nonlinear structure sprang in part out of the sporadic nature of the shoot. But Nolan saw how it offered a new way of constructing a thriller.* "

With all potential avenues for funding exhausted (Thomas spent her lunch hours firing off hopeful missives), the twenty-eight-year-old Nolan took the bold step of striking out on his own. Starting with little more than a work bonus, the Film Society gang reunited, working for free, with the old equipment at the ready.

Introducing the film on the festival circuit, Nolan would joke that there were few productions that could fit cast, crew, *and* equipment into the back of a London cab. All the actors were Film Society members, while Nolan served as director, producer, screenwriter, cinematographer, camera operator, and editor (with Gareth Heal). The final budget was somewhere in the region of £3,000 (it was hard to be precise), with film and processing the largest outlay.

Following follows a nameless would-be novelist, known only as The Young Man (Jeremy Theobald), who has taken to picking people out of a crowd and following them for kicks, and maybe to spark his muse into life. Like many protagonists to come, he is a distortion of Nolan. As the film begins, we see him wander past the steps of the Bloomsbury Theatre. There is something shabby and Dostoyevsky about him. This is how he falls under the spell of Cobb (Alex Haw), a serial burglar, but cultured, handsome, chilling, and the first of Nolan's characters to come armoured in an impeccable steel-grey suit. As Cobb tutors The Young Man in the art of break-in, and the thrill of disrupting lives, his new accomplice will meet The Blonde (Lucy Russell), who fits the mould of the femme fatale rather too conveniently. The finely tuned clockwork of a long con begins to turn.

Of the actors, only Russell turned pro. Theobald would take cameos in *Batman Begins* and *Inception* for old time's sake, but is now an editor. Haw, arguably the most impressive to the trio, slick and preened like a demonic yuppie, left for Australia as the shoot

▲ Jeremy Theobald as a nameless young man who gets his kicks from trailing strangers along London streets in *Following* – shots grabbed, guerrilla style, without permits and with very little planning.

▶ The signature image of *Following* in crisp black and white – Theobald dressed up to the nines yet still anonymous in the crowd, a man without an identity.

wrapped, before studying architecture at Yale, and now works at a prestigious firm in New York.

'We'd shoot one day a week and kept that up for most of a year,'[18] recalled Nolan. It tended to be a Saturday as they all had jobs to go to. It was like making a short film every week.

Everything was hustle. They scrounged locations, as well as filming in Nolan's parents' home, using a friend's restaurant for the bar scenes, and Theobald's flat as his character's shabby rooms. Exteriors were grabbed without permits. The crowds are real crowds. For the police interrogation scenes – with the director's uncle John Nolan, a professional actor, as the police officer – they shot in the old Film Society coop, using the ancient dolly track, which was in no condition to be transported. It is the only sequence in the film not to be

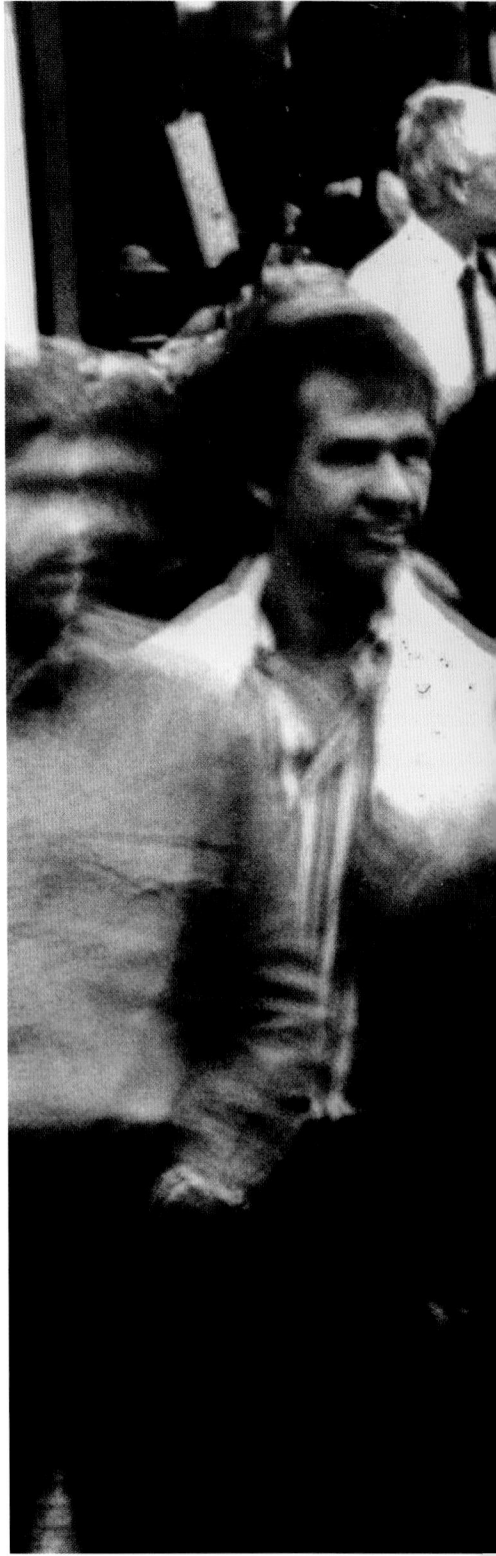

FOLLOWING

handheld. Nolan took advice from his Uncle John on how to handle actors. He was advised to read Stanislavski to understand what his cast needed of him.

Everything was strategy. Nolan had it all worked out. They rehearsed for six months beforehand, as if they were putting on a stage play. That way the actors knew each scene verbatim, with the schedule more a matter of convenience than design. If a location became available, they sprang into action. Besides, Nolan only had the time and money for one or two takes, so the cast needed to know their parts backwards.

The costumes were their own clothes, the props their own belongings. The typewriter we see on The Young Man's desk had been a twenty-first birthday gift to Nolan from his father, on which he'd written the script. The prophetic sight of a Batman sign just happened to be stuck on Theobald's front door.

A pattern emerged. Within the bones of Nolan's first feature film lies a blueprint for future blockbusters, made on the largest scale possible. How a tincture of real life would stir thought experiments, which began to grow into possible films. Outside influences would then make their presence felt: books and films and paintings; locations and architecture, a growing sense of style; plus the urge to press against his limitations. Right from the beginning, he loved the discipline of real locations. Soon he could see it in his mind's eye, edited into the strange rhythms of Nolan time. Films that on some fundamental level were about the nature of films.

▼ Suave, dangerous burglar Cobb (Alex Haw) rummages through the personal items of his latest victim. With next to no budget, all the props in *Following* were things that belonged to Nolan and his actors.

Shooting in black and white was a conscious, practical choice. 'It was a cheap way of applying an expressionist style,'[19] laughed Nolan. There is an eeriness that comes with the ultra-low-budget film, a spareness, which he leaned into. He positioned actors beside a window to save on lighting, loving how he would follow them with the camera on his shoulder, writing the film as he went. Right from the start, he knew he was fashioning a film noir and researched the genre accordingly, throwing himself into Hitchcock (with *Strangers on a Train* as the first port of call) and the chiaroscuro intensity of Jacques Tournier (particularly *Out of the Past* with its web of flashbacks). Borges and Chandler inevitably played their part. The MacGuffin is a set of pornographic pictures, as it is in *The Big Sleep*. At the time, Thomas was working as an assistant at Working Title. There she got her hands on the script for *Pulp Fiction*, which was doing the rounds of production companies. Nolan had been enormously impressed by *Reservoir Dogs*, and was electrified by how Quentin Tarantino planned to zigzag between storylines, ripping the rules of chronology. Effect need no longer follow cause.

Following's ingenious, now tell-tale nonlinear structure sprang in part out of the sporadic nature of the shoot. But Nolan saw how it offered a new way of constructing a thriller. He noticed how little of our lives ran chronologically. Even simple conversations retraced their steps. You could say that Nolan makes films in the same way we describe them to each other, rewinding to add a forgotten detail.

So here's the twist, *Following* runs on three different timelines. In the first, The Young Man is being interrogated by the police, recalling his encounter with Cobb in flashback. In the second, he meets The Blonde, who claims she is being blackmailed. In the third, he is being beaten up on a rooftop. Each will crisscross the others, throwing the sequence into cunning, deterministic disarray. The title becomes both irony and instruction. Events will become extremely difficult to follow. Within the whirlpool of narrative, which we vaguely thread together by location or haircut, deceptions are played out, and identities shift and reshape. In the final scene, as we see Cobb vanish back into the crowd, we are left to wonder if he was a figment of the young writer's imagination all along – or the director's.

Nolan admitted *Following*'s structure was a somewhat unusual choice. 'But it's those things that are the strength of the project.'[20] Unusual became a philosophy. To bring something to the craft that no one else would have thought to do. Where directors like his beloved Scott added visual layers you could return to again and again, finding something new, he wanted to 'put layers into the storytelling approach itself.'[21]

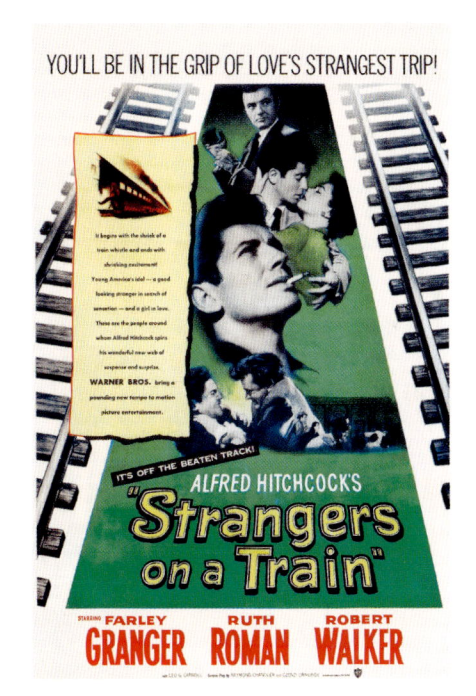

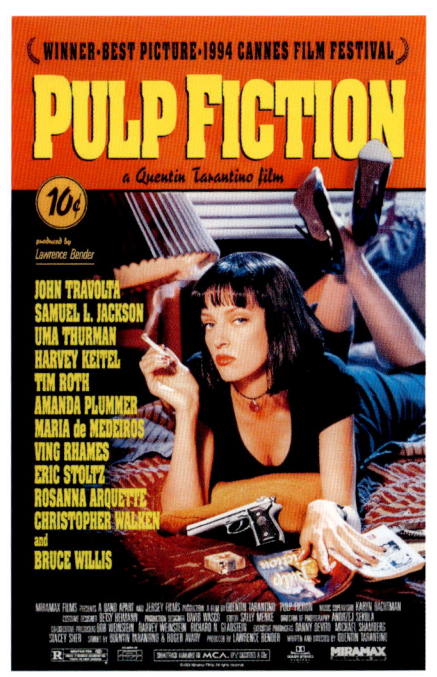

▲ Two classic influences on Nolan's debut: Hitchcock's *Strangers on a Train* for the concept of a stranger being lured into a trap; and *Pulp Fiction*, for how Tarantino wilfully messed with the chronology.

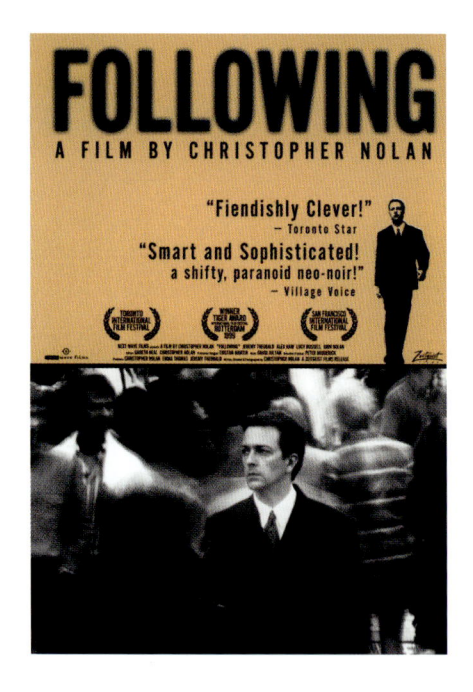

▲ A poster for *Following*'s small but profitable release in American cinemas, heralded by critics as the arrival of a major new talent.

◤ Christopher Nolan and wife Emma Thomas arriving at a screening of *Following* at Los Angeles' Grauman's Egyptian Theatre in 2002. As the director's reputation later surged, so did interest in his curious debut.

Premiering at the San Francisco Film Festival in 1998, *Following*'s reputation soared on the American film festival circuit, landing a token theatrical release with Zeitgeist Film, though making only $50,000 (actually a healthy return when you consider its slender budget). Critics quickly took notice. 'That the movie succeeds as thoroughly as it does – getting deeper and creepier as it goes along – is evidence of a far-seeing creative imagination,'[22] wrote Mick LaSalle in the *SFGATE*, declaring Nolan to be a compelling new talent.

Having been panhandling to get something, anything made along the streets of London, America – his other home – suddenly beckoned. Six years of grift turned into overnight success. Such are the distorted timelines of Hollywood careers. And he was about to radically shake up the prevailing indie film scene of the late 1990s, still under the loose, pop-expressive influence of the video-store renegades Tarantino and Kevin Smith. Things were about to get serious.

In hindsight, for all the shortcomings of budget, there is much Nolan still admired about his first effort, now a cult totem for fans. The textures were so good: the peeling wallpaper, the chipped skirting, flimsy curtains spilling muzzy light into cramped rooms. They looked real because they were lived-in and worn-out spaces. He laughed. 'I think I've spent every other film, spending massive resources, to get back to where we had nothing.'[23]

'*Following* is that rare debut in which a formidable creative personality seems to have sprung upon the scene fully developed,' said Scott Foundas, director of the Film Society of Lincoln Center in New York. 'All of Nolan's abiding obsessions are in evidence: the boldly nonlinear chronology, the liquid sense of identity, the involuntary spasms of memory.'[24]

It is not like we weren't warned.

Micro Nolan

The mysterious short films of Christopher Nolan

Space Wars (1978)
One of a series of homemade science fiction films Nolan shot with the family Super 8 camera. Using *Star Wars* and Action Man figures, egg boxes and toilet rolls, and flour to create explosions, he replayed scenes from George Lucas's galactic saga in rudimentary stop-motion. At the time, he confessed, he was 'obsessed with anything to do with space and spaceships.'[1] Viewing his first attempts from the perspective of a grown-up filmmaker, he admitted they were pretty crude, but here were the basics of shot progression. He would use similar techniques – spaceships against star fields – with a slightly bigger budget and level of expertise in *Interstellar*.

Tarantella (1989)
Made with childhood friend Roko Belic (now a documentary maker) between school and university, the four-minute *Tarantella* is as close as we come to a Nolan horror movie, with a real sense that this is the inception of *Inception*. An uncredited Jonah Nolan awakens in his bed (we assume this to be the actual family home used as a setting), but it is unclear if he has really awoken at all, given the procession of nightmare images that follow ... including a tarantula, a screaming man, Luis Buñuel-style close-ups of eyeballs, Jonah running through an underpass (Chicago's Lower Wacker Drive, which later featured in *The Dark Knight*), and Nolan himself looking positively vampiric as he sits, expressionless, at the head of the dinner table.

Larceny (1996)
Essentially a dry run for his debut feature *Following*, this nine-minute crime story was shot over a weekend in Nolan's flat, with Emma Thomas as production assistant, and using the University College London Film and Television Society's limited store of equipment. Nolan served as a one-man band of director, writer, cinematographer, and editor. While it played at the Cambridge Film Festival in 1996, and gained strong reviews, *Larceny* has long been withdrawn from public view. Little is known about the plot, beyond what star Jeremy Theobald described: 'A man breaks into a flat, startling the occupant (me). They argue about the new girlfriend of the "burglar", who's come to get her stuff. Then a third man bursts out of the cupboard...'[2]

Doodlebug (1997)
With its recursive, Escher-style structure, literary allusions, and expressionist style, *Doodlebug* is arguably the most revelatory of the UCL-era shorts. Within this three-minute, black-and-white, Kafka-like tale, Theobald's paranoid young man chases an unseen vermin through his ratty apartment. When he finally catches the creature, it is revealed to be a miniature version of himself. And as he smashes his shoe down on his tiny doppelganger, a giant shoe descends on him.

Quay (2015)
Returning to his roots, Nolan produced, directed, shot, and edited this documentary short between *Interstellar* and *Dunkirk*. It covers the work of the animator brothers Stephen and Timothy Quay (*Street of Crocodiles*, *Nocturna Artificialia*), revealing the twin stop-motion filmmakers at work in their studio, creating their inscrutable works with eerie dolls. It is a brief, eight-minute ode to two fringe artists who come at storytelling in a very particular, lo-fi way towards which Nolan clearly feels a great kinship.

◀ Plucked from obscurity: stop-motion marvels Stephen and Timothy Quay (seen directing *Institute Benjamenta*, or *This Dream People Call Human Life*) were the subject of a loving tribute from Christopher Nolan in 2015.

THROUGH THE LOOKING GLASS

Memento (2000) & *Insomnia* (2002)

For his second trick, he made an L.A. murder story, only the story ran backwards so that the viewer shared the hero's amnesia. For his third, he deprived a detective of sleep, blurring his senses as he tracked a killer through the midnight sun of Alaska

It began when two brothers simply ran out of things to say to one another. In 1996, Christopher Nolan was taking the family's battered Honda Civic from Chicago to Los Angeles, the long haul with half a continent on view, and his brother volunteered to join him. Jonah was studying at Georgetown University in Washington, D.C. at the time. Unlike his brother, he was educated in America and speaks with a relaxed Midwestern accent. By the second day of travelling along the endless American highways, roads stretching into infinity, conversation had drawn to a halt. Both Nolans, handsome young men with faraway eyes, were thinkers rather than talkers.

Apart from the wheeze of the air conditioning, the car was as silent as the grave. So it was to break the monotony more than anything that Jonah decided to tell his brother about an idea he had for a short story. Inspired by a psychology class on anterograde memory loss, and eventually published in *Esquire* as *Memento Mori*, it opens with a striking image. A man wakes up in a motel room. Looking into a mirror, he sees that his entire body is covered with tattoos. Rather than designs, they are sentences – notes to self. One of them reads, 'John G. raped and killed your wife.'[1]

We learn that a violent blow to the head has left the protagonist with this very particular form of amnesia. Everything before the injury remains stored in his memory as normal (the certainty of who he was). Thereafter he can cling onto nothing for longer than ten minutes, leaving him trapped in a perpetual present. His brain simply cannot form new memories. In effect he has been cut free from the flow of time, orientating himself via instructions inked into his own flesh, with a set of Polaroids in his pocket providing a vital who's who to identify those who come calling. Plot revelations come with the turn of a sleeve.

To give the story an emotional kick – and somewhat ironically – Jonah drew upon a vivid memory of being robbed at knifepoint late one night in Paris. He kept going over and over it in his mind, plotting a revenge that could never be meted out. It was a primal response. His protagonist (named Leonard in the film) would feel that same urge for retribution, even though he couldn't remember who the perpetrators were. It was a detective story that kept rubbing itself out.

▲ Leonard (Guy Pearce) and Natalie (Carrie-Anne Moss) dare to glance into the looking glass. The whole film works as a mirror of a standard thriller.

MEMENTO & INSOMNIA 27

28 CHRISTOPHER NOLAN

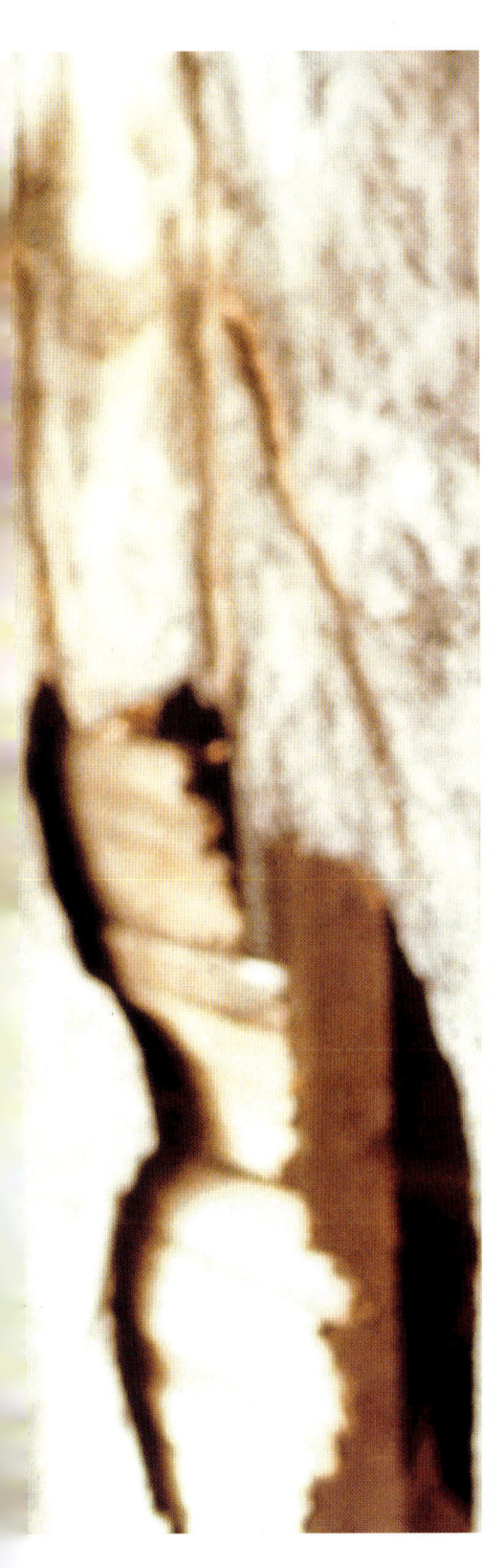

> " *A case can be made that Nolan's entire career has remained encased in the chambers of noir.* "

Jonah knew his brother to be a sharp critic who'd be quick to sniff out the flaw in a story, the cog that didn't fit. But Christopher didn't raise a single objection. There was only more silence, before he finally spoke. 'That's a terrific idea for a movie.'[2]

The beat-up Honda barely made it to L.A. But that idea flew. Nurtured by Nolan over the coming months, and renamed *Memento*, this was the story that would transform his career.

What struck Nolan from the moment his brother told him the story was that this was a classic film noir, but with a twist that was almost Lynchian in its transgression. As he had with *Following*, to get into the right headspace he immersed himself in the genre, fascinated by how the 'application of complexity had a purpose.'[3] You were *supposed* to get lost in the plot. 'Forget it, Jake. It's Chinatown,'[4] ran the famous last line of the Jack Nicholson classic. Nolan was twisting that particular epithet too. Remember it, Leonard.

◀ One of the brilliant concepts that drives the mystery of *Memento* is that in lieu of memories, Guy Pearce's Leonard tattoos clues across his body and keeps Polaroids of significant acquaintances.

It's Chinatown. *Double Indemnity*, *The Maltese Falcon*, *The Big Sleep*, and *Marathon Man* all offered up their deceptions. A case can be made that Nolan's entire career has remained encased in the chambers of noir.

With its disorientating backwards tilt, *Memento* has the intensity of a dream. However, it breaks with the tradition of amnesia movies – Hitchcock's *Spellbound*, say, or Ronald Colman in *Random Harvest* – in that the protagonist knows his identity. He has a past, what he lacks is a present. Alan Parker's bayou horror *Angel Heart* hinged on a more relevant identity crisis. 'It took you by surprise,' recalled Nolan. 'But it played fair with you.'[5] When you found out the truth, it changed your relationship with the central character. And *Blade Runner* was a river that never ran dry. 'There's so much concern with memory and identity that I carried over from that film,'[6] he said.

Following the path laid down by his brother's story, Nolan worked on the screenplay, and worked on it again, trying to fathom how he could bring the existential shockwave of anterograde amnesia to life on screen. One morning, sitting in his Orange Street apartment in L.A., a little overstimulated by caffeine, it came to him. The key was not simply telling a tale about an amnesiac, but

MEMENTO & INSOMNIA 29

having it *told* by an amnesiac, the ultimate unreliable narrator. Nolan was going to put us into the protagonist's damaged head, withholding knowledge from the audience in the same way it is withheld from the protagonist, by running the story backwards. Individual scenes play as normal, but always end where the previous one began. The film would rewind toward a revelation. Is it pertinent that Nolan is left-handed, and always leafs through magazines back to front?

Nolan wrote *Memento* while listening to the ambient, digital-age paranoia of Radiohead's *OK Computer* – to this day he struggles to recall what song comes next – staying in a succession of cheap motels along the Californian coast to soak up the deadbeat atmosphere. Interestingly, he put it on page exactly as he wanted the audience to experience it – in reverse. There was no conventional first draft tipped on its head: he wrote a scene and then followed it with the scene before it. 'It's actually the most linear script that I've written,'[7] he laughed. Each scene depended on the one that ran before it, with cunning visual and sonic overlaps. What Nolan called echoes between scenes.

The anterograde head in question belongs to Leonard Shelby, to give his full name, who is out to find and kill the man who raped and murdered his wife, and delivered the head trauma that has left him bereft of new memories. What evidence he has is stored in various maps and files, with serious revelations committed to skin. After a curious Brad Pitt found his schedule too full, Australian actor Guy Pearce gives a vivid rendition of Leonard beneath a flare of blond hair (Nolan with bed head) and plaintive self-possession, with Carrie-Anne Moss as local bar tender Natalie and Joe Pantoliano as Teddy, an undercover police officer, in close proximity.

Neither is exactly trustworthy. But then Leonard has no way of trusting anyone. Ten minutes later they are a stranger.

There is a later DVD extra that played *Memento* forwards, and the film clarifies into a grim tale which is, as Nolan said, 'literally just a couple of characters torturing someone.'[8] A bent cop and a bartender manipulate an amnesiac with a secret into doing their dirty work – that's the plot. Only travelling backwards, motive evaporates and the film breeds a shoal of red herrings. Critics would liken *Memento*

▼ Arriving in 1999, *The Matrix* heralded an era of reality-twisting thrillers into which critics would group the more visceral *Memento*.

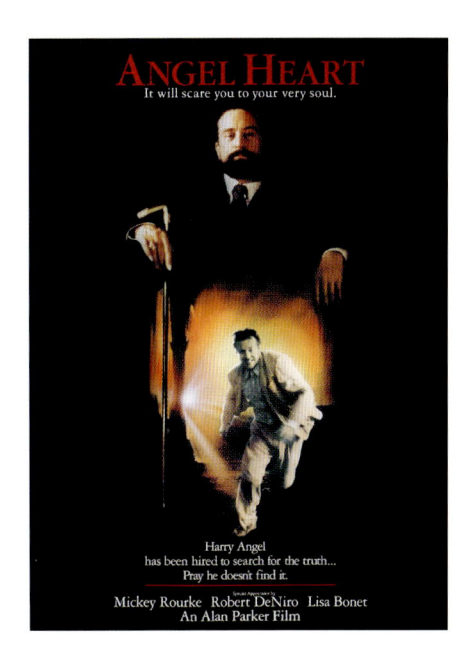

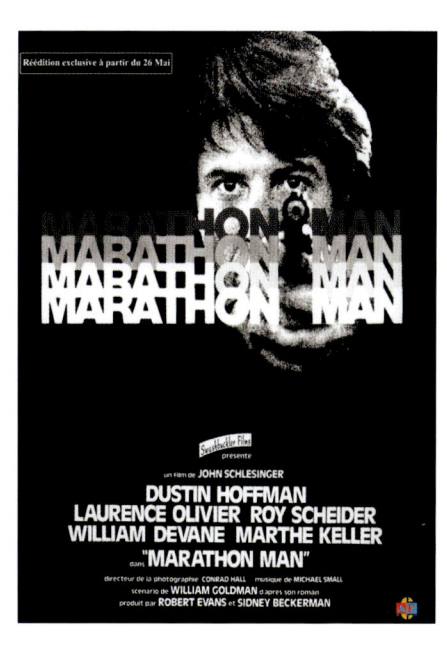

◀ The idea of film as deception – that the audience has no idea what is really going on – had been inspired by such thrillers as *Angel Heart* and *Marathon Man*.

to the deviousness of *The Usual Suspects* or *Fight Club* or *Being John Malkovich* – a taste for deviant narratives was certainly in the air. Only now the entire film functioned as a twist.

'The whole idea was to make a film that bled into your mind a little bit, spun your head, that you constructed very much yourself,'[9] said Nolan.

In fact, there are two timelines flowing through *Memento*. As the main plot ticks backwards, scenes alternate with a subplot, helpfully demarcated in black and white like *Following*, and moving forward in time… though *when* it is taking place is a mystery. Here we find Leonard in a familiar motel room on the phone to an unknown person, recounting the tale of Sammy Jankis (Stephen Tobolowsky), another victim of anterograde amnesia, who he encountered in his former life as an insurance investigator. Jankis, we learn, accidentally killed his wife with an insulin overdose. Insurance investigator also happens to be the same job as that of Walter Neff, the sap played by Fred MacMurray in *Double Indemnity* – told in flashback,

and written by Raymond Chandler.

Potential backers tended to either love the material or hate it, subdividing into those that finished the script and those that couldn't make head nor tail of it, or indeed tail nor head. Thankfully, Emma Thomas had managed to get it to Aaron Ryder at Newmarket Films, who thought it the most innovative thing he had ever encountered and offered a budget of $4.5 million. People tend to think that the shift into studio filmmaking – upgrading to big budgets, A-list stars, and pensive executives – was the big leap, but for Nolan nothing compared to going 'from *Following*, which was a group of friends wearing their own clothes and my mum making sandwiches to three and a half to four million dollars of somebody's money…'[10] He had a crew. Trucks and trailers were parked outside. Deadlines and permits were in effect. Actors were being paid. It was small fry in Hollywood terms, but a defining moment for the young filmmaker.

Twenty-five days of production began on 8 September 1999, passing

through Burbank, Pasadena, Sunland, the Hill Crest Inn in North Hills (for the Mountcrest Inn) and the Travel Inn in Tujunga (for the Discount Inn). The geography is as haphazard as Leonard's brainwaves. Such is the Nolan method – to place a story on familiar ground, then tell it in the most unfamiliar way. The setting was what Nolan classified as 'fringe urban.'[11] What could have been the outskirts of any midsize, sun-bleached American town where dive bars and scuzzy motels take root, the ones where movies tell you crooks hole up.

The central motel room was built on a soundstage in Glendale, where production designer Patti Podesta strangulated the space. Cinematographer Wally Pfister would shoot with shallow lenses, reducing the background to a blur, and blocking out the windows. The camera is kept as close as possible to Leonard, within the tractor beam of his subjectivity. The effect is almost tactile, as if his senses are compensating for the lack of recall. Nolan sat beside the lens, close to the action, beginning the

MEMENTO & INSOMNIA   31

habit of a lifetime. 'Watching with your eyes things are much clearer than on a monitor,'[12] he said. You caught dimensions you would never see.

Disorientation had become his M.O. The swift gait of the film is vital. We never get time to work out where Leonard's head's at. With every new scene it's like he's just woken up. It's impossible to tell how much time has elapsed. Days? Weeks? Nolan is drawing our attention to how all films distort time.

It should be the most self-conscious film ever made, yet we become absorbed in the storytelling. There is an underlying momentum, gaining pace the closer we get to an answer, the closer we get to the beginning. We are conditioned to the way that films work, their natural cadence, and Nolan required us to tune into our instincts. 'It actually has a three-act structure,'[13] he contended. The mood lightens in the middle as Nolan starts having fun inverting convention. The motifs of noir are still carefully upheld, only though a looking glass. At one stage we cut to the middle of a chase scene and Leonard isn't sure if he is the one being chased or doing the chasing. Think about Natalie for a second. She's a femme fatale in reverse order: betrayal to manipulation to seduction. Leonard is the ultimate embodiment of someone watching a

◀ The truth is out there – Leonard (Guy Pearce) and not-so-friendly acquaintance Teddy (Joe Pantoliano) get close to the beginning.

Nolan film – trying to figure a way out of the maze.

Eagle-eyed critics noted the casting of one veteran of L.A. Confidential (Pearce) and two from The Matrix (Moss, Pantoliano). L.A. noir meets time-bending sci-fi. Nolan noted how the script had spoken 'to something paranoid'[14] in Pearce's soul. The actor had a fantastic memory, repeating specific movements with unerring precision. All the actors grasped the concept with ease. After all, the film's discombobulating chronology was close to the typical day-to-day challenges on movies – which are rarely shot in sequence. It was the cast's job to plan for not knowing what comes next. Pearce in particular was a great 'logic filter,'[15] said Nolan, probing things that didn't make sense to him. 'We were both doing the same job,'[16] he laughed.

Pearce loved how Leonard vainly tries to 'retain some stability.'[17] It was essential for the character to be a tragic figure. 'I lie here not knowing how long I've been alone,'[18] he tells Natalie. Without memory, grief is impossible. He doesn't even know if he can trust himself. What happens if you turn out to be the villain? Leonard can be viewed as pure Chandler: the outsider, the private eye, the crushed romantic

▲ Ironically, Guy Pearce put his great memory to use in the part, keeping a mental tally of everything Leonard would or wouldn't know in any one scene.

soul, walking the same streets, stalking the same crimes. That instinct for vengeance is driving him – something that runs deeper than memory, like the insistent pull of the universe. 'Facts not memories,'[19] he iterates, contemplating his notes and diagrams like a director mapping out his narrative. The Polaroids matched those taken by the make-up team to chart his recuperation – he needed to become less harried with each retreating scene, the scratches on his cheek returning to open wounds.

Look at him, shot to hell. He wears a good suit and blue shirt, which don't seem to fit (Pearce thinned down for the part). Battered and bruised perhaps, but he resembles the director. On set, Nolan had already settled on the same uniform he'd had as a student, a habit that lingered from the daily diktats of Haileybury. A blazer and cotton shirt, eggshell blue or white, open at the collar. On later productions, if the elements were testy, he would add an overcoat. There was also a black suit and waistcoat. He remembered that without fail Hitchcock had turned up to set in suit and tie.

With the film's completion, Newmarket had confidently put on a screening for potential distributors, and the response was shock and awe. They all praised Nolan, shook his hand, handed over the statutory embossed card, asked what else he had in mind. *Memento* was still too clever by half. Audiences wouldn't get it. 'We got turned down by everyone,'[20] sighed Nolan, and his film sat in limbo for a year. His career started to feel as if it was moving backwards in time. Like many fellow filmmakers, Steven Soderbergh had been blown away by Nolan's audacity. Cracking open the most fundamental aspect of film narrative – that it moves forward in time. '*Memento* was a quantum leap forward,'[21] he insisted. As far as he was concerned, if a movie this good couldn't find distribution then the independent film scene was dead.

Such was Newmarket's belief in the film that they formed their own distribution arm to get it into cinemas. That's when things began to happen. Not for the last time, critics were stunned. A gauntlet had been thrown down. '[It's] like an existential crossword puzzle!'[22] clamoured the *New York Times*. 'Delectably disturbing,'[23] championed *Variety*. 'With each revelation, the big picture changes radically,'[24] marvelled the *Washington Post*. Some cried gimmick, but the majority saw a radical new direction for thrillers. 'Given the choice between a movie so smart that it leaves me feeling like an idiot and a movie that was made by idiots in the first place, I know which I'd take,'[25] concluded Anthony Lane in *The New Yorker*.

▲ Christopher Nolan on set with Guy Pearce – the director still regards the leap in scale between *Following* and *Memento* as the biggest change in his career.

◀ Nolan confers with Carrie-Anne Moss, a femme fatale played in reverse order – betrayal to seduction.

MEMENTO & INSOMNIA   35

Word got out. Were you up to *Memento*? Audiences returned again and again, determined to get to the truth. Somehow coming away knowing less the more they saw it. The film moved counter to box office gravity, rising week by week. Starting out in only eleven cinemas – the arthouse folly – before culminating in over 500, on its way to a worldwide gross of $40 million.

Nolan's belief that you could challenge an audience on a large scale became a conviction. He had experienced reactions first hand as he toured the festival circuit. People were responding, he said with satisfaction, 'in a very mainstream way.'[26] At Venice, as the film finished with that sharp skid of tyres on L.A. tarmac, there was a stunned silence. They were taking a breath, unscrambling their brains, before rising to a standing ovation. From now on he would trust his own mind. By the time the film was nominated for Best Screenplay and Best Cinematography at the Oscars, studios and independents were clamouring at his door for more of his arcane magic.

When we finally get the beginning of *Memento*, the timelines combine. Answers emerge, but the puzzle remains. We learn that the black and white sequences are a flashback to before the events of the film, but not who is on the other end of the line. Teddy launches into a rant. That Leonard's wife was raped, but it was Leonard who killed her by accident via an insulin overdose. Leonard is no hero. He stinks of guilt. Or is that just another of Teddy's lies? Leonard (and we) have no way of knowing.

Maybe we're asking the wrong question. *Memento* isn't about who killed Leonard's wife. That's a distraction. The real question is why – and, more to the point, *how* – does Leonard remember to kill Teddy in the opening scene? As Scott Tobias reasoned in *The A.V. Club*, 'the astonishing payoff takes the film to another level entirely, unleashing a battery of existential questions that shed new light on everything that precedes it.'[27]

'[There] are ambiguities in the film, but the ambiguities themselves

◤ Losing the plot – the memory-deficient Leonard (Guy Pearce) tries to figure out if he has ever even known bar owner Natalie (Carrie-Anne Moss).

▲ The iconic release poster for one of the most talked-about films of its generation.

▶ Sleepless in Alaska – Al Pacino's guilt-stricken LAPD detective Will Dormer is trapped in the never-ending daylight of *Insomnia*.

are answers,' I supposed,' teased Nolan, beginning a career's-worth of evasion. 'It's very clear to the audience the things that they can't know. You have to feel there's a person behind the film that knows what's going on.'[28]

Nolan's third film opens on a scale we had never seen before: a frozen landscape, ridges of glacial ice repeating into the distance, ribboned in blue as bright as Nolan's eyes, and a twin-propped plane banking into view. In actuality, this is Columbia Glacier near Valdez in Alaska, though it might as well be one of *Interstellar's* distant worlds. A striking pattern is established whereby Nolan offers images that echo forward in time: *Memento* begins with a bullet springing back into the gun from which it was fired, as bullets will one day flow backwards in the inverted entropy of *Tenet*. Here too is the widescreen promise of what he would soon bring to Batman.

When Nolan saw the original *Insomnia* in 1997, he liked it so much he saw it again on the same day. There was something about the graven textures that spoke to him – an early chill of Nordic noir. He loved the way it reversed the poles on film noir. Norwegian director Erik Skjoldbjærg's murder mystery did away with the chief component of what we consider to be film noir – nightfall. The midnight sun is what is troubling Stellan Skarsgård's detective. Rather than mentally out of kilter, this was a character environmentally out of kilter, which is sending his body clock is all over the place.

Nolan loved how *Insomnia* was 'swimming against cliché,'[29] and when he got wind that Warner Brothers were developing an English language remake, he pushed his agent to get him a meeting. To no avail: at that point he was still untested as a director, a nobody still one film away from becoming a somebody.

While Nolan turned to *Memento*, Jonathan Demme briefly flirted with *Insomnia*, with Harrison Ford to star as his weary detective. But like so many projects floating in the Hollywood think tank, inertia took hold… until Steven Soderbergh, having seen *Memento*, took matters in hand, crossing the Warner backlot, walking straight into the head of production, and demanding that they give this young filmmaker the time of day. That he and partner George Clooney also offered to serve as executive producers really got things moving.

So Nolan was already deep into *Insomnia* when *Memento* had its moment. Which was a relief. 'I wasn't put into a position of everybody saying, "Oh, you've done this very different, extreme thing. What are you going to do next? How do you top that?"'[30] He was establishing the steady flow of his career, rarely finishing a film without the next already filling up the horizon. Dictating his own terms.

Insomnia is often categorized as the outlier of Nolan's filmography, the straight arrow: it is a remake, based on a pre-existing screenplay, and runs along chronological rails from start to finish. But don't be deceived into thinking it's conventional. This $44 million studio thriller still coheres to the conceptual highwire acts that define him as director.

▶ Christopher Nolan and star Hilary Swank on location in Alaska, where the landscape would come to reflect the inner torment of the characters.

Relocated from Norway to the Alaskan town of Nightmute, Nolan's version begins with a teenage girl who has been found beaten to death, but no suspect has come to light. LAPD veterans Will Dormer (Al Pacino in the Skarsgård role) and Hap Eckhart (Martin Donovan) have made the trip north to assist the local police, including awestruck young detective Ellie Burr (Hilary Swank). But they are not a happy team. Dormer's revered career has fallen under the shadow of an internal affairs investigation, with which Eckhart is threatening to co-operate. Guilt pulls at Dormer like gravity. Tormented by the crack of light that squeezes between his blinds, he won't sleep for six days.

This was Nolan's first taste of a Hollywood production. He had much more money and less time to think. They would block out scenes the night before shooting, reacting to locations. The film feels more organic, hemmed in by the terrain as they ranged for three months, from April to June 2001, across Alaska, British Columbia, and Vancouver. With cinematographer Wally Pfister, he strove to give the northerly locations the same oppressive texture he had admired in the original. There's a damp that seeps into the bones. We glimpse distant, forested mountains, but the foreground is clogged up with rubbish tips, processing plants, seedy bars, alleyways, and gloomy motel rooms. Civilization looks jerry-built like a movie set.

Both *Memento* and now *Insomnia* offer a unique refraction of America into these liminal zones, the outskirts of society. Geography as psychology. The ambient light is set permanently at overcast, except when a fog rolls in like the breath of a fairy-tale, or the elemental expression of Dormer's blurring senses and delivering a twist well ahead of schedule. As a stakeout goes badly awry, and the killer escapes, he shoots his partner. A tragic mistake, or a deliberate act? Even he is not sure. Once again, we are thrust into the alien world of a fragmenting psyche.

Although the screenplay is credited to Hillary Seitz, Nolan made it clear that he 'collaborated with [Seitz] on several drafts.'[31] He can't see or feel a film unless he is part of the writing process. All the while, he was banking on negotiations for Pacino working out. That is how he pictured Dormer, with the deep pools of Pacino's eyes. *Insomnia* had similarities to the cop-criminal dynamic of Michael Mann's *Heat* – the De Niro-Pacino neo-noir classic was never far from his filmmaking thoughts. The way that detective and quarry circle one another, each trying to outwit the other like the warring magicians in *The Prestige*, more alike than they know. It's a pleasingly Hitchcockian set-up – both men have evidence of the other's crime. 'We're partners in this,'[32] announces his gleeful foe.

'[Nolan's] disoriented heroes are all trying to regain control of their lives in the face of malevolent, manipulative antagonists who turn them away from their intended goals,'[33] wrote Philip French in the *Observer*, which is a fine précis of Nolan's early career.

Like Leonard Shelby before him, Dormer is vainly attempting to impose order on chaos. Exactly as a director attempts to compel the structure of story across the turmoil of reality. And again Nolan brings his camera uncomfortably close to his lead's weathered face – the whole film is written on Pacino's reptilian skin – amazed at how the great New York actor, emblem of moral uncertainty in *The Godfather*, *Serpico*, and *Dog Day Afternoon*, remains oblivious to its interrogation. The result is a brilliant, concentrated study in the corroding power of guilt. Dormer's increasing weariness is as much existential as it is physical. 'He's on the edge of madness,' relished Moira Macdonald in the *Seattle Times*, 'and Pacino isn't afraid to totter.'[34]

◄ Nolan was amazed at how Al Pacino – the first major star he had worked with – remained oblivious to the camera's unremitting stare.

▼ Local hero – Swank shines as impressionable Alaskan detective Ellie Burr, *Insomnia*'s only true innocent.

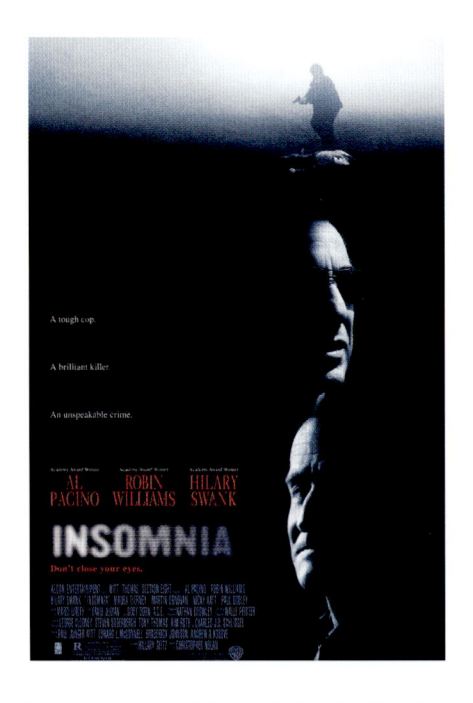

▼ *Insomnia* was Nolan's first studio film, beginning a highly successful relationship with Warner Brothers that would last for nine films in succession.

▲ Detectives Ellie Burr (Hilary Swank) and Will Dormer (Al Pacino) consult the evidence – but as this is film noir, we learn that evidence is a slippery concept.

◄ The duel of fates: Pacino's Dormer meets his match in the psychopathic Walter Finch (Robin Williams). The two men are far more alike than the cop wants to admit.

◀ Christopher Nolan marvelled how Williams really found something in himself to play Finch, a character light-years from his usual loveable comic persona.

As his opposite, Walter Finch, a dime-store thriller writer (he invents crimes rather than solves them) and fully fledged psychopath, Robin Williams doesn't make his entrance for nearly an hour, though we catch his deadpan voice on the phone. If Pacino was symbolic, Williams was an inverted piece of casting: he was firmly established as Hollywood's Peter Pan, a hyperverbal man-child. He was Mork, Mrs. Doubtfire, and John Keating, scattering inspirational maxims before his adoring class in *Dead Poets Society*. 'He really found something in himself,'[35] appreciated Nolan. For a superstar hankering to be taken seriously, 2002 was a pivotal year in every sense. In the double dose of *One Hour Photo* and *Insomnia*, he was cultivating a creepy recalibration of his comic innocence. '[Robin] Williams is a shockingly effective counterweight,' wrote David Edelstein in *Slate*. 'The key is what he doesn't do: those rubber features remain rigid, that madcap energy harnessed.'[36] How adept Nolan was at exploiting A-list baggage.

Likewise, *Insomnia* is our first sample of a highly distinctive and metaphorical approach to action. The confusion of a shooting engulfed in blue fog. A chase across the slippery skins of an Alaskan logjam that sees Dormer plunging into the ice-cold water and trapped beneath slamming logs. He has slipped beneath the surface of his own nightmare. The syntax of the edit establishes a familiar rhythm: long dialogue sequences into swift cuts, with shards of sensation, memory, and bloody detail intruding on the flow of events. Fractured time.

As well as furthering the possibilities of neo-noir and the subjective swerve of a personal style, *Insomnia* marked the immediate transition from indie prodigy to polished studio phenomenon. 'As a picture of a driven cop, and as a vision of a personal hell, it's unmissable stuff,'[37] concluded Peter Bradshaw in the *Guardian*. Critics and fans were gratified that Nolan's idiosyncratic traits hadn't been crushed by studio pressure. Taking a profitable $114 million at the box office, Warner were so pleased they asked Nolan to think about an existential superhero.

Readying himself for studio concerns, Nolan had shot two endings. In one, Dormer survives his ordeal. But at Soderbergh's behest he let Dormer die. This was the John Ford ending, they agreed, in which the moral order is re-established. Incredibly, Warner didn't interfere. It's a moving moment, the fatally wounded Dormer finally letting go. 'Just let me sleep,'[38] he whispers to Burr. He means the big sleep.

MEMENTO & INSOMNIA   41

THE INTIMIDATION GAME

Batman Begins (2005)

For his fourth trick, he reinvented a comic-book icon, bending the demands of blockbuster filmmaking to his will, and beginning the trilogy that would change Hollywood forever

Sir Michael Caine had thought he was the courier. When the doorbell to this country manor rang, there stood this polite young man, blond hair flopping into eyes, a script clutched in his left hand. It was called The *Intimidation Game*. Sceptical this was another wearisome rehash of British gangster clichés, Caine told the stranger to leave it with him – after fifty years in the business, a bona fide legend, he wasn't in any hurry. But the young man insisted that he read it right away, while he *waited*. The script was so secret it would have to leave with him. That was when Caine realised this was the director, and the title was the codename for a new rendition of an iconic comic-book character.

'I want you to play the butler in *Batman*,' explained Christopher Nolan.

Which did nothing to allay Caine's reservations. 'The butler? What do I say, "Dinner is served?"'

'No,' Nolan implored, 'he was the godfather of Batman and it's a much bigger part.'[1] Alfred was a pivotal role: the moral force in Bruce Wayne's double life, mentor, co-conspirator, and the rock on which the complicated hero rests. He was the film's heartbeat and chief source of humour.

Caine would be convinced to take the part, beginning a creative partnership that has taken in every film Nolan has made since. The very famous actor, the very rational director would often remark, is his lucky card.

'The thing about Nolan is you don't always know what's going on in the scene, as an actor,' laughed Caine. 'And you ask him, and he says, "I'll tell you after you've done it."'[2]

This story illustrates several things. That the director was revolutionizing the *Batman* saga to such an extent that even Alfred, the hero's faithful English butler, had gained unprecedented breadth. The ease with which he bonded with his actors. His almost obsessive secrecy. That his gnomic responses weren't limited to interviews. And quite how extraordinary Nolan's career path had been to this point – within four films he was ringing Michael Caine's doorbell with $150 million dollars warming his pocket.

▲ A superhero is reborn – Christian Bale arrives as a new, deeper, darker Batman. Christopher Nolan insisted to the studio that he wanted to combine comic-book mythology with psychoanalysis.

BATMAN BEGINS 43

◀ Bruce Wayne (Christian Bale) with his faithful butler Alfred (Michael Caine) – now more of a godfather and moral force in his charge's life.

Stop and consider what had happened in five years. Nolan had gone from unknown to indie darling to gaining creative control over one of the biggest properties in Hollywood, and (perhaps unwittingly) fomenting the genre that would redefine the entire industry. His ascension to mainstream director had the propulsive nature of one of his own plots.

'You know how you're supposed to have a character arc in a screenplay? My brother would not make a good character,' said Jonah Nolan. 'There's no arc. There's a straight vector line, straight out of the womb: *filmmaker*. Didn't waver, didn't wrestle with any of the doubts that plague the rest of us.'[3]

Visiting the set of *Batman Begins*, which was shot through the spring of 2004, Warner Brothers CEO Alan Horn was staggered by how calm Nolan remained while corralling hundreds of extras as helicopters scoured the skies like angry hornets. Furthermore, he didn't appear to consult any storyboards, or even have so much as a notebook about his person. 'It was all in his head,'[4] said Horn. This might be the most salient point in any analysis of Nolan's career – more than in the screenplay, the films exist in his head. In that Hitchcock fashion, they are precisely tailored to his own sensibility

long before a camera rolls, making it next to impossible for studio chieftains to interfere.

Warner were a good fit for an aspirant auteur. They were known in the industry as 'filmmaker-friendly'[5] – it was their general policy not to interfere. This was a relative distinction, but it was under the aegis of the venerable studio that Kubrick had worked his fiendish magic. In his way, adept at managing upwards, Nolan was studio-friendly. On *Insomnia*, Steven Soderbergh had advised him that the best way to deal with executives was not to be defensive. 'We're brought up being told how bad the studio will behave and that expectation can actually create those problems,' reflected Nolan. 'So it was a valuable lesson to be able to talk to the studio and gain people's trust and then you can work more easily.'[6]

To fans' initial dismay, Nolan came to Batman thinly versed in the strata of DC comic-books that dated back to 1939. Which was the reason he sought the aid of David S. Goyer to help him write the script alongside Jonah. Goyer had written the *Blade* trilogy, a trailblazing foray into superhero adaptations featuring a gadget-rich vampire hunter (effectively a Marvel spin on *Batman*), and his personal comic collection ran to 13,000 editions.

The critical and commercial success of the *Blade* films, combined with the first *X-Men* and Sam Raimi's *Spider-Man*, had convinced Warner, who owned DC (the stable of Batman, Superman, and Wonder Woman), that the time was ripe to rescue Gotham's night prowler from his descent into camp. His last outing, the woeful *Batman & Robin* in 1997, had arrived done up like a Christmas tree. Radical pitches had come and gone: Boaz Yakin's *Batman Beyond* (an older Wayne mentors a young apprentice, much like *The Mask of Zorro*), Darren Aronofsky's *Batman: Year One* (also featuring a mature Wayne returning to Gotham and based on Frank Miller's graphic novel, which would influence Nolan), and Wolfgang Petersen's earlier take on *Batman vs. Superman*. Through his agent, Nolan had simply been asked what he would do with the brooding superhero. Begin again, he told them.

'Creating a recognizably real scenario was the overriding drive,' he said. 'Addressing the origin story that hasn't been told in film before.'[7] Why does Bruce Wayne become Batman? There was, he said, a gap in pop culture for psychoanalysis *and* Batmobiles. A new breed of blockbuster.

For weeks Goyer and the Nolan brothers conceptualized their rebirth

> *" Stop and consider what had happened in five years. Nolan had gone from unknown to indie darling to gaining creative control over one of the biggest properties in Hollywood... "*

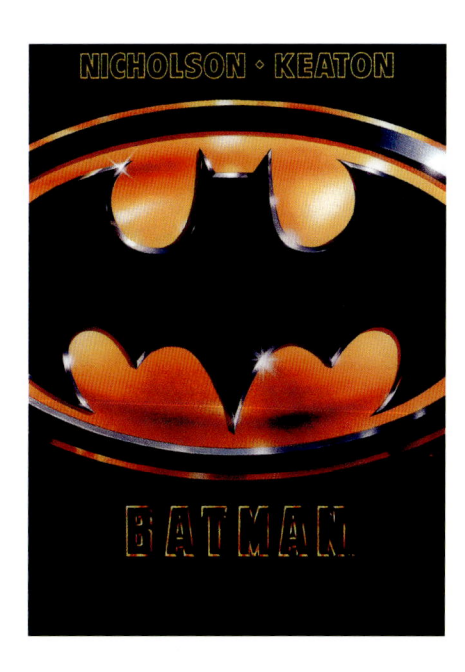

▲ The recent success of the darker superhero styles of films like the *Blade* trilogy convinced Warner Brothers that the time was right to reinvent their more theatrical approach, which began with Tim Burton's *Batman* in 1989.

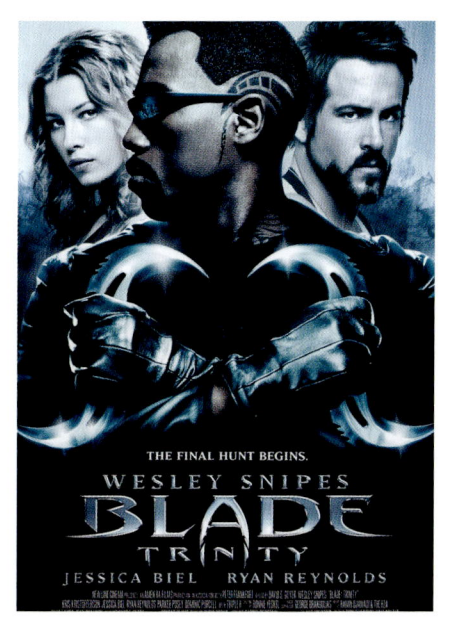

of *Batman* in the director's garage, converted into a filmmaking nerve centre – a reboot of the old Film Society den, Nolan's Batcave. Production designer Nathan Crowley joined them, formulating early concepts for those essential props of the mythology: the Batsuit, the Batmobile, and Gotham, the labyrinthine, crime-stricken city which he called home. It was crucial for Nolan that he present Warner with a holistic approach, design and script as entwined as DNA. He wouldn't relinquish control of any element of the production; he still shoots his own second unit. Goyer was there to protect the DC legacy, Nolan wanted to assert his filmmaking authority.

After the success of *Insomnia*, Warner learned to trust in their well-spoken young protégé, cultivating a relationship that would last for decades, giving life to that Hollywood chimera: rich rewards and complex, original filmmaking. He became their new Kubrick, self-sustaining, brilliant, and aloof. The terms of engagement were simple: he agreed both his ideas *and* approach with the studio ahead of time, and they left him alone. He earned that trust, and with it his obsessive freedom, by coming in on budget, if not under-budget. That in itself took control.

'These guys were totally, genuinely on board,' insisted Nolan, when it came to pitching *Batman Begins*, 'I know it sounds like BS but they really got the movie. I think we had a huge advantage in that the 1989 *Batman* film that Tim Burton did has defined comic-book movies. Because we're doing a *Batman* film, something new, fresh and different, they were looking for a reinvention.'[8]

Even the superhero movie was slave to the dark, cerebral currents of Nolan's imagination. This was Batman

BATMAN BEGINS   45

◀ Trust issues – Wayne Industries company man Earle (Rutger Hauer) introduces himself to the young Bruce (Gus Lewis), beneath the suspicious eye of Alfred (Michael Caine).

▼ The long journey home – Bruce Wayne (Christian Bale) ventures out into the wilds of Asia, where he will be taken in by the sinister League of Shadows.

jutting his firm chin into the realms of film noir: crime and punishment, a Halloween Dostoevsky, capes *and* realism. 'It was about taking this beloved character and recontextualizing the character,' said Nolan, 'setting this extraordinary figure in an ordinary world, or a seemingly ordinary world.'[9] What you might call Nolan reality: tales as tall as skyscrapers grounded in taut, objective filmmaking.

With a familiar restlessness, we flashback to Bruce Wayne's boyhood, and in and out of dreams, with the sprawling Wayne Mansion (in fact, Mentmore Towers in Buckinghamshire, England) as intimidating an old pile as Haileybury. The question of wealth had troubled the director. Why would anyone root for a billionaire? We had to get inside his head. The key, and central theme, was fear: Wayne embracing his phobia of bats, overcoming the trauma of witnessing the murder of his parents as a child, and confronting the soaring crime rate in downtown Gotham.

The story splits into two halves: Wayne (Christian Bale) far from home, a lost soul in the frozen wastes of central Asia, as brutal as Alaska but more robustly epic. Nolan is drawn to colder climes, bleaker places. Landscapes that reflect and challenge his heroes. He shot on the stratified glaciers of Vatnajökull National Park in Iceland for Wayne's proving ground, where he will be found and trained by the elusive League of Shadows, led by Ducard (Liam Neeson) and Ra's al Ghul (Ken Watanabe), whose clandestine devotion to ridding the world of injustice tends toward the megalomaniac. As Ducard extols, they are 'a check against human corruption.'[10] Top of their list is wiping out Gotham.

When it came to casting a hero with a complex, a parade of names soon began to grind through the rumour mill: that Guy Pearce, Billy Crudup, Henry Cavill, Jake Gyllenhaal, and Cillian Murphy had all read for the part, with the director impressed enough by Murphy to offer him the smaller part of Dr. Jonathan Crane, an oleaginous shrink with his own mask issues. Bale brought intensity. The British actor had a taste for the theatrical, darting unpredictably between roles as varied as *American Psycho* and *Captain Corelli's Mandolin*, keeping to the fringes of the A-list, renowned or notorious for his Method approach (he would hold onto an accent right through to interviews) and a capacity for physical transformation. He liked extremes, and came to *Batman Begins* having rapidly bulked up from the ravages of *The Machinist* – a distinctly Nolanesque tale of a guilt-stricken factory worker who hasn't slept for a year, for which he got down to a skeletal 110 pounds. Bale, like Nolan, responded to the idea of unpeeling Batman like an onion. He was intrigued by the notion of 'multiple personalities.'[11] That Batman was the character's true identity and Bruce Wayne the performance. For all the action and suspense and comic-book paraphernalia, *Batman Begins* is the fourth in line of Nolan's studies in guilt. Wayne can't shake his responsibility for what happened to his parents.

◀ Dark designs – Ra's al Ghul (Ken Watanabe, centre) challenges Wayne (Bale) to mete out deadly justice on the man who has wronged him.

◀ Fresh foes – rather than the familiar array of villains, Christopher Nolan delved deeper into the mythology to find weirdos such as The Scarecrow (Cillian Murphy).

▶ Cape fear – Christopher Nolan was determined his Batman might have swooped in from a horror movie, scaring criminals out of their wits.

Before Batman came into view, Nolan was in the thick of writing a biopic about the orphan-turned-eccentric-American-billionaire Howard Hughes: aircraft designer, movie producer, recluse, opiate addict, and agoraphobic nutball. He had Jim Carrey attached, and was promising to rip up the old, biographical rise-and-fall formula. *Citizen Kane* was in his sightlines. 'It will have strong connections to the films I have already made,'[12] he said, considering it the best thing he had ever written, only to be blindsided by two of his heroes. When producer Michael Mann and director Martin Scorsese slid *The Aviator* into production, with Leonardo DiCaprio as Hughes, that was that. But the script didn't go to waste. Nolan would model Wayne seizing control of his father's company with Hughes's combination of dashing spirit and unsteady psyche.

Needing gravitas, Nolan filled out his array of supporting characters with a strong mix of American and British character actors: Caine, of course, as Alfred; Neeson as mentor-turned-nemesis Ducard; Morgan Freeman as gadget guru Lucius Fox; Gary Oldman as Detective Jim Gordon; Tom Wilkinson ripening things up a bit as Gotham hood Carmine Falcone; *Blade Runner's*

▲ Crusading lawyer Rachel Dawes (Katie Holmes) confronts edgy psychologist Dr. Jonathan Crane, the alter-ego of Murphy's Scarecrow.

executive Earle; and Katie Holmes as Wayne's childhood sweetheart-turned-crusading-lawyer Rachel.

Across a 129-day shoot, he preached innovation – take the core proposition and add sophistication, root out what makes Batman tick, but never let go of the need for big, bombastic action. Without pandering to nostalgia, the second half was all about bringing Gotham to life.

As Batman returns home to thwart the League's plans, fear abounds in the seething city. Murphy's true guise as the Scarecrow, one of a coterie of elaborate if not top-tier DC villains, floors his foes with a hallucinogenic gas, which stirs psychedelic visions out of a victim's worst fears like a weaponized version of the psychological torments of Leonard Shelby and Will Dormer.

In parallel, Wayne adopts the mantle and cowl of Batman, Bale affects a voice like lawnmowing gravel, and Nolan's first ostensibly heroic character sets about scaring the criminal class out of their wits.

'The concept was always to present him from the criminal's point of view,' he said. 'I always liken Batman to the first *Alien* where you just glimpse it. So he's frightening, threatening, and elusive. You understand why they're afraid of him.'[13]

There's a startling sequence in which we first see Batman in action picking off crooks one by one amid Gotham's maze-like container port. Nolan had been struck by the sight of shipping containers on the quayside when he visited the Hong Kong (China) Film Festival with *Following*, storing it up as a backdrop for an action scene.

But these were the infectious moves of a horror movie.

One of the great attractions for Nolan in shouldering the weight of expectations that come with Batman was the 'opportunity of walking in a particular genre.'[14] But it was never about making a darker film. The opposite, in fact. Away from his habit of esoteric inspiration, Nolan was jazzed by the chance to make a film he would have loved as a kid: his variation on *Raiders of the Lost Ark* or *The Spy Who Loved Me*. He likened the return of Wayne to *The Count of Monte Cristo*. The windswept opening drew upon his love of John Huston's sterling 1975 Kipling adaptation *The Man Who Would Be King*, which starred Sean Connery and a younger Caine.

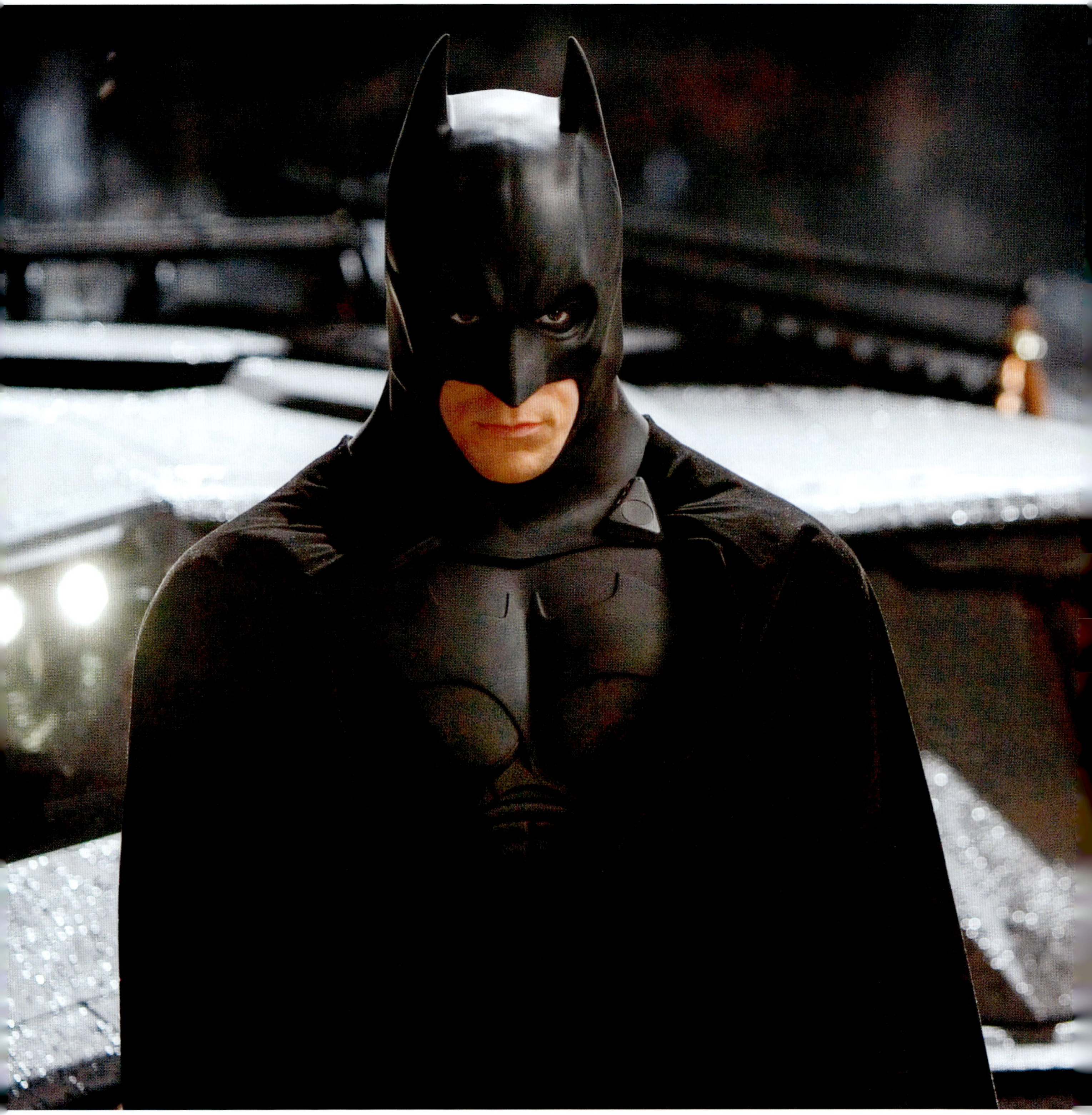

▲ As *Batman Begins*' spin on 007's Q, Lucius Fox (Morgan Freeman) gives Bruce Wayne (Christian Bale) a tour of a radically reinvented Batmobile – known as the Tumbler.

◀ Back in black. The realism of the Batsuit was all-important – its dark smudge of Kevlar body armour with a cape of parachute nylon allowing the hero to plummet from on high.

In effect, he was making his James Bond movie – undercover hero unpicks the plans of extravagant villains, with gadgets for every occasion. He wanted that 'global footprint,'[15] to show the world beyond Gotham, expanding the studio-bound fairgrounds of earlier iterations. Nolan had come to the legendary fictional spy through the movies, then later read Ian Fleming's books, appreciating how Connery came close to 'the selfishness'[16] of the character. That vanity was something else Bale invested into Wayne.

'We decided money was his superpower,'[17] said Crowley. While physically adept, Batman is still human. Significantly, there is nothing super in any of Nolan's superhero films. The rational prevails. Wayne armours himself with futuristic equipment to carry out his supra-legal crusade. Freeman's Fox, with his slew of gadgets cooked up in the Applied Sciences Division of Wayne Enterprises (a collection of plot-enabling devices thought up by the director), was an unabashed homage to Bond's Q. But there is something of a post-9/11 persuasion to the emphasis on military hardware, with tech-heavy chat about Kevlar bi-weave body armour and microwave emitters. The concept of a War on Terror resonated through the movie, even as Nolan denied it was anything conscious.

The suit, a smudge of darkness against the night, was designed to look more animalistic, the gauntlets scalloped in blades, the cape cut from parachute nylon and unfurling into bat-like wings thanks to a network of air tubes, allowing Bale to glide like Dracula from rooftop to rooftop. More radical still, the Batmobile was flipped from a pimped-up Corvette into a high-speed tank crossbred from a Hummer and a Lamborghini, delivered in soot-black armour plating. When cornered, Batman would simply drive over his enemy. Christened the Tumbler, it was built from scratch by the practical effects team, led by Chris Corbould – a fully-working Batmobile and solid-state emblem of Nolan's commitment to practical effects. 'It became a real mission,'[18] noted Corbould.

CGI was resisted like the plague, with the director only relenting when the laws of physics or safety got in the way, or for the few wide-shots of places that didn't exist outside of a comic-book. 'We did some pretty outrageously ambitious things in making the film,' said Nolan, as the grown-up boy who had once made stop motion films with his brother 'built what I believe is the biggest set for any movie.'[19]

Gotham becomes the purest vision yet of Batman's schizophrenic metropolis and Nolan's thematic thunderstorms. Like the circuit board of the director's imagination, it is a citywide maze where real locations jostle with fantastical sets, at once vast and confined. He wanted to

BATMAN BEGINS

▶ Part tank and part getaway-car, the now iconic new Batmobile hits the streets of Chicago, used for exteriors.

build a world like Ridley Scott or Fritz Lang, where the streets doubled as an allegorical space. 'No whimsey'[20] had been Crowley's mantra, but Gotham has its romantic side, calling upon *Blade Runner's* luminous dystopia, Fritz Lang's expressionist Berlin in *M* and the fathomless futurescape of *Metropolis*, and Giovanni Piranesi's etchings of infinite imaginary prisons, gothic derangements of Escher's mathematical purity. Giant sets were built across London studios, and at the 200-foot-tall former airship hangars at Cardington in Bedfordshire, where an entire Gotham block was housed – as intricate and impossible as a funhouse maze. Nolan thought of it as 'New York on steroids.'[21]

Cinematographer Wally Pfister was impressed by how Nolan still treated each scene in much the same way he had *Memento* or *Insomnia*. 'We could be sitting on the set with 150 people and huge setups, but when the camera rolls, it's just Chris sitting next to me with a little monitor, and the actors right there in front of us. His entire universe is in that twelve-foot area.'[22]

Three weeks of location shooting on Lower Wacker Drive and The Loop in Chicago provided the gleaming flanks of van der Rohe skyscrapers and avenues wide enough for Tumbler derbies, with the Board of Trade Building doubling as Wayne Enterprises. This is the gritty urban atmosphere of Sidney Lumet and William Friedkin: the corrupt quarters of *Serpico* and *The French Connection*. And Mann's *Heat*, always *Heat*, that mythologized Los Angeles in ribbons of shimmering lights. During his peripatetic childhood, Nolan would remember the sight of the Sears Tower soaring into the future as his plane banked into O'Hare. He would position Batman high on Chicago's ramparts, gazing down on Nolanville – the electric tapestry that lies behind his eyes. Also sewn into the fabric of the city is the architecture of his student years, such as St Pancras Station, and Senate House, part of his old alma mater, University College London.

Meanwhile, the crashing monorail, fog-bound Dickensian slums, and Arkham Asylum with its intake of wacky prospects, represent a little give in the direction of Warner and genre tradition. The action-packed last act is as conventional as Nolan had been in his career. 'With *Batman Begins*, we very specifically wrote it in the biggest way possible,'[23] he accepted. It is a film often caught in two minds, or dual identities – a Nolan blockbuster.

Released into cinemas on 16 June 2005, *Batman Begins* emphatically pulled off the required U-turn in a superhero's fortunes to a profitable if not head-turning $374 million worldwide. 'People like the film a lot, but it wasn't as successful as we expected it to be,'[24] he said. These were not yet the transformative numbers that would redefine popular culture. Nevertheless, an icon was reborn to the murky ambience of Hans Zimmer's score (with the aid of James Newton Howard), which eschewed anthems for a rising wave of tonal pressure somewhere between music and assault, and began another career-long creative partnership, something we will return to.

▶ Christopher Nolan pursues his expanding vision – to be helming a major blockbuster by only his fourth film marked an incredible success story for the precocious director.

▼ In the moment – Nolan shows exactly what he wants while shooting within the League of Shadows' secret sanctuary.

BATMAN BEGINS 53

▲ Fans and critics were gratified that *Batman Begins* proved to be a superhero film that could only have come from the director of *Memento* and *Insomnia*.

▶ Christopher Nolan wanted the audience to perceive Gotham City as a character in itself – at this stage, still a mix of the gothic comic-book streets of old and the sleek Nolanesque metropolis to come.

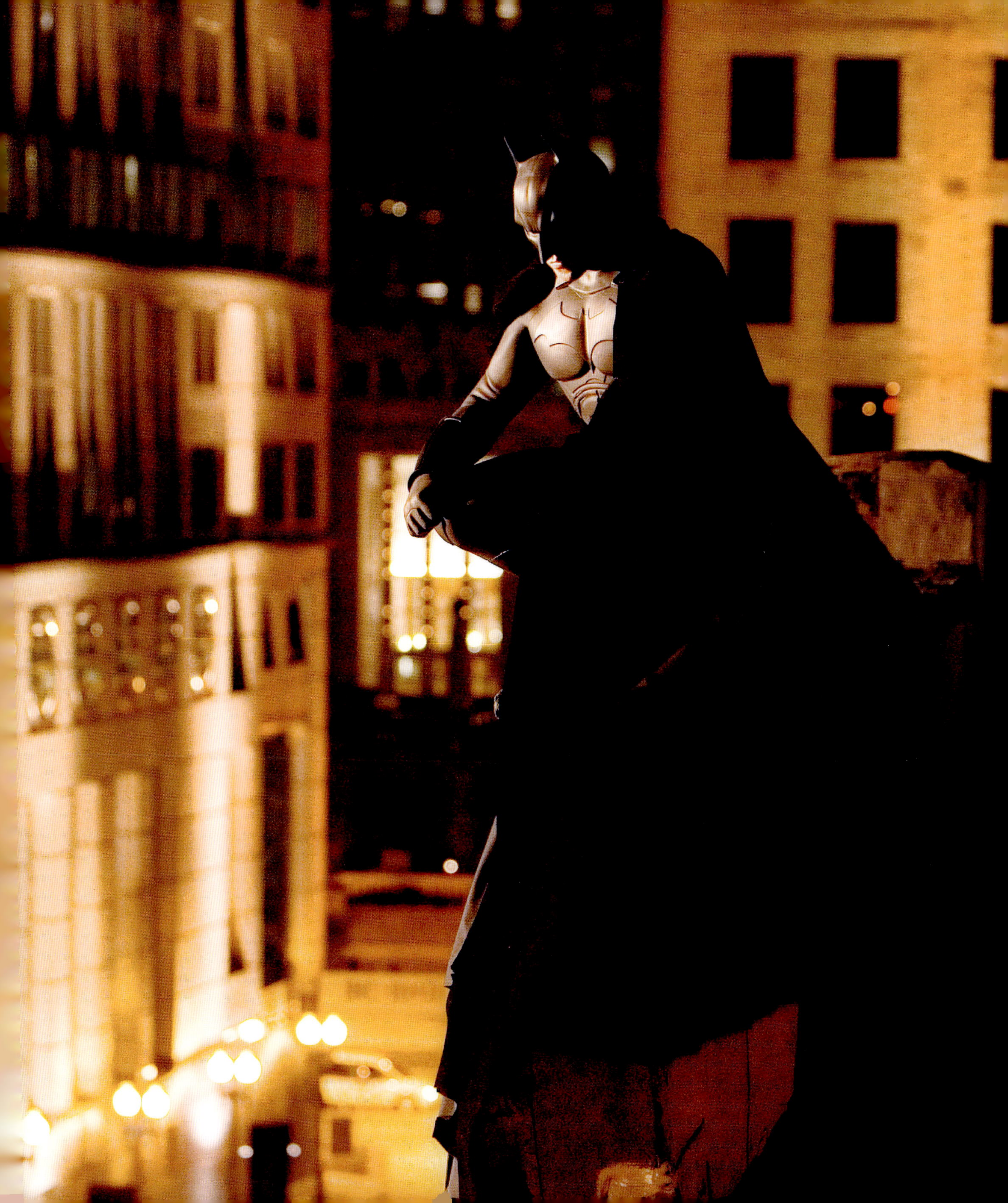

▲ Signs and wonders – as the film finishes, Detective Jim Gordon (Gary Oldman) ignites the Bat-Signal to tell Gotham's guardian angel of a strange new foe in town. Cue: sequel.

Critics were again relieved to find this was indeed a Batman film by *Memento*'s maestro. Nolan hadn't been corrupted by the League of Studios. 'An unexpectedly intense and disturbing affair,'[25] trumpeted *Time Out*, which they deemed a positive. 'There was a soul behind the special effects,'[26] sensed David Ansen in *Newsweek*, approving of the film's gesture toward psychological realism. Yes, it bent toward the mainstream, but the director's ambition stood out. Kenneth Turan in the *Los Angeles Times* saw that Nolan's intention was 'to create a myth grounded, as much as myth can be, in plain reality.'[27] As the director said, the story of a superhero who 'really is just a guy that does a lot of push-ups.'[28]

Nolan had made a big, broad, pulpy movie bound to a bold new realism that accessed the rich depths that ran beneath the Batman legend like the cave system beneath Wayne Manor. There was something universal and even autobiographical in the hero's struggle between vengeance for the senseless slaying of his parents and the quest for greater good. To make a better Gotham. 'Because Batman is limited by being an ordinary man,' said Nolan, 'there's a constant tension between pragmatism and idealism.'[29]

So having answered the question of how Batman began, what next for both earnest hero and determined director? To make a better Hollywood?

Psychic Scenery

Christopher Nolan doesn't build sets – he creates symbols.

◀ Dream factory – the spinning corridor set from *Inception* is one of Christopher Nolan's most iconic images.

THE MOTEL ROOM – *Memento*
The central location, and metaphor for Leonard's leaky memory, was built as a set. There was never an actual motel room to match what Nolan had in mind: everything about the room had to appear both grittily realistic yet imprecise. 'If M.C. Escher was going to design a motel room, this would be it,'¹ he said on the DVD commentary.

THE GOTHAM STREETS – *Batman Begins*
For his first *Batman* film, Nolan built an entire city street, complete with working monorail, on the massive soundstage of Admiralty Hangar 2 at Cardington in Bedfordshire. This is street-level Gotham, a labyrinth dubbed the 'Narrows,' and based on the cluttered streets of *Blade Runner*. More

THE SPINNING CORRIDOR – *Inception*
Surely the central image of Nolan's career, the spinning corridor built on giant gimbals at Cardington is a dream in physical form. Which is an ironic endeavour, when you think about it, for Nolan was making the surreal real. Here is the perfect marriage of the director's trademark dream imagery and genre – a fight scene with unreliable physics.

THE SINKING SHIP – *Dunkirk*
When the soldiers are trapped in the belly of a sinking destroyer, the scene becomes a microcosm of Dunkirk itself. To capture it, Nolan doubled a real destroyer with a forced-perspective set built in a tank. It is a set he is especially proud of in terms of desired effect. By attaching the camera to the 'boat', the water seems to rise sideways. 'It's not unlike some of the imagery of *Inception*,' he

THE TRANSPORTED MEN

The Prestige (2006)

For his fifth trick, a tale of rival Victorian magicians, each carrying their own dark secrets, and bent on perfecting the illusion of making a man disappear

The two brothers met in a graveyard. The gothic tableau of sleeping angels, tilted crosses, and ivy-choked headstones set a fitting scene. Concealed on a quiet hillside in North London, near to where they grew up, Highgate Cemetery could easily double for the 1890s. But this was the autumn of 2000, and Christopher Nolan was in London to promote *Memento*, and put a proposition to his brother Jonah. There was a book he was itching to adapt, only with pre-production underway on *Insomnia* he didn't have the time. It was something he could only entrust to his brother. Jonah had never attempted a screenplay at this point, but Nolan knew he had 'the right type'[1] of imagination for the challenge it presented. Brotherhood numbered among its many themes.

On this occasion it was Nolan who told Jonah the story. Written by Cheshire-born author Christopher Priest, who had a psychoanalytic way with genre, *The Prestige* centres on two Victorian stage magicians gripped in a manic rivalry that will consume the lives of those around them and leave them – variously – destitute, maimed, jailed, and (repeatedly) dead. The driving force in their enmity is the trick they both perform – The Transported Man, in which the magician manages to disappear, only to reappear moments later at an impossible distance. Each pulls off the deception in his own way. And each is driven to the borders of insanity trying to discover the other's secret.

Nolan had been handed a copy of Priest's book by the producer Valerie Dean. 'You'll see a film in this,'[2] she told him. After *Memento*, anything seemed possible. Why not magicians, and the ultimate exercise in misdirection? He convinced Aaron Ryder at Newmarket Films, who had kept faith in *Memento*, to option the rights. At which stage Nolan didn't realize he had a rival. Having seen *Following*, Priest had chosen him over Sam Mendes. He felt this would be a 'meeting of minds.'[3]

The plan was to make it before *Batman Begins*, when his Howard Hughes project had run aground. But the book didn't bend easily into a screenplay. It would take Jonah five years to find the film in *The Prestige*. Part of the problem was that on page the story took off in so many different directions – including a contemporary framing device – that there were ten

▶ Before the rift – illusionists Alfred Borden (Christian Bale) and Robert Angier (Hugh Jackman) while still on speaking terms.

THE PRESTIGE 59

different films you could make from it. However, the bigger challenge was how to convey a sense of magic on film without dwelling on the magic itself. Nolan was conscious that the thrill of a trick would be rendered futile, because filmmaking was already a process of illusion with its own special effects. It would be an illusion of an illusion.

'We decided to use the narrative itself, the story, to create a sense of magic,'[4] he explained. Let's put it this way, a story of magic tricks is a magic trick of a story. Essentially the film is about a series of doubles: two magicians, two tricks, and two twists. But the way it is told, locking away four different timelines inside one another, *The Prestige* may be the most complex piece of movie engineering that Nolan has ever pulled off – more so than *Memento*, more so than *Inception*, certainly until *Tenet*. Draped in pristine period dressing, lit up by the scientific eagerness of the age, it just doesn't feel that way – which is a classic piece of misdirection. We are conditioned to trust period stories. Mix all of Nolan's existing films together – devious narrative strategies, intense rivalries, the theatricality of Gotham – and you end up at the footlights of *The Prestige*.

'What is unique about it is you have no idea there is another magician called Christopher Nolan who is the writer-director, who is working behind you,' said Sir Michael Caine, returning in the guise of Cutter, the ingénieur, who builds magical contraptions – the production designer in a sense, and, like Alfred before him, the voice of reason. 'The whole movie you're seeing is a two-hour trick, and I've never seen that done before.'[5]

▲ The magical cast of *The Prestige* is filled out with the likes of Michael Caine as master set-builder Cutler and Scarlett Johansson as treacherous assistant Olivia.

▶ Christopher Nolan specifically wanted Hugh Jackman to play the natural showman Robert Angier because of his experience on Broadway.

THE PRESTIGE 61

▼ Everything is misdirection – the affection shown toward Olivia by Christian Bale's Alfred Borden may or may not be all part of the act.

With the success of *Batman Begins* still warm, the project sprang swiftly into production, backed by a double act of rivals in Disney and Warner Brothers (Ryder stayed on as a producer). This was at a conservative $40 million, less than a third of the budget of his previous film. After ironing out a few creases in Jonah's final draft, Nolan took off for Victorian London.

Here we meet Alfred Borden (Christian Bale) and Robert Angier (Hugh Jackman), the foremost stage magicians of their day. Yet as things begin, with barely an introduction, we find that Borden is on trial for Angier's murder. This is the effect from which the story will dance back and forth through time in search of a cause. 'Are you watching closely?'[6] utters a disembodied voice. Borden? Angier? Nolan? All is not what it seems.

Indeed it is never the same film twice. Among the layers of narrative our sympathies keep shifting (both men are guilty and innocent). At different points, each will decipher the encrypted diaries of his opponent. Could it be

◀ Star turn – Borden (Christian Bale), like his rival, rises to become one of the foremost stage magicians of his day.

that what this tale of duplicity and sleight-of-hand offers is the codex with which to unravel the workings of Nolan's tricks? 'Secrets are my life,'[7] says Borden. Without them, he adds, he would be ordinary. Do these two obsessive magicians represent the director's two halves? One is British, the other ersatz American; Angier's accent is part of the act. Angier is a great showman, hungry to taste the applause; Borden a technical genius, devoted above all to perfecting the trick. 'The Prestige is very much about filmmaking,' acknowledged Nolan with a rare smile. 'It is very much about what I do.'[8]

The Prestige is a film about devotion to art bleeding into obsession. Which again draws us back to Nolan himself as master magician. When Priest wrote the book, what intrigued him wasn't simply the era and the mastery of stage magic, it was the combination of 'obsessive secrecy' and 'obsessive curiosity'[9] in the performers – which speaks rather loudly to the filmmaker's predilections. Doing something different, maybe even better, than your fellow filmmakers. Could it be that the two magicians are metaphors for the growing ranks of Nolan obsessives, driven to understand the secret behind the story?

Although Emma Thomas had wanted to take a back seat with the birth of their third child (Oliver, who cameos as Borden's baby daughter), Nolan required her wisdom. She was vital in stretching the budget, and pushed him to give the female characters, who fall victim to the rivalry, more credibility. First Julia (Piper Perabo), wife to Angier, whose death after failing to escape from a water tank causes the initial rift between the magicians, back when both were stagehands. Angier blames Borden for tying the wrong knot in her bonds. Like Dormer in *Insomnia*, he implores his friend that he doesn't know if he is guilty. Then *he* may not have tied the knot. Then Rebecca Hall as the tragic Sarah who falls for Borden only to be driven to suicide by the conviction that there would be days when she knew he didn't love her. She was effectively married to a schizophrenic. And Scarlett Johansson as Olivia, the lovely assistant who will betray them both. Like the complementary men in *Heat*, Angier and Borden have more in common with each other.

THE PRESTIGE   63

> *"Mix all of Nolan's existing films together – devious narrative strategies, intense rivalries, the theatricality of Gotham – and you end up at the footlights of The Prestige."*

Nolan had no actors in mind as he and Jonah worked on the script. He tends not to. You inhibit developing characters if you imagine them with specific faces or builds. That came later.

When Australian actor Jackman, star of *Swordfish* and *X-Men*, first met Nolan, the director asked him which of the magicians he preferred. 'Angier,'[10] he replied, surprised at how instinctually that came to him. But it made sense. Both are very fine magicians, the cream of their day, but there are essential differences between them.

'Borden is kind of a genius magician, a better magician ultimately than my character,' said Jackman. 'But my character is much more a natural showman.'[11] Does that not chime with the two actors? Both had played superheroes, certainly, but Jackman was a Broadway veteran, a song-and-dance man. In turn, Bale's concentrated methods were the stuff of legend. And like Borden, he wasn't comfortable on stage. He had canvassed for the part, worried that his Nolan connection would count against him. But Nolan liked the contrast with Jackman.

There is a clear class tension at work – Bale's Borden is the Cockney commoner, while Jackman's suave Angier is closer to Bruce Wayne, the son of wealth. Nolan took inspiration from *Chariots of Fire* with its fierce Olympians from different walks of life.

The most curious stroke of casting was the presence of David Bowie as real-life Serbian-American scientist Nikola Tesla, father of electricity, whom Angier seeks out in Colorado Springs with unexpected results. Quite apart from the music, which he loved, Nolan adored Nicolas Roeg's Bowie-as-E.T. film *The Man Who Fell to Earth*, and he wanted Tesla to strike a similarly otherworldly aura – he is, as we are informed by Cutter, a real wizard. There are no tricks to Tesla's machinations – he creates a device for Angier that does exactly what he bids it do. But it will be a Faustian agreement. Tesla's Real Transported Man machine, spitting lightning like the birth of Frankenstein's monster or the arrival of a Terminator, brings a terrible price. Sealed within its pyramid-shaped container, it looks like one of the tombstones at Highgate Cemetery.

For the only time in his career, Nolan wouldn't take no for an answer. Bowie had politely declined, but the director returned to his agent and asked for a meeting at least, so he could explain himself. They met in New York – and, as he had once persuaded a sceptical Caine, he won over the enigmatic singer.

Bowie is remote, strange, and a trifle wooden in the part – the accent doesn't bear too much scrutiny either. But it is his sheer exotic presence that counts – the electric baggage that Nolan wanted to plug into. Versatile British actor Andy Serkis plays Alley, his assistant, and a curious fellow. He gets far more screen time than his master, which may well be to maintain Tesla's enigmatic aura, or because Bowie's availability was still minimal… but, as with all things Nolan, there runs a curious theory. That it is Alley who is really Tesla; that Bowie's version is merely a stooge, a distraction. Watch closely, and it is Alley who explains the experiments and tests the machine. Then again, Serkis's opinion was that he was a mirror to Caine's old ingénieur. Duels and dualities are everywhere. Tesla, we learn, has his own rival in the unseen Thomas Edison, keen to steal away his inventions.

Something Nolan holds to be true is that genre is not defined by the most 'superficial aspects.'[12] He never thought of *The Prestige* as a period piece. God forbid they should open scenes with the noise of carriage wheels against cobbles. The Victorian age had too often been mischaracterized as repressive and glum. This was an era of profusion and science, quackery and deceit. If anything, London feels more

YOU MUSTN'T BE AFRAID TO DREAM A LITTLE BIGGER

A 'chronolanology' of the major works

1998

2000

Following
Director, producer, writer, cinematographer, editor

A lost soul is drawn into the sinister games of a career criminal.

Memento
Director, producer, writer

An amnesiac tries to find the man who killed his wife.

2002

Insomnia
Director, producer, writer

A guilt-ridden, insomniac cop hunts a serial killer in the permanent daylight of Alaska.

2005

Batman Begins
Director, producer, writer

The origin story of how billionaire Bruce Wayne became Batman.

2017

2017

Dunkirk
Director, producer, writer

The evacuation of Dunkirk seen from land, air and sea.

Justice League
Executive producer

Batman teams up with Superman, Wonder Woman, Aquaman, The Flash and Cyborg to prevent apocalypse.

2020

2023

Tenet
Director, producer, writer

Spy thriller with the technology to invert time.

Oppenheimer
Director, producer, writer

Biopic of the father of the atomic bomb.

◀ Olivia (Scarlett Johansson) takes to the streets of what the director decreed to be a *modern* city of the past.

▼ The big idea – Angier (Jackman) puts his plans for the perfect trick to Tesla (David Bowie, centre) and Alley (Serkis).

THE PRESTIGE 65

▶ Christopher Nolan and Hugh Jackman shooting on a street set built on the Universal studio backlot – creating the *illusion* of Victorian London.

▼ Screenwriter and brother Jonah Nolan was the only person Nolan could trust to find a movie within the complex novel.

abundant than Gotham, though he only had $40 million at his disposal. *The Prestige* has the abundance of Ridley Scott's approach to period. Visual layering, sumptuous woody colours, set decoration as rich as Renaissance art, pierced by spotlights. There is something here too of the obsessively sparring Napoleonic officers in Scott's *The Duellists*. And that antique quality of *Blade Runner*.

The future burned bright in the 1890s. Electricity was about to spark a cultural revolution. Scientists were the new magicians, while magicians, fearing their acts looked out of date, adopted the terminology of science. Cinema was about to be born – a new magic, which would sweep away the old vaudeville houses. In his research, Nolan found that many of the earliest filmmakers had begun as magicians, moving into the strange new world of moving pictures as electricity allowed. Georges Méliès, inventor of special effects, grandfather of genres, was originally an illusionist. 'But I think that cinema has over the years co-opted an enormous amount of the pop appeal of magic, which is why this is a period film – magicians in the Victorian era were like the filmmakers or even the movie stars or rock stars of their day. The stakes

66   CHRISTOPHER NOLAN

are much higher; fame and fortune and all the rest,'[13] said the director.

Such is the looking-glass world of Nolan's filmmaking that where he'd largely shot Gotham in England, he would shoot Victorian London in Los Angeles. It's all an illusion, after all. Back and forth across the Atlantic with each film. They shot for three months from 26 January 2006, and being in Los Angeles helped escape that dreaded aroma of BBC costume drama. For the stage shows, they found four rundown theatres in Los Angeles's Broadway district – the Los Angeles Theatre, the Palace Theatre, the Los Angeles Belasco, and the Tower Theatre – which for a fleeting moment were revived from their slumber.

They converted the Universal backlot into Victorian London, and even moved behind the façades among a warren of wooden stairways to emulate the backstage catacombs of London theatres. A movie set was doubling as a movie set. Tesla's lair in the Colorado mountains (in fact Redstone) reinforces the steampunk veneer – a fetish for contraptions amongst the period detail, a hint of bigger, stranger things beyond the edge of the screen.

'What I ended up with is strangely a much bigger film than I realized,'[14] recalled Nolan. He had thought this was on the arty side. They shot predominantly with a handheld camera, following the actors rather than tying them down to marks. For all the reality-bending within his films, Nolan refuses trickery in his filmmaking. 'I won't fly the walls on sets,'[15] he said, as it was always so obvious when the walls parted to allow a camera to pass. The audience can sense you've cheated. Especially with *The Prestige*, Nolan wanted that feeling of constriction. 'You want to feel you're in the space.'[16]

'Where's his brother?'[17] sobs the small boy, Sarah's nephew, who senses a little yellow bird has died for the sake of a trick and the one Borden is holding is a double, which of course it is. So here is the thing… not once does Nolan lie to us. In fact, he puts the film's secrets in plain sight right the way through – only, with his subtle games of misdirection, the shifts in time, and the distraction of genre, we don't see a thing. Moreover, there was a book ready and waiting to reveal the answers if we so chose. 'Don't read the book before you see the film,' Nolan would implore journalists. 'It spoils everything!'[18] He managed to stall the release of the movie tie-in edition in America to dissuade those hungry to know its secrets ahead of time.

'The audience knows the truth: the world is simple,' says Angier in a line written by Jonah that Nolan loved. 'It's miserable, solid all the way through. But if you could fool them, even if just for a second, then you can make them wonder, and you get to see something very special.'[19] Isn't it the same with films? We know they are artifice, but we *want* to suspend disbelief. That is what is magic. Films cast a spell. But Nolan both heightens and tests our powers of disbelief by giving us glimpses behind the curtain.

We are told in the voiceover, with the familiar rough-edged eloquence of Caine as Cutter, that a great trick can be divided into three parts. And the film we are watching is subtly divided along these very lines, like a magician's variation on the classic three-act structure. First comes The Pledge, when you are shown something that is apparently ordinary, like a deck of cards or Victorian London. Then comes The Turn, when the ordinary becomes extraordinary. 'Now you're looking for the secret,'[20] says Cutter. And finally The Prestige – the final flourish.

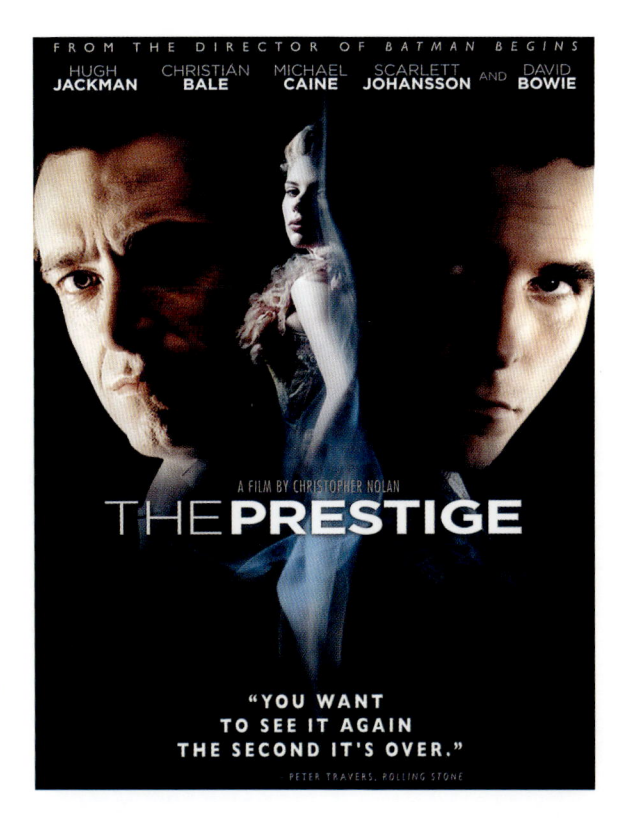

◀ *The Prestige* defied pessimistic studio predictions to open at number one at the US box office, giving Nolan a third hit in a row.

THE PRESTIGE 67

◀ Rebecca Hall as Sarah, wife of Alfred Borden, and one of the victims left in the wake of the magicians' obsessions.

▼ The ties that bind – Christian Bale's Borden readies Julia (Piper Perabo), Angier's wife, for the fateful trick.

▲ The master magician – Christopher Nolan subtly directs the performances of Olivia (Scarlett Johansson) and Robert Angier (Hugh Jackman).

▶ Michael Caine is once again the film's moral centre – as was his Alfred in Nolan's *Batman Begins* – and provides many clues to the film's riddles.

▶ Christopher Nolan had specifically sought out David Bowie to play the enigmatic Nikola Tesla – he wanted that feeling of a visitor from another planet.

'A film doesn't make sense until you get to the end,'[21] said Nolan. Only when you think back over it in the light of revelation do you realize what it is you have seen. Your emotional response changes. The dénouement should make what you've seen into a better film. With the end of The Prestige, the two tricks will be explained and we realize the truth had been right before our eyes.

Borden's 'Transported Man': Cutter gets it straightaway. 'He uses a double,'[22] he tells Angier. But Angier won't listen – like us, he thinks it's so painfully obvious a solution he refuses to accept it. But Cutter is right. In fact, Nolan doesn't suggest otherwise. It is the only possible solution. What is so sly is that we never see the Borden trick in action – the camera always averts its gaze. So we're distracted from thinking about it. Borden is indeed two characters, not one... (almost) interchangeable twins, each of whom has hidden the other's existence for the sake of their life's work. Always lurking somewhere nearby, the silent figure of Bernard Fallon isn't a stagehand or partner, but Bale in disguise as his twin. His name is a simple-enough near-anagram of Alfred Borden. What is so startling in the reveal is not how Borden did it, but what he is willing to sacrifice in order to keep it secret.

How Nolan has us in the palm of his hand! Even Angier tries out a double act at one point, finding his spitting image – almost a 'twin' – in alcoholic actor Gerald Root (also Jackman – each of the lead actors plays two roles). But it's a formulation that leaves Angier under the stage while Root takes the applause.

Angier's 'Real Transported Man': again, Cutter provides the answer early on (he's the film's guiding light). 'It has no trick,' he explains. 'It's real.'[23] It's right there on the poster. Halfway through the film, sent on a wild goose chase by Borden, Angier encounters Tesla, who agrees to build him a machine that, amid a tangle of lightning, will *really* pull off the trick. QED: it is like the teleporter in David Cronenberg's The Fly or the transporter beam in Star Trek. But there is one problem: the magician is replicated, like all those top hats we see in the opening shot, unaware we are being let in on a secret.

The mechanics of Tesla's invention go unexplained because they are inexplicable – made up. And to some viewers this is bad faith (though it was there in the book). We can't guess it. QED: Nolan cheats. 'The aggregate affect of The Prestige is that you can't believe what you're seeing,'[24] complained Walter Chaw in Film Freak Central. Meanwhile, cultural critic Darren Mooney seizes on this as a masterstroke. 'Nolan has fooled us into believing we were watching a period mystery, a parlour game, but this is a story device right out of science fiction.'[25] Had we misplaced the genre? But Nolan never lets the mask slip. Like all of what you might consider fantastic elements within his films (to wit: the dream invasion of Inception, the wormholes of Interstellar, and time reversals of Tenet), this isn't science fiction so much as fictional science. In the flash of possibility in his *modern* Victorian age, electricity *is* magic. With each execution of the trick, the old Angier is executed, left to drown in a water tank while his replacement takes a bow.

More metaphors! Deeper symbolism! That the Tesla machine can replicate things ad infinitum draws an amusing parallel with Hollywood's propensity for copycat movies. The superhero genre was proliferating by copying Nolan's trick of taking it seriously. More immediately, there was even another period piece about magicians underway, *The Illusionist*, starring Edward Norton.

There was a genuine perception within Disney (who distributed it in the USA) that the film was about to prove Nolan's first flop. Who cared for magicians and Victoriana? There was no clear protagonist. It was dark stuff. The tracking (a form of studio box office prognostication, reading the tea leaves of opinion) was poor. But Nolan was about to repeat his favourite trick – confounding expectation. Defying box office logic, *The Prestige* opened at number one, before finally making $109 million worldwide. Hollywood marvelled that this magician could keep pulling rabbits out of his many hats.

▲ Tricks of the trade – Robert Angier (Hugh Jackman) and assistant Olivia (Scarlett Johansson) toy with the audience. All parallels between stage magic and moviemaking are entirely deliberate.

WHY SO SERIOUS?

The Dark Knight (2008)

For his sixth trick, the sequel that became a phenomenon, returning to a gleaming Gotham and the trials of Batman, and a showdown with the most iconic villain of all

For once, it was a trick he pulled on himself. The playing card that Gary Oldman's stalwart police officer James Gordon reveals in a Ziploc at the end of *Batman Begins* – the Joker, naturally – was intended as a tingle of anticipation and possibility to send the audience home with, no more than that. Christopher Nolan had no intention of maintaining a franchise; he had done his superhero bit, bringing Batman back from his decline into camp, and wanted to be away to pursue more personal, original material. This was only a tease, or at best a departing offering to the studio – the enticing question of what a revamped (as far as fans were concerned, a *Nolanized*) Joker might resemble. 'We wanted to suggest possibilities for how the story would continue,' he claimed, 'not because we were going to make a sequel.'[1]

Nolan was innately resistant to the notion of repeating himself, or conforming to Hollywood norms, or genre norms, swapping out the villain with each movie. Inevitably you have to write with the returning actors in mind. And there was no contractual obligation. But there was an irresistible force emanating from the stalls. Jonah Nolan recalled watching *Batman Begins* on a sell-out opening night at Grauman's Chinese, in the very heart of Hollywood. He was nervous as hell. Will it work? It worked – and then they got to his brother's little send-off. 'Gordon flips over the Joker card at the end and the audience erupts like they're going to tear the place apart,' he said. 'I've never heard a noise like it.'[2]

As Warner Brothers pressed, the director stalled for time. 'You need to let the ideas you set up in the first film sit for a while,' he insisted; 'go off and do something else, returning to see how it looks.'[3]

The creative worms began to squirm in his head a little sooner than expected. He had barely begun pre-production on *The Prestige* when his thoughts turned to the concept of 'escalation'[4] posited by Oldman's Gordon – that the very existence of Batman would have an equal and opposite effect among the criminal class of the midnight city: flamboyant villains in the grand tradition would emerge from the shadows. The next of whom had already been announced. He seriously tried to picture the Joker through the realist prism of what he had done in his first *Batman* film. A paradoxical concept was becoming inevitable – he was going to make an original sequel.

'When you're dealing with questionable notions like people taking

▶ Heath Ledger creates a villain for the ages as the iconic Joker – for Christopher Nolan the idea of a true agent of chaos, without any motive, was utterly terrifying.

THE DARK KNIGHT 73

the law into their own hands, you have to really ask, where does that lead?,'[4] he said.

This wouldn't simply be a progression of setting and character, an expansion of the comic-book mythos, it would be a progression in realism. Using the doctrine of genre as cover for his own agenda, he was 'going a little bit more into the crime story, a little more into the epic city stories of films like Michael Mann's *Heat*.'[5] Such is Nolan's dedication to that neo-noir, in September 2016 he would host a 20th anniversary Q&A reunion at the Directors Guild, with Mann, Robert De Niro and Al Pacino, a flicker of fanboy eagerness to his questions. For now he was going to pay tribute with an entire film.

In a subsequent industry dominated by interlocking superheroic universes riveted to house style, such a shift in tone would be unthinkable. Nolan was basically telling the studio that he, the filmmaker, was the prize asset, not Batman. His demands to Warner were knowingly stringent. Four years to make his film, with absolute creative control. They didn't think twice.

Then he met producer and co-writer David S. Goyer for lunch. 'Okay, let's talk about a sequel,'[6] he said. Their discussion would stretch for three months as they figured out the story, putting the main beats down on index cards. Then, while he gave himself up to the world of *The Prestige*, Jonah set to work on the script. They were still refining their story as they went into production, trying to compress a 'dizzying'[7] array of subplots and action sequences, a vortex of moral conundrums, into a satisfying movie. They named it *The Dark Knight*, provocatively removing the word 'Batman' from the title.

It was never about the Joker for the Joker's sake. It was about figuring out the best story to tell about Bruce Wayne and then determining which villains from the canon fitted into that story. *Alien* and *Aliens* were always the story of Ripley, not the creature. 'It was a much more holistic approach and completely flies in the face of the way that a lot of other superhero films are developed,'[8] said Goyer, and something the Marvel machine has struggled to understand.

The Dark Knight put the characters and story ahead of paying service to the comic-books.

'I liked the [Tim] Burton films, a lot,' said Goyer, recalling that director's fantasias *Batman* and *Batman Returns*, 'but the one bone to pick with film, television, anything: I just never felt that the Joker was scary. Chris and I wanted the Joker to be scary.'[9]

Not simply scary, but thematically diabolical. He wasn't so much a character as a catalyst – a dark philosophy for a new kind of *Batman* movie. 'The Joker is what I am afraid of more than anything,' declared Nolan, 'more than any of the villains, these days particularly, when you feel civilization is very thinly lined. I think the Joker represents the id in all of this.'[10]

A returning Christian Bale as Batman was the constant, forever the troubled hero. It was his eccentric foe that would set the temperature of the new film. The Joker's warped energy would, said Nolan, be the 'engine of the movie.'[11]

The debate over casting began almost at the moment *Batman Begins*

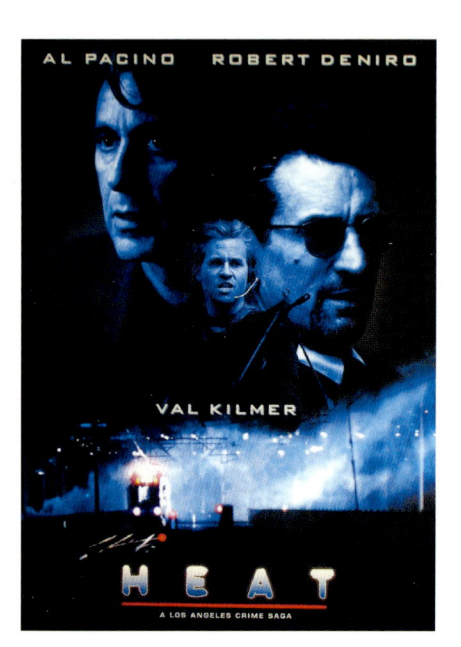

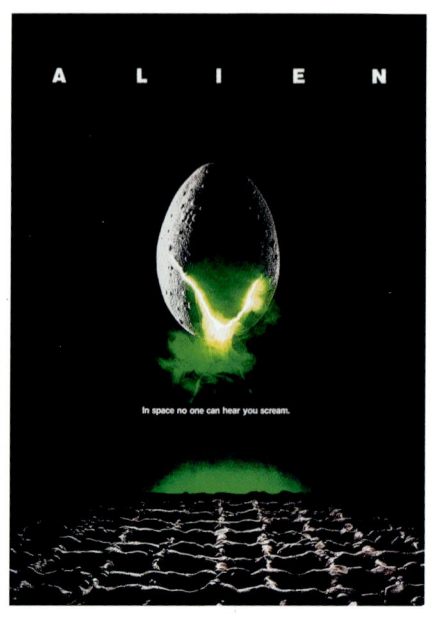

◀ Christopher Nolan drew on two very contrasting but key films for *The Dark Knight*: Michael Mann's ultra-modern crime thriller *Heat*, and the science-fiction intensity of *Alien*.

◥ Criminal mastermind – Christopher Nolan checks the bank vault for his opening heist scene, which will set the tone for a very modern thriller.

made its farewell reveal. Paul Bettany was mentioned, Sean Penn insisted upon. A young Gary Oldman would have been a natural choice. But it was always Heath Ledger for Nolan. They had met when the young Australian actor had come in for an informal chat about playing Batman in the original. But he soon dropped out of the reckoning, disillusioned by such a rote genre. 'I would never take part in a superhero film,'[12] he announced to the press. That resistance told Nolan all he needed to know.

They met again in Nolan's office on the Warner lot, chatted for a couple of hours. The script was still being assembled on Jonah's laptop, but Nolan produced an outline of the story. By the time they parted, he said, Ledger was 'determined to do it.'[13]

The choice shocked a few. Ledger was good at discomfort and self-doubt (burdened with his choices in *Brokeback Mountain* and a soulful outlaw in *Ned Kelly*) – but demonic? In interviews he was softly spoken, if anything a little diffident (though there had been flashpoints with paparazzi). Cast early in the process, he took the opportunity to dig deep. Locking himself away in a London hotel, he experimented with voices and mannerisms, keeping a written log of things the Joker might find funny, like 'land mines' or 'AIDS' or 'brunch'[14] alongside lines from the screenplay scrawled in his own handwriting. He put together a mood board of inspirations: Alice Cooper, Sid Vicious from the Sex Pistols (long ago given the full blast of Oldman's jagged charisma in *Sid and Nancy*), and Alex from Stanley Kubrick's *A Clockwork Orange*. For the body language, he watched Charlie Chaplin and Buster Keaton – he was, after all, playing a clown – affecting a lopsided totter, an exaggerated heave of the shoulders.

For their part, the Nolans delved into comic-book history, discovering to their satisfaction that the first iteration of the Joker in 1940 had been heavily influenced by gaunt German silent star Conrad Veidt in *The Man Who Laughs*. Nolan also reacquainted himself with the great Berlin director of the silent era, Fritz Lang, especially *The Testament*

THE DARK KNIGHT

of Dr. Mabuse about the citywide intrigues of a hypnotic villain, which he had forced his brother to watch with him when they were young. 'I fight the feeling that he's been planning this project since we were kids,'[15] laughed Jonah. That may be true of all his films.

One thing Nolan appreciated about the eventual *Dark Knight* trilogy was that it set a standard for the casting of superhero films. It was something he drew from Richard Donner's original *Superman* (1978), which had Marlon Brando, Gene Hackman, and Ned Beatty alongside Christopher Reeve. 'So we set out to put that kind of cast together and we did,'[16] he said. In *Batman Begins*, he had placed Sir Michael Caine, Gary Oldman, and Morgan Freeman alongside Bale, all of whom were returning for the sequel. It was about a certain kind of integrity. And now he had the addition of Ledger, elevating Cesar Romero's sixties television-show prankster or Jack Nicholson's eighties wacko uncle to formidable heights.

Watching Ledger at close quarters, cinematographer Wally Pfister said it was 'like he was busting blood vessels in his head,' he was so intense. 'It was like a séance, where the medium takes on another person and then is so completely drained.'[17]

The story would ripple out from the opening salvo – a stunning IMAX-tall heist sequence. The Joker arrives in Gotham unannounced (perhaps he has been there all along), first seen from behind, the hunched anarchist, ready to rob a bank *Heat*-style, a clown in a clown mask identical to those worn in Kubrick's clockwork-clever heist flick *The Killing*.

When we get our first good look at him, he's a horror, even for the Joker. Lank, mildewed, puke-green hair, flaking white face paint, smudged

▲ The real deal – Christopher Nolan was intent on depicting the Joker in reality, turning his clown make-up into a sick extension of his warped but brilliant mind…

▶ … and it was also vital there was never a backstory for the character. He is like a force of nature, something conjured up by the universe in reaction to Batman.

racoon eyes, and a smear of red lipstick to cover the curving welts of a Glasgow Smile. The paintings of Francis Bacon were a starting point. In the litany of confected anecdotes about how he got the scarred imprint of a grin, we realize he has no origin story. Nolan had seen how iconic villains like Hannibal Lecter or Darth Vader had been reduced by the loss of mystery.

The tatty purple frock coat of comic-book legend is worn thin. The key point for costume designer Lindy Hemming was that he really dresses like this. He is not putting on a costume – there is no alter ego. Licking his lips with serpentine relish, he is armed with no more than a pocket knife and diabolical cunning.

He was, the director accepted, like Anton Chigurh in the *No Country for Old Men* – a killer not only without remorse but without explanation. With the whiplash energy of *Fight Club's* Tyler Durden. Yet Nolan never saw him as a monster. '[His] only real amusement comes from tearing down the structures around him,' noted the director, 'that's a very human form of evil.'[18] Jonah saw their scabrous devil in more mythological terms (he tends toward a classical analogy) – a trickster character such as Loki in the Norse mythos.

Nolan ultimately likened the Joker to *Jaws* – he is as much plot device as character. 'He's a force the other characters have to react to,'[19] he said. In other words, the Joker is the equivalent of the backwards chronology of *Memento* or the inside-out tricks of *The Prestige*, Nolan's latest, confounding plot dynamic rendered in the body of a psychopathic clown.

There is this beguiling idea that he doesn't so much strategize plans as conceive of lethal jokes. The Joker will put a series of witty tests before Gotham and its dark knight, probing the limits of Batman's ethical gambit. Can he save the city without taking a life? Moreover, can Gotham rid itself of its own corruption? Gangsters and lowlifes are back in circulation again, and with the exception of the stoic Gordon, the cops are on the take. 'Compared to *Batman Begins*,' confessed Nolan, '*The Dark Knight* is a cruel, cold film.'[20] He is often surprised it proved as popular as it did.

'In *The Dark Knight* (Nolan must have been tempted to add "of the Soul" to the title), the Joker might be [Batman's] shadow or his evil twin. In some sick way, they need each other,'[21] proposed Tom Charity for *CNN*. Is he an extreme variation on Nolan too? Turning up to set in his neat suit, the wrecking ball director, smashing through convention. Like *The Prestige*, we are left wondering if the lead duo match the hemispheres of Nolan's brain in furious opposition.

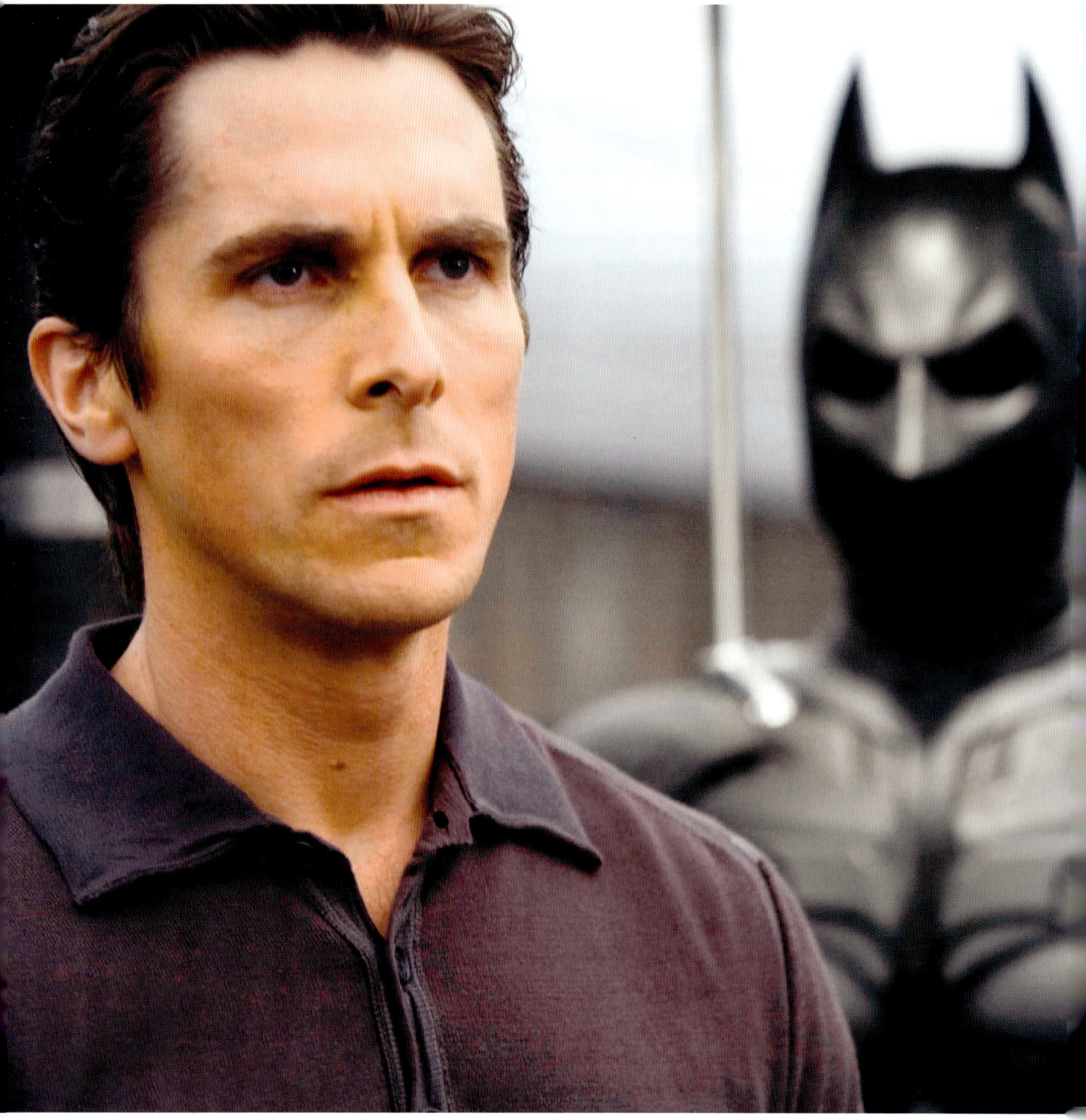

Bale must have been confounded, if not a little put out. These were the extremes he was famed for. What trauma did that leave for Wayne and his shadowy double life? Well, if his ink-black suit boasted improved flexibility, he was as uptight as ever.

'With Batman, it's a question of what's the tragedy?' Paul Levitz, president of DC Comics, had impressed upon Nolan over dinner. 'What is it that moves Batman?'[22] As an origin story, in *Batman Begins* this had been clear – the murder of his parents. With the sequel it was more complicated. While dealing with an outbreak of chaos in Gotham, his dual identity is taking its toll. 'This escalation has now meant that he feels more of a duty to continue,'[23] was Bale's perspective. He is burdened by power, responsibility, the whole superhero deal. He has also seen his childhood sweetheart Rachel (Maggie Gyllenhaal replacing Katie Holmes, who declined to return) turn her affections to square-jawed DA Harvey Dent (Aaron Eckhart).

On an equivalent crusade to rid Gotham of crime by legal means, Dent is the film's white knight. Even Wayne backs him – spying the chance to retire Batman. There is a school of thought that the real story of *The Dark Knight* is the rise and fall of Harvey Dent. When Rachel falls victim to the Joker's tricks, both Wayne and Dent will embrace their darker selves. The title signifies them both. We're back in the territory of *Memento* and *The Prestige* (and the same will go for *Inception*) – the curse of dead lovers.

To bring down the Joker, Batman must cross the boundaries of civil rights, connecting every phone in the city to create a sonar tracking device, with the film breezing close to satire. 'It's the Joker's film for so much of the movie because he's such an electric sort of presence,' said Nolan. 'And with Heath's performance, he's such a motor for that film. But right at the end Batman just takes it back. Bruce takes it back to himself.'[24]

More immediately, Dent is maddened by grief and left hideously scarred by the Joker's explosive party trick. So enter, late on, the film's second villain: Eckhart's Dent as Two-Face, his split personality made literal – half his face handsome, half a CG-assisted horror story of charred bone, sinew, and a lidless eye. He embarks on a killing spree of those he holds responsible. On the inevitable second viewing, you suspect he wasn't quite as bright a light as we first thought. Was he as much narcissist as idealist? Was Two-Face already somewhere inside? As ever with Nolan, clear moral distinctions get blurrier the closer you look.

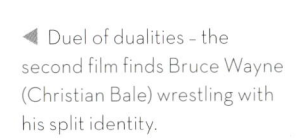

◀ Duel of dualities – the second film finds Bruce Wayne (Christian Bale) wrestling with his split identity.

▶ In many respects *The Dark Knight* is not the story of Batman or the Joker, but crusading DA Harvey Dent (Aaron Eckhart), determined to rid Gotham of crime by legal means.

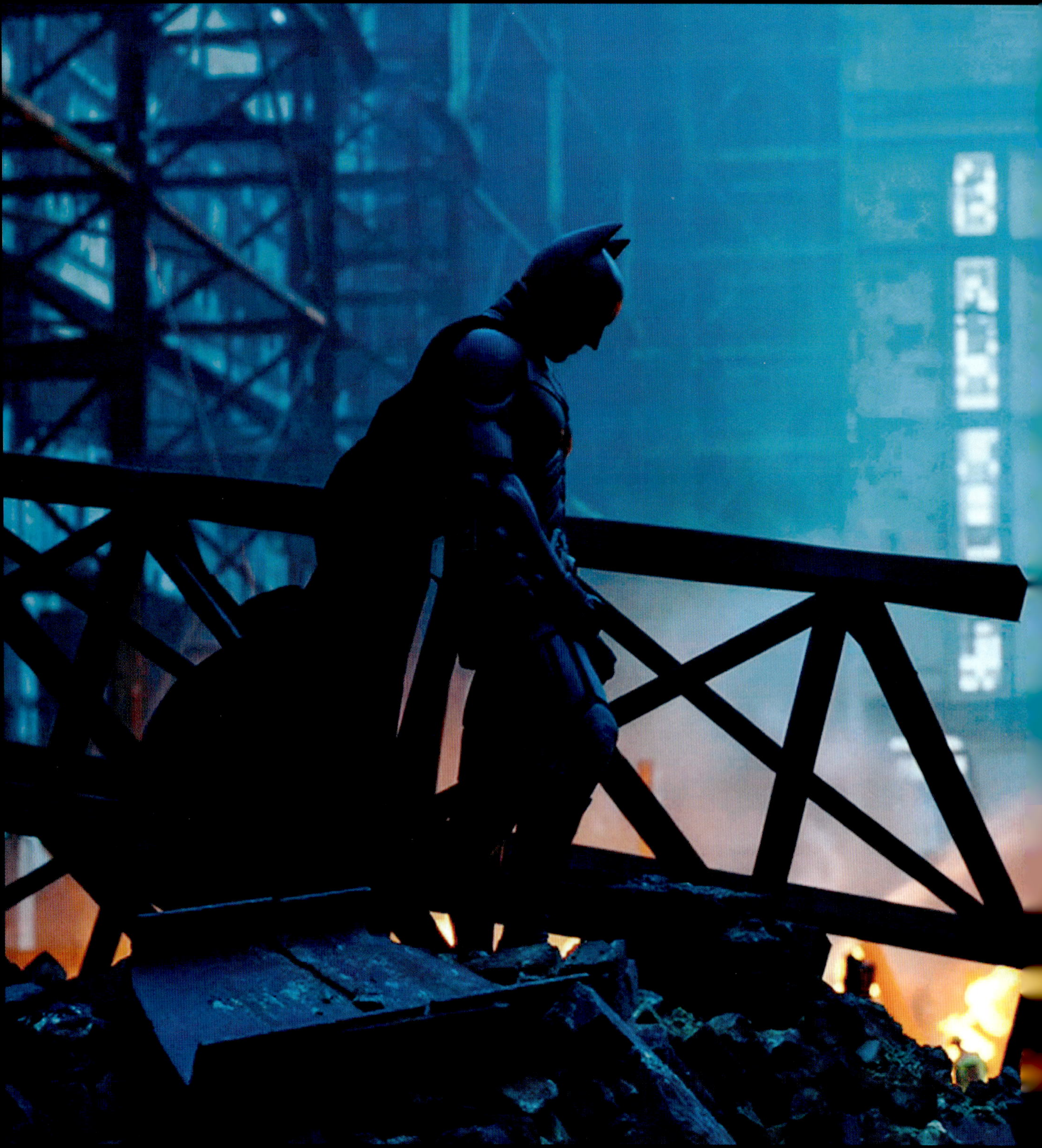

▲ *The Dark Knight* wouldn't simply be successful, it would become a bona fide phenomenon, ushering in the new era of superhero dominance.

◄ *The Dark Knight* in crisis. Batman (Christian Bale) stands outlined against the smouldering ruin of the joker's handiwork, knowing he must depart Gotham. For now.

THE DARK KNIGHT 81

◀ Clowning around – a gatecrashing Joker (Heath Ledger) confronts Rachel Dawes (Maggie Gyllenhaal, replacing Katie Holmes).

Even the score has a split personality with the returning duo of James Newton Howard, providing Dent's heroic themes, and German-born composer Hans Zimmer, who conjured up a siren's call for their jester. 'How much can I stretch the meaning of a single note?'[25] he had wondered, and ended up using two. The son of a musician mother and engineer father, Zimmer would become increasingly integral to Nolan's filmmaking process, beginning a score (if that term even applies) as the script was being written.

While morally skewed, this remains Nolan's most linear film. Time proceeds in an orderly fashion, even as disorder rains down on the streets of Gotham.

Another pull for Nolan was the chance to redefine Gotham. As counterpoint to the untethered antics of the Joker, he cut away any trace of the first film's neo-gothic romanticism – the monorail now demolished – to shoot almost entirely on location in Chicago. There are no Gotham sets, and only a few CG-assisted wide shots. Clean lines were the order of the day. City streets, underpasses, and panoramic views: this was reality. As well as Mann's synthesis of myth and city in *Heat*, Nolan wanted to give his new approach to Gotham the concrete grind of seventies New York in *Dog Day Afternoon*

▲ Morgan Freeman returns as gadget maestro Lucius Fox, who helps Bruce Wayne (Christian Bale, left) devise a plan to track down the Joker.

▶ Another of Batman's all-too-few allies, Lt. Jim Gordon (Gary Oldman) unveils some of the Joker's handiwork.

82 CHRISTOPHER NOLAN

> " ...the Joker is the equivalent of the backwards chronology of Memento or the inside-out tricks of The Prestige, Nolan's latest, confounding plot dynamic rendered in the body of a psychopathic clown. "

and *The French Connection*. The interiors followed suit: the Batcave and Wayne Manor were replaced with minimalist Mies van der Rohe boardrooms and sleek glass-walled penthouses. Nolan was removing the comic from comic-book. He wanted his city to have weight and breadth and depth.

'One of the fun things about shooting in Chicago, where I grew up partly and have a great love for, is that it's not as instantly recognizable as New York but it has this great architecture and all kinds of great geographical features in terms of underground streets and all kinds of amazing skyscrapers,'[26] said Nolan. What he had always liked about the Batman mythos was how Gotham came to symbolize the entire world – the drama was entrapped in this forever city, peeling away into the bluish dark.

During the seven-month, $185 million dollar shoot, the only escape valve from the prison of Gotham came in a brief foray to the urban heights of Hong Kong (China) to snatch a corrupt banker. Nolan shoots from on high, with Bale in his Batsuit, oblivious to the vertiginous depths. Across the film, the action was even more expansive and daring, and ever more averse to the convenience of CGI. The film itself was *escalating*.

THE DARK KNIGHT

In the midst of the Joker tracking Dent through the streets, Nolan decided to flip an eighteen-wheeler truck in the heart of Chicago's banking district, with the aid of a remote-controlled piston. Curving through the traffic on his natty new Batpod, a motorbike-scale reworking of the tank-like Tumbler aesthetic, Batman wraps a steel cable around the front wheels, sending the juggernaut tail-over-top (an apt metaphor for the entire film). And there Nolan was in the middle of his city-sized film, thirty-seven years old, waistcoat and dark blazer, a thermos of tea to hand, still standing as close to the camera as he could get.

Still six months from release, the film would be overshadowed by tragedy, when Ledger died from an overdose of prescription drugs in his New York apartment on 22 January 2008. Once the headlines had quieted, Nolan found himself suddenly burdened with a 'massive sense of responsibility'[27] to do right by his performance. Any insinuation that the role had taken its toll was dismissed – Ledger had been expressing his eagerness to return (the Joker's fate is left ambiguous). 'The truth is, Ledger's death was a surprise to everybody, and *The Dark Knight* neither hints at it nor makes sense of it. Nothing could,'[28] said Mick LaSalle in the *San Francisco Gate*. Indeed, Ledger's bravura antics as the Joker provide a fitting tribute for which he would be honoured with a posthumous Oscar for Best Supporting Actor.

Nolan's career is to an extent overshadowed by *The Dark Knight*. It is his most acclaimed film, and still deemed the high watermark in superhero filmmaking. Critics exemplified the startling effect the movie had. As well as the statutory thrills of the genre, said Scott Foundas, a Nolan advocate writing in *Village Voice*, 'it will occupy your mind, too, and even lead it down some dim alleyways where most Hollywood movies fear to tread.'[29] Those alleyways were regular haunts for Nolan. As Keith Phipps in *The A.V. Club* concluded, this was a film with 'the unapologetic density of a good crime novel.'[30]

▲ The real deal – Batman hurtles his newly fashioned Batpod through the streets of Chicago, with the city now fixed as an ultra-modern version of Gotham.

▶ Among the towers of Hong Kong (China) – with the sequel, Christopher Nolan was intent on shedding as much of the comic-book texture as possible to give the world of Batman a sleek neo-noir sheen.

THE DARK KNIGHT 85

▶ Street-wise – cinematographer Wally Pfister and Christopher Nolan on location in Hong Kong (China).

▼ Hitting new heights – Nolan looks on as Bale braves the vertiginous edge of a Hong Kong (China) skyscraper. Not a green screen or stunt man in sight.

86   CHRISTOPHER NOLAN

▲ The cast of *The Dark Knight* poses for photographers at the premiere. From the left: Chin Han, Michael Caine, Gary Oldman, Christian Bale, Maggie Gyllenhaal, Aaron Eckhart, Morgan Freeman, and director Christopher Nolan.

Audiences swept to the cinema to partake of the darkness, as it opened to a staggering $158 million on its first weekend, going on to break the billion mark at the global box office, and become the second biggest film of all time (after *Titanic*). Event numbers. Industry shifting numbers. And still provocative and challenging.

Behind all of the masks and make-up lay a question. What could a superhero film say about the real world? Plenty, it seems. Even more than its predecessor, Nolan and his brother Jonah wrote the film (Goyer takes a story credit) against the backdrop of George W. Bush's War on Terror. It was there on their television screens every night – terrorism as a global game changer. Under the cover of a superhero movie, Nolan was again intent on taking the temperature of his times. To the Joker's catastrophic disruption came Batman's overbearing response.

'You're trying to be relevant,' said Nolan. 'But I think if you try to do that in any conscious political sense you're going to be somewhat violating the terms of the type of entertainment you're trying to make.'[31] Nevertheless, he did refer to 'Batman's war on crime.'[32] To be fair, despite some sensationalist reactions in the media, the inflamed cause of League of Shadows from *Batman Begins* makes a far better corollary for modern terrorism than the Joker's anarchic spin through Gotham.

Touching on hot-button issues such as the surveillance state, civil liberties, social disparity, and those that stand as figureheads, *The Dark Knight* is both authoritarian and antiauthoritarian at once; a shakedown of modern American ethics. Nolan is venturing into the ironic terrain of Alan Moore's *Watchmen* comic series. Are these caped crusaders such a good thing for society? There remains a thin line between a fractured Batman and his insane counterparts.

'By the end, the whole moral foundation of the Batman legend is threatened,'[33] wrote Roger Ebert in *Chicago Sun-Times*. Batman takes the fall for Dent's corruption, leaving the DA to stand as a symbol of virtue and hope – even if it is a lie. 'You either die a hero,' he tells Gordon, 'or live long enough to see yourself become a villain.'[34] He rides back into the wilderness like *Shane* or Ethan Edwards in *The Searchers*, slipping into another genre entirely, astride his Batpod, cape fluttering in the wind. In effect, Nolan was doing the very opposite of what he had done with *Batman Begins*, suggesting there would no further sequels. Who was he kidding?

HEAD SPINNING

Inception (2010)

For his seventh trick, he constructed a strange, sci-fi inflected heist movie, to be set in dreams instead of a bank

From the very first time he experienced *2001: A Space Odyssey*, Christopher Nolan had been obsessed with the centrifuge. Kubrick had devised a cinematic trick to make it appear as if a Jupiter-bound astronaut was jogging a loop-the-loop of his circular living quarters, defying gravity. An extraordinary set by any measure, it was built by Lockheed to the director's specifications, a giant rotunda 38 feet in diameter (details that Nolan could reel off by heart), spun on an axis fooling the camera that the actor was moving and the set was stationary: the crew soon dubbed it the centrifuge. In truth, the actor was basically a hamster on a wheel; a visual challenge had been met by reason and geometry.

Nolan dreamed of creating cinematic magic as the master magician Kubrick had done – without the aid of wires, the ones plugged into computers, which generated the impossible like layers of paint. He wanted to build his own centrifuge and defy gravity. That desire, to bend reality to his will using filmmaking architecture, was one of the seeds planted in his imagination that grew into *Inception*, his most byzantine concept since hitting reverse on *Memento*. This would be a movie set in a world of realistic dreams.

You could argue, as Nolan does, that *Inception*'s true inception point was the dormitory of his boarding school, Haileybury, where he would listen to film soundtracks on his Walkman after lights out. Beneath the sheets, he conceived of a horror film made up of an interconnected nightmare. When he finally put pen to paper in 2002, shortly after finishing *Insomnia*, he produced an eighty-page treatment for a horror story not so very far from the *Nightmare on Elm Street* films. Nolan remembered a TV spin-off called *Freddy's Nightmares*, where characters would wake up from a dream only to discover they were in another dream. 'I found that pretty terrifying,'[1] he admitted. But he sensed something was missing – or that he wasn't ready – so he left it to stew in his imagination, where other forces were at work.

The endless tributary of Nolan's dreams readily serve as building blocks in his filmmaking. 'I first dreamed the end of *The Dark Knight Rises*,' he said, storing up the image for the film to follow, 'the idea of somebody taking over Batman and being in the Batcave.'[2] Back in his student days, he would set his alarm for 8am, regardless of how late he had been up talking film and philosophy the night before. He

▶ City of Dreams: Leonardo DiCaprio's Cobb (centre) and his team of dream thieves in a poster image showcasing *Inception*'s mind-bending imagery.

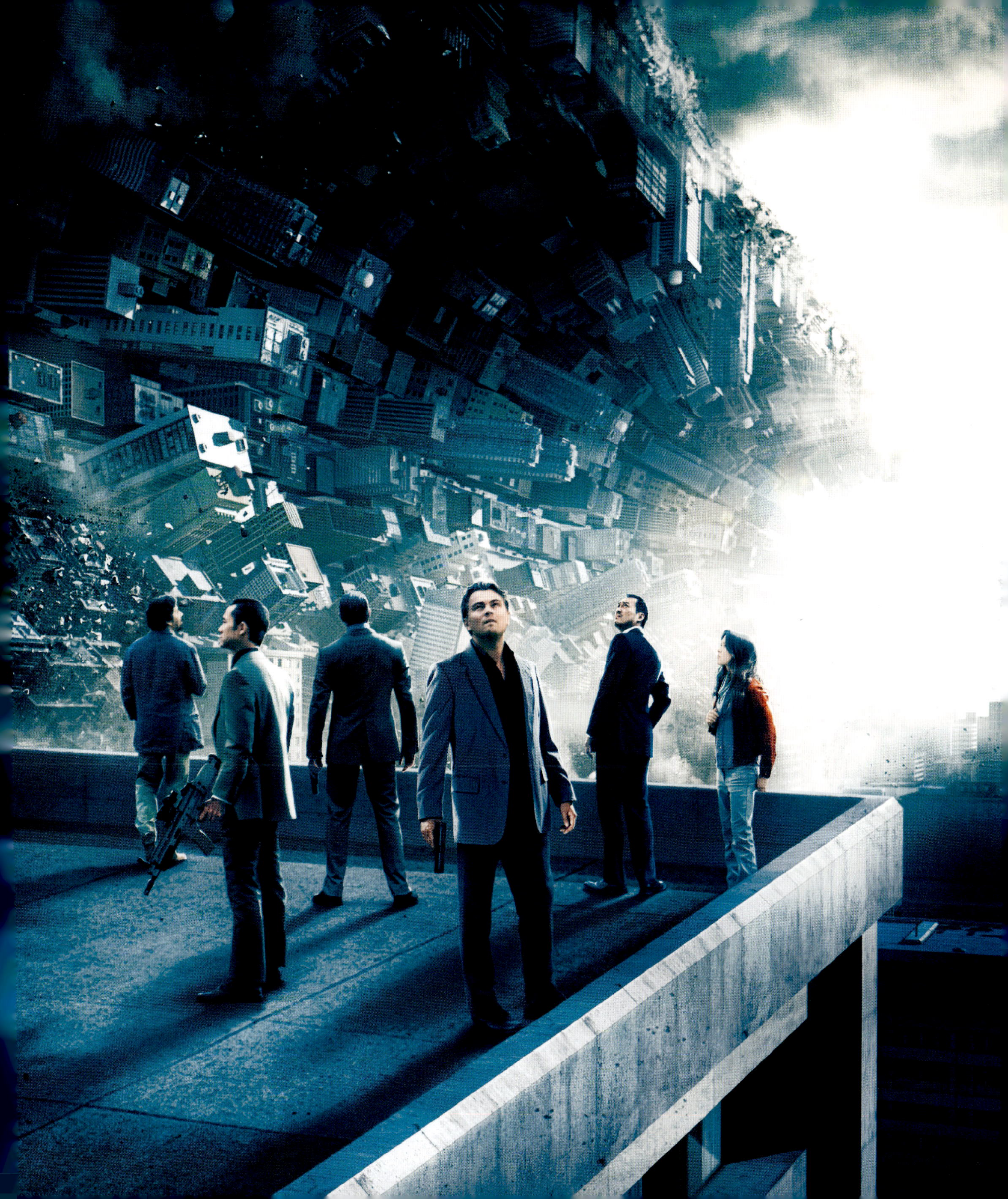

wanted to make sure he got his free breakfast from the University of London refectory, and would then go back to bed. But that second phase of sleep would always draw forth lucid dreams – dreams in which he was aware he was dreaming. In one, he recalled walking on a beach, knowing that his own mind had created every single grain of sand.

Two things fascinated Nolan about his subconscious creativity. First, that his dreams were not in the slightest bit like the cluttered surrealism with which movies tend to burden dream sequences. Outlandish stylists like David Lynch, Luis Buñuel, or the Coen brothers loved to warp reality into uncanny tableaux of mutant babies, eye-slitting, or Jeff Bridges gliding above LA on a magic carpet in *The Big Lebowski*. Second, how once you were within the grip of a dream, time became distorted. You might be dreaming for seconds, but it would always seem so much longer. Of course, he was already well aware that dreams were rather like movies.

Following the success of *The Dark Knight*, which had left Nolan in a position to make anything he wanted, it was the first time in eight years he hadn't known where he was headed next. Taking a month-long holiday on the island of Anna Maria near Florida, with its long beaches of white sand, his thoughts returned to his dream film, and he found that it was now Kubrickian in scope.

Drawing faith from the fact that *The Matrix* had become a sensation by pulling the rug out from beneath reality and selling an audience on 'a complex philosophical concept,'[3] he had a brainwave about brainwaves. 'It is in dreams our most valuable ideas take root,' he reasoned, 'and where they can be stolen.'[4] What if a dream space could be shared? Or, more to the point, *invaded*. So he switched genres, and over six months wrote the screenplay for his next film. Not coincidentally, it was his first solo script since *Memento*.

From one angle, *Inception* is what would happen if Nolan finally got to make his precious James Bond movie. Call it a thought experiment in blockbusting espionage. 'This is *absolutely* my Bond movie,' he laughed. 'I've been plundering ruthlessly from the Bond movies in everything I've done, forever.'[5] But not for Nolan the dash of international intrigue – the world is not enough. The very fact that groups of people could share the same dream created, he said, 'an infinite number of shared universes.' Each had their own rules and 'dramatic consequences.'[6] He sets a spy movie, or heist film, while it's certainly a thriller and arguably a love story – Nolan more eager than ever to slip between genres – in their quarry's subconscious.

'It's about the architecture of dreams,'[7] announced producer Emma Thomas, which was a perfectly rational pitch from the angular conceptualist to whom she was married. Though she had worried how they were going to pull this one off. Architecture is the central motif – buildings dreamed up by human minds, cities both real and imagined. 'Our minds create and perceive the world simultaneously,'[8] he mused, happy to put some distance between his film and the slew of

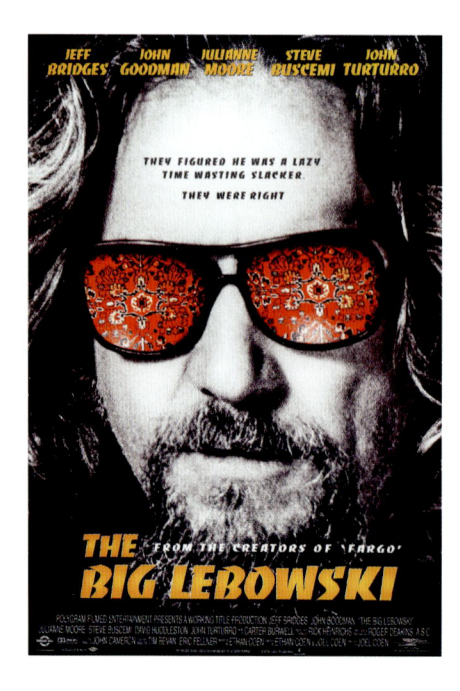

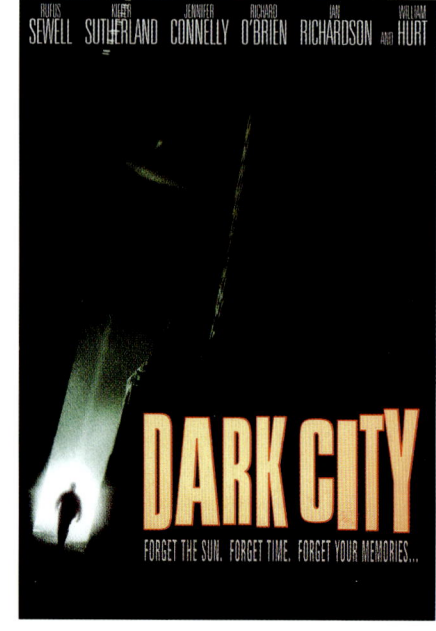

▶ The surreal deal – there is a long Hollywood history of dream sequences in films as diverse as *The Big Lebowski* and *Dark City* which Christopher Nolan felt bore very little comparison with 'real' dreaming.

◀ Nolan with wife and producer Emma Thomas attend the premiere of Inception in London, the town where they met.

alt-universe noirs that burst onto the surface of *The Matrix* like mould: *Dark City*, *The Thirteenth Floor*, *Equilibrium*, *Æon Flux*, et al. We are left to wonder how the pitch meeting went down, but Warner were transfixed by his flights of fancy. That the studio was willing to take a gamble on such an elusive plot – whose true nature may never become clear – spoke volumes about how Nolan had become a self-sustaining brand. 'Chris brings a lot to the party,'[9] reported Jeff Robinov, sanguine president of the motion picture group at the studio. He was as big as Batman.

And this was against a background of increasing conservatism among the studios. Perpetually risk-averse, by the mid-noughties they had become entrenched. 'IP' was the catchphrase hanging in the smoky air over Power Point presentations – the manna of a pre-existing intellectual property, much of it dumbed down to widen the appeal. Individual blockbusters were costing more, but the studios were making less. In March 2009, Disney purchased Marvel and accelerated the accumulation of its superhero catalogue on screen – this was no longer a franchise, it was a universe, as interconnected as it was relentless. Nolan was partly to blame. *The Dark Knight* had taken the genre seriously, and Marvel was mining that credibility.

So Warner happily rolled the dice on a $160 million thriller, about which they were expressly instructed to reveal nothing. Audiences genuinely had no idea what was in store. Nolan's film was being pre-sold on the strength of his reputation alone. Of all his films until *Tenet*, none came cloaked in greater secrecy than this tech-noir mind bender. Trailers sowed hints of sleek action, handsome stars in tailored suits, and phantasmagorical shifts in the laws of physics. Whole corridors began to spin.

That secrecy was its own language of hype. The less we knew, the bigger the film became in our imaginations. It turned out that *Inception* was (and remains) the apotheosis of Nolan's vision – a Bond movie by Borges.

At its outermost level, *Inception* is a heist movie with shades of corporate espionage. Cobb (Leonardo DiCaprio) and his crack team of specialists use a clandestine technology to penetrate the mind of a specific target. Typically, they want to steal information. But a more daring challenge is afoot. Cobb has been hired by business titan Saito (Ken Watanabe) to plant the idea of breaking up a company within their chosen target, Cillian Murphy's Fischer, heir apparent to a rival global corporation with soon-to-be-visualized Oedipal hang-ups. Nolan was surprised how few critics picked up on the fact he was satirizing the Murdoch dynasty long before the television series *Succession*.

INCEPTION 91

> *“Audiences genuinely had no idea what was in store… Of all his films until Tenet, none came cloaked in greater secrecy than his tech-noir mind bender.”*

▶ Establishing a dream logic – Leonardo DiCaprio and Christopher Nolan confer on the set of *Inception*.

▼ The casting of DiCaprio as head dream-thief Cobb was the first time Nolan had felt the need to employ an A-list star. Highly detail-orientated, DiCaprio would work on the script with his director for an entire year.

Access to the script was strictly controlled. Actors had to come to Nolan's office, or, if high enough on the Hollywood totem pole, have it delivered to their home with a guard on hand to take it back as soon as they were finished reading. Nolan had longed to work with DiCaprio, who represented a kindred anomaly. The Los Angeles-born actor was a superstar free of convention. He had shed the boyish appeal of *Titanic* mainly by becoming Martin Scorsese's muse of choice in *Gangs of New York*, *The Aviator* (as Howard Hughes) and corkscrew thriller *The Departed*. He and Nolan had talked over the years, promising to work something out. 'He sure as hell knows what he is doing,'[10] the star appreciated. When Nolan approached him in earnest for the central role of Cobb, dream thief and flawed hero, the actor had recently completed Scorsese's *Shutter Island*, which also played fast and loose with perception, madness and dead wives.

Nevertheless, the actor was intrigued by *Inception's* connection to Nolan's earlier films *Memento* and *Insomnia* in its fusion of psychological enquiry, genre and fractured storytelling. In fact, the new film completed an unofficial 'dark night' trilogy, reconnoitring the human psyche (not coincidentally, Cobb was also the name of the thief in Nolan's debut *Following*). 'It was cerebral,'[11] he appreciated.

Populated with distinctive, unusual actors, the gang of 'extractors' have the feel of seasoned, high-class crooks: sourpuss intelligence gatherer Arthur (Joseph Gordon-Levitt), identity thief Eames (Tom Hardy), and master of sleeping potions Yusuf (Dileep Rao). Most intriguing is new recruit Ariadne (Elliot Page), a dream architect whose mythological namesake provided the thread that guided Theseus from the Minotaur's lair. And the Minotaur in question is one of Cobb's making: the unwelcome psychic apparition of Mal (Marion Cotillard), his dead wife, who has a habit of disrupting the mission like a chic, mournful Joker.

Over the year leading up to production, DiCaprio worked closely with his director, easing a complex script in the direction of performance. He stressed the need for emotion, to emphasize the love story at the film's kernel in which Mal offers the temptation to remain forever within the illusion of the dream world. It was a fraught period, but Nolan could see the film becoming more resonant, more intense, and more tragic, a spin on Orpheus and Eurydice descending into the underworld. It also became more personal. A photo of young Nolan and Emma Thomas with their heads lain on the tracks of a railway line during a Californian holiday became a memory of Cobb and Mal, lying on rails. Trains will run through *Inception* – even in so-called reality.

There are rules that govern the film's fantasies, struts of logic that Nolan puts in place lest his movie fritter into nonsense. Within his conceptual architecture, the film will submerge and then resurface through a multi-story of dreams. Five different levels running concurrently, each at a different tempo, and each conjured up – to Ariadne's specifications – by a separate member of the team enclosed within the psyche of Murphy's target Fischer, whose subconscious generates armed bodyguards to fend off attack. Back in what we take to be reality, they are all connected via the tubes of Cobb's intravenous dream tech, lying back in the first-class seats of a 747 like heroin addicts.

Nolan's rules are both abstract and precise. Each level physically influences the one below, each sleeper is 'kicked' awake from above when the time comes. Each extractor carries with them a personal 'totem' which can determine if they are conscious or unconscious. Cobb uses a spinning top – if it topples, it's proof he's no longer dreaming. If you

INCEPTION 93

◀ Ariadne (Elliot Page) receives an initiation into the world of dream manipulation from Cobb (Leonardo DiCaprio).

die in a dream, you descend into Limbo, a deep, collective, Jungian subconscious where eons pass in minutes; we see it, via Cobb's crumbling subconscious and nine months of conceptual drawing, as a vast, mutant cityscape of gullies and ravines, sat on the edge of an ocean with a long, grey beach.

Here was a director trusting that his audience was sophisticated enough. We didn't need spoon-feeding. He believed in our imaginations. As Jonah Nolan perceived it, 'Now the level of audience scrutiny has roughly reached parity with what he is doing.'[12]

Effectively, Cobb and his dream-making cohorts are an allegory of filmmakers. Nolan admitted that the make-up of his fictional characters parallels a crew: Cobb is the director; Arthur the producer; Ariadne the production designer; Eames the actor; Saito the studio, backing the enterprise; Fischer the audience, and so on. One line of interpretation is that *Inception* is not a film about dreams at all, but movies.

From the very first, the dual propositions of film and dream were interlinked. Hollywood became the dream factory. Films were the nearest thing we had to a translation of our sleeping state. Leastways, they shared similar rules: cutting between scenes, constructing narratives from images, twisting reality, distorting time, stories often sparked by anxiety. In turn, critics used Freudian techniques, psychoanalysis, to decode a director's intentions.

Inception is a film built from films. Watching it, said Scott Foundas in the *SF Weekly*, is 'like taking an illustrated tour of Nolan's cinematic subconscious. Shamelessly plundering the films that have inspired him.'[13]

'I didn't set out to make a movie about movies,'[14] insisted Nolan. The imagery simply needed to resonate on a shared level. Cinema, he knew instinctively, worked as a collective memory, shared dreams. It was like a spinning top – a film about dreams being like films.

So it wasn't only Bond and Kubrick: here were Michael Mann's slick contemporary cityscapes of crime and punishment and Ridley Scott's gaunt realism, even the streets of Nolan's own Gotham City. 'I'm mindful of the great directors I carry with me,'[15] he said. From further afield, he called upon the rich noir antecedents of *The Maltese Falcon*, the strangeness of Hitchcock's *Vertigo* and *North By Northwest*, the slick criminal brotherhood of *Ocean's 11*, and the urban dystopia of anime classic *Akira*. This was surrealism delivered by a master surgeon.

Within the unbounded filmmaking of *Inception*, M.C. Escher serves as concept artist as Haussmann's Parisian boulevards are bent back on themselves like colossal origami (literally blockbusting). 'You never remember the beginning of dreams, do you?'[16] Cobb says to Ariadne. It is as if the dapper heroes gatecrash movies already underway. A.O. Scott in the *New York Times* would grumble that these weren't dreams at all, but 'different kinds of action movies crammed together.'[17]

'What Chris accomplishes here,' said DiCaprio, 'besides the emotional journey, is the constant, unrelenting feeling of suspense and infinite possibility. You never know what is going to happen next.'[18]

▶ Team member Arthur (Joseph Gordon-Levitt), whose job it is to procure intelligence ahead of the mission.

▼ Reality or phantasm? Arthur (Gordon-Levitt, left) and Cobb (DiCaprio, right) strike a deal with industrialist Saito (Ken Watanabe) in an exaggerated Japanese setting.

▲ The famous Parisian city blocks are bent back on themselves like an M.C. Escher sketch.

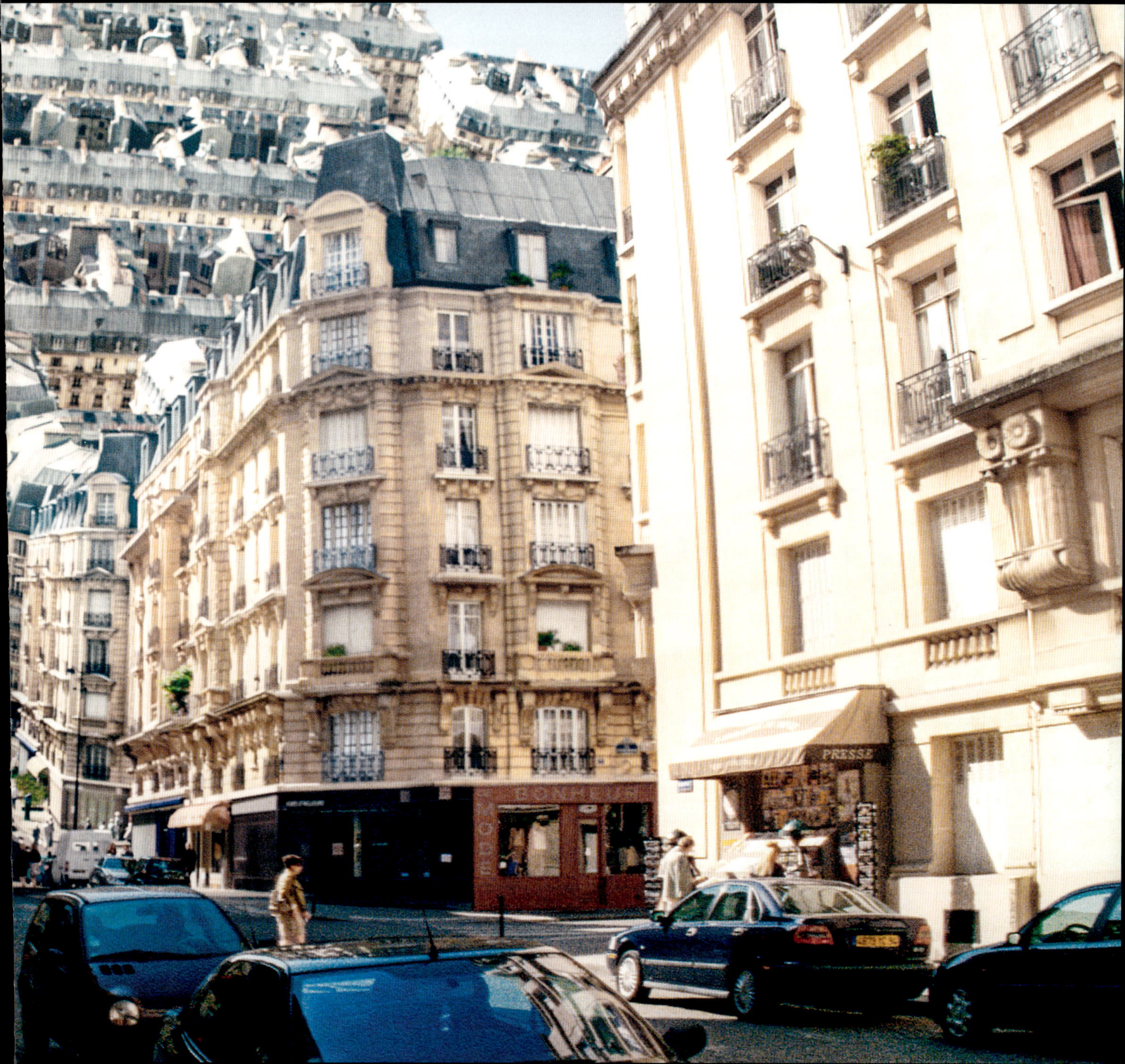

▶ Dreams within dreams – Arthur (Joseph Gordon-Levitt) stays 'awake' on the hotel complex, the second level of *Inception*'s tiered structure of dreaming.

Nolan was free to, well, dream up anything he wanted. The levels of *Inception* are knowingly constructed in the taut, super-charged noir of Nolanesque: they have the same hard clarity, the symphonic greys, the Brutalist architecture, and bursts of extravagant action.

With shooting commencing on 9 June 2009, this required seven months of circling the globe: Tokyo; the outskirts of London; Paris, Tangier, Los Angeles, and the icy mountainsides beyond Calgary in Canada. Indeed, exactly the lavish flight-plans that came with a Bond movie. 'It has to feel like you can go absolutely anywhere by the end of the film,'[19] said Nolan.

What we take to be reality featured Tokyo – where the deal is struck with Saito, hovering over the sprawling city in a helicopter – and Tangier, with its cluttered, discordant streets. Yet nowhere ever feels wholly present. Nolan told cinematographer Wally Pfister he wanted the validity of the real world throughout. 'No superfluous surrealism.'[20] At the same time, every location needed to evoke an unsettling aura, as if something was out of joint. It was about atmosphere. There would be no space for the bulky IMAX cameras, with dizzying handheld shooting the cornerstone of their approach. The audience should be uncertain about the difference between dream and reality.

We learn that Cobb is a fugitive, on the run for allegedly killing his wife, unable to return home to his children. Pull off this one last job and Saito can use his influence to clear his name. In Paris, where he tutors Ariadne (and us), we learn the rules and limits of dream manipulation. We learn about the plan.

The first level of dream was filmed in Downtown Los Angeles in a downpour (dreamer Yusuf has forgotten to empty his bladder), where a train crashes though a city street without rails. The full-sized locomotive was constructed over the chassis of an eighteen-wheeler, with Pfister up close and shaking the camera by hand. The propulsion of vehicles with fluid grace is now a mainstay of Nolan's aesthetic. 'I wanted every shot moving,' he said. 'Putting the audience into the experience.'[21] Like early James Cameron, he poeticizes the clichés of a worn-out genre.

Whether they buy into his ideas or not, Nolan wants his audience to feel the effort. To know that the filmmakers have poured everything into it. 'I want that effort there – I want that sincerity.'[22]

98   CHRISTOPHER NOLAN

INCEPTION 99

◀ Inflight espionage: Cobb (Leonardo DiCaprio) eyes up the team's quarry – Cillian Murphy's Robert Fischer, heir to a media empire.

Take the dazzling second level, set in a sleek, modernist, Nolanesque hotel, all steel and glass, which was constructed in the former aircraft hangars turned gigantic soundstages at Cardington, Bedfordshire, where he had once erected Gotham. It was here he finally birthed his version of the centrifuge: the film's signature image, a spinning hotel corridor, 100 feet long, rotating on its axis eight times a minute as the integrity of the heist breaks down and the dreams become more dreamlike.

This was not only a take on Kubrick's *2001* Ferris Wheel, but on Fred Astaire dancing on the ceiling in *Royal Wedding*, for which the set could spin like a tumble drier. 'I was interested in taking those ideas, techniques, and philosophies and applying them to an action scenario,'[23] said Nolan.

The spinning hallway rotated through 360 degrees like a rotisserie, the camera moving independently on a crane or mounted on a specially designed rail, as the van containing the sleeping Arthur is spiralling through the air toward a river in the level above. A second identical hallway stood vertically on its end, with the camera gazing up as actors and stuntmen were raised or lowered on wires. Cardington's voluminous sheds also housed an entire hotel bar which could be tilted to thirty degrees, and a horizontal elevator shaft. It was a dream factory.

Nolan is a 'brilliant engineer-artist,'[24] said Chris Corbould, special effects supervisor. He doesn't simply design shots, he conceptualizes the means and apparatus to make them happen.

'Anything he can think of, anything, he can do it,'[25] marvelled Gordon-Levitt, who had to train for weeks to partake in a stunning zero-gravity fight sequence.

The third level of *Inception's* dream sequences was found in Fortress Mountain, a ski resort near Calgary, where, 7,600 feet above sea level, a full-scale neo-Brutalist fortress was built while the production made its lap of global cityscapes. The air was bitingly cold, the winds getting up to 100mph, as the dream turns hostile. And amid the grand tradition of ski chases and shoot-outs, the team attempt to gain access to the fortress and the vault in which they plan to plant their idea. Here, Nolan was drawing direct inspiration from his favourite of the suite of 007 films – *On Her Majesty's Secret Service*. 'It's a hell of a movie, it holds up very well,'[26] he laughed, well aware the single George Lazenby entry is an unorthodox way to go. He loved the balance of romanticism and action, scale and tragedy. 'Of all the Bond films,' he said, 'it is the most emotional.'[27] And it had ski chases to die for.

With forty sticks of dynamite and eighty barrels of gasoline, they would eventually blow up their fortress, with the wreckage tumbling down the mountain. Even in dreams, you still need explosions. Interiors of the fortress were built on the Warner Brothers lot in Los Angeles, and nearby Universal Studios, including a raised set so that the floor could collapse using giant pistons.

'In retrospect, I wouldn't have been able to do this film until I had done the *Batman* films,' Nolan later reflected, 'because it's on such a massive scale.'[28] Which was why the film had to wait until Nolan had become a prestige director. Each level needed a distinctive look and feel, as he would increasingly crosscut between characters and dream levels as the film reached its crescendo, with Hans Zimmer's throbbing, growling score surging in unison. The colour palate changes from the cold sterility of Calgary to the warm hues of the hotel corridor. You should immediately know where you are.

Almost to a critic, the reviews claimed this to be a film that could

▶ Fred Astaire famously dances onto the ceiling within the rotating set of *Royal Wedding*, which served as inspiration for...

only have sprung from the forehead of Nolan. The entire movie serves as a metaphor for his entire ethos – *immersion*. We plunge into his films, and accept every level as reality. Certain now of his signature, the hot, strange currents that flow around his films, where psychological insight is as much a venue as a trait. Good films get into the minds of their characters.

Précising the plot was a trial, but reviews were quick to praise provocative ideas nestled within the skin of a mainstream movie. The twistiness! The scale! The pounding score! The labyrinthine concept! A suggestion lingered that many critics really hadn't a clue what was going on.

'Like *Memento*, the most intellectually demanding of Nolan's previous films, *Inception* demands and rewards our total attention as well as our emotional engagement,' wrote Philip French in the *Observer*. 'You'll want to see it again but not, I think, on the same day.'[29]

Not all were so sure that the fabulous intricacies hid anything at their core. David Denby of *The New Yorker* saw a director driven unheedingly to construct great celluloid puzzles out of his own cleverness. 'But why? To what end?' he wondered. 'His new movie, *Inception*, is an astonishment, an engineering feat, and, finally, a folly.'[30]

Audiences were ready and willing to be baffled. In a summer of duds, *Inception* was heralded as a saviour, an original film making $836 million at the worldwide box office, reinforcing Nolan's global appeal. But that was only the beginning.

▲ ...Christopher Nolan's now iconic spinning corridor, a real spinning set, and arguably the signature image of his entire career.

INCEPTION 101

▲ Less is so much more: despite (or maybe down to) its wilfully obscure marketing material, *Inception* would become a massive worldwide hit.

▶ Master dreamer - Christopher Nolan briefs DiCaprio and Page on what lies beneath.

▶ Boulevards of broken dreams – Ariadne (Page) and Cobb (DiCaprio) shelter within an exploding Paris street.

▼ Dream team briefing – from the left: Cobb (Leonardo DiCaprio), Ariadne (Elliot Page), Eames (Tom Hardy), Arthur (Joseph Gordon-Levitt), Yusuf (Dileep Rao), and Saito (Ken Watanabe).

INCEPTION 103

▶ Cobb (Leonardo DiCaprio) concentrates on his dream totem – if it stops spinning he must be in reality.

At its heart, protested Nolan, 'it was a big action movie.'[31] He hadn't set out to bamboozle audiences. But therein lies the rub – his films continually propose questions he refuses to answer. He waves away the protests. These things are background radiation, the thread in the suit, they shouldn't affect our cinematic pleasure. But fans were never likely to let things rest. Indeed, this stand-off between creator and followers has spawned an industry of Nolan deconstruction, with cabals of internet extractors tunnelling into the director's psyche, and *Inception* standing as the *ne plus ultra* of fan exploration.

Why is it Cobb who shapes Limbo? What is it the ancient Saito whispers to him at the end? Where do the never-ending staircases come from? Why is Mal haunting his footsteps? It goes on… riddles wrapped in mysteries inside enigmas encased in a sleek, populist action movie.

On a more general level, you can read *Inception* as a film about the pursuit of originality; a pointed crack at Hollywood's homogenization. Like a mantra, characters are pushed to dream new dreams, embrace new possibilities. 'Always imagine new places,'[32] Cobb instructs Ariadne. It is nostalgia that entraps the hero. Dreams and memories are different things; combine them and you could lose your grasp on what is real. Is this what has happened to Cobb? And by default to us? While we watch we believe the film to be real.

Leaving the cinema, our heads still spinning, we whispered uncertainly about the meaning behind the final image – Cobb's brass totem still spinning on the table top. Is it wobbling? Ready to fall? It took days for Nolan and his editor for find exactly the right, ambiguous frame. The happy ending, it hinted, might be another illusion. A convincing theory abides that Nolan's ultimate gambit is that *all* of *Inception* takes place inside a dream. Think of the strange alley that narrows to a slit as Cobb is chased through 'real' Tangier. Why haven't his children aged? Why is everyone so weirdly friendly at the airport? Can it be that film has no reality? Then, of course, it is a fiction conjured up from Nolan's imagination. The thing about spinning tops, he said, 'is that they do destabilize and stabilize.'[33] Cut. Time to wake up.

▶ Ghosts of the subconscious – Mal (Marion Cotillard), Cobb's dead wife, in a vision from happier times...

▼ ...but she is a figment with an agenda – Mal (Cotillard) threatens to disrupt Cobb's plans as Saito (Ken Watanabe) looks on. Notice that the setting is the same as for Saito's meeting in so-called reality.

THE BIG GOODBYE

The Dark Knight Rises (2012)

For his eighth trick, he would bring his grand Batman saga to its triumphal conclusion, with an epic tale of revolution and redemption, though its reception would be more mixed

The opening sequence could have graced any James Bond movie. In truth, Christopher Nolan was now working on a level not even 007 could aspire to. It is also worth noting that the recent Daniel Craig incarnation of the beloved British spy – tougher of bark, wounded of soul – had fixed its compass on Nolan's school of brooding realism. In any case, without a lick of CGI, high over the Scottish highlands a daring mid-air hijack takes place, magnified by IMAX (half of the new film would be shot in Nolan's prized format, compared to only twenty-eight minutes of its predecessor). The quarry are two hooded CIA prisoners: a scientist (with the know-how to drive a fusion reactor, one of the film's plethora of MacGuffins) and a mysterious figure revealed to have a shaven head, the shoulders of a bison, an elaborate respirator clamped to his face, and the designation of Bane. Via extended cables, one plane will grapple another like a bird of prey. The smaller CIA turboprop will lose its wings, its tail, and plummet to the earth, but not before the cabin is tipped vertically like one of the disorientating dreams in *Inception*. The two prisoners finally abscond through the air, clinging to a cable reeled in by a C-130 Hercules. It is trick worthy of *The Prestige*… if the magicians had had $250 million at their disposal (darker rumours put the budget at $300 million).

'It doesn't matter who we are,' intones Bane through his mask like a Shakespearean grandee with a head cold, 'what matters is the *plan*.'[1]

No truer sentence has ever been said of the Nolan way. The plan is everything. And where *The Dark Knight* was about escalation, the follow-up was about *expansion*. Everything was bigger: the budget, the running time (two hours forty-five minutes!), the quota of villains, the stunts, the vehicles (there would be no less than three Tumblers crashing through the streets), the Batcave (now with its own waterfall), and the nefarious plot to bring down Gotham once and for all.

If Nolan had fretted about sequels, part threes were anathema. 'There are no good third sequels,'[2] he insisted. Though Warner were always pressing for sequels, the security of a franchise, there was within the ongoing saga this sense that Bruce Wayne's story was finite. But his endgame had not yet been fought. Back in Nolan's garage, his creative cavern, as he and David S. Goyer tested ideas, he knew that this was not a sequel but the conclusion of a trilogy.

▶ Batman in crisis – a promotional image for *The Dark Knight Rises* suggests a hero about to face his ultimate test.

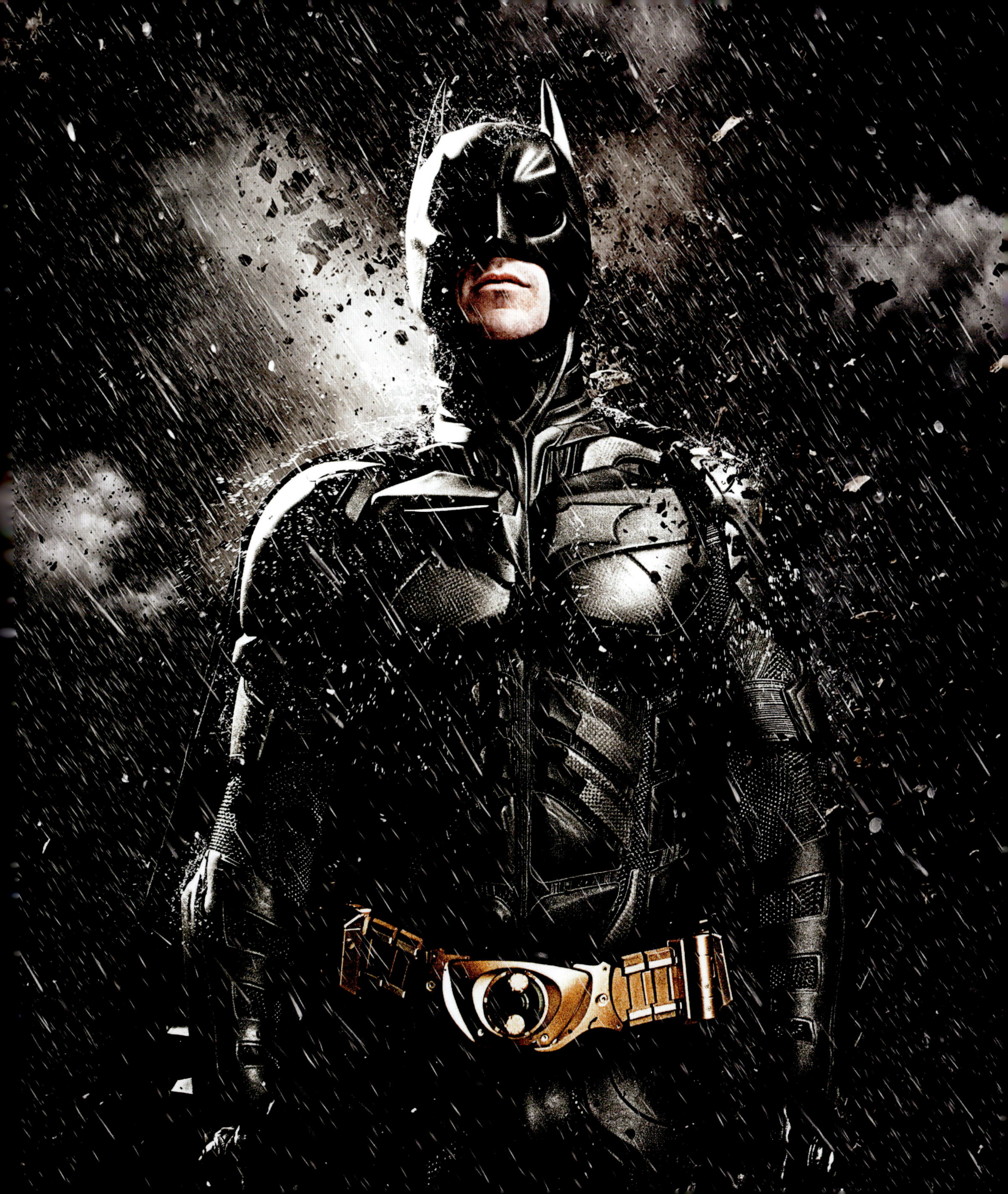

When Jonah suggested they use Charles Dickens' *A Tale of Two Cities* as the basis for a new Batman adventure, Nolan's contrarian juices began to flow. Fundamentally, he realized that events had to be bigger this time. There was no going back, the audience wouldn't accept a reduction in scale (Batman trapped in a motel room). As Jonah advised, they needed to think of this as a third act, and they were going to see what would happen when the villain's diabolical plan for the city actually came to fruition. The French Revolution would be transplanted to Gotham, adding spice to the trilogy's social commentary, and thousands to the cast list. 'We felt we had a story to tell,'[3] concluded Nolan.

So he was shifting genres again into the epic mode (with Jonah citing *The Iliad* and *The Odyssey* as guiding lights). He wanted the ancient flamboyance of DeMille (biographer Tom Shone called him the 'DeMille of disorientation'[4]), the history and romanticism of *Doctor Zhivago*, and the disaster-movie extravagance of *The Towering Inferno*.

'When you take on these icons,' said Nolan, talking about the exaggerations of comic-book characters, 'you are allowed to indulge in this grand-scale storytelling that you can't in other genres.'[5] He was going to miss that operatic quality. This world allowed very large emotions.

And what is Batman's latest trauma to keep the wheels of drama turning? Well, he and Gotham, their natures always aligned, are chilled by winter's touch. The rivers freeze, snow falls on troubled streets, a film noir is underway in daylight like *Insomnia*. There is a temporal arc across the three films for when we see Batman at large: from the depths of night in *Batman Begins*, through a mix of night and magic hour in *The Dark Knight*, to broad daylight. Which was partly down to improvements in the design of the Batsuit and partly about how much our hero is willing to show himself to the people of Gotham.

For now Bruce Wayne is a recluse, abjectly hobbling around the new Wayne Manor (shot at Wollaton Hall in Nottinghamshire) like Howard Hughes in his Las Vegas phase, his body and spirit broken, wrestling with his demons as Alfred fusses. 'There is this idea that he hasn't moved on,'[6] said Nolan. Batman is no more than a rumour, a myth.

▲ The Batcave is reborn – Alfred (Michael Caine) and Bruce Wayne (Christian Bale) investigate the rise of their new foe beside the dramatic new water feature.

▶ If the suit fits ... Wayne (Bale) contemplates having to come back out of retirement.

THE DARK KNIGHT RISES 109

▲ A promotional image of the mighty Bane (Tom Hardy) – Christopher Nolan reimagined the comic-book thug as a modern, masked Robespierre fomenting revolution in Gotham.

Eight years have passed since the events of *The Dark Knight* (there was barely a year between the first two films). Time enough, Nolan decided, to see the results of the sacrifices made at the end of that film. Gotham's criminal leanings are being kept in check by the Dent Act – granting the police added power to stifle organized crime. To some it's martial law, a police state. And there is a growing suspicion that Dent may not have been a paragon. The underclass is growing restless.

To allow space for the coming storm, and add the bite of winter, Nolan moved Gotham to a new venue. With specific locations captured in Glasgow, London, New Jersey, and New York, the majority of filming took place in Pittsburgh. Each film brings a different emanation from the city. Now it was a hard grey light, something of the bleached-out quality of *Memento* when it hit the streets, and what Nolan saw as the pulp ambience of James M. Cain and Dashiell Hammett's fiction.

The Joker's whereabouts go unmentioned. Nolan had no intention of recasting the part, though there were various propositions from Goyer that had involved a hunt for the deadly clown in a potential third film. How could they ever hope to catch lightning in a bottle like that again? The role belonged to Heath Ledger's legacy. So the director needed a new ringleader. A brief creative debate was had with Warner Brothers, with the studio all for the arrival of the Riddler (and Leonardo DiCaprio's name springing into the gossip columns). But the Riddler is in essence just the Joker in a leotard.

Bane was relatively new to the comic-book mythology: when he debuted in 1993, he was no more than a thug in a wrestling mask. In the lamentable *Batman & Robin* (1997), he had been played by the wrestler Jeep Swenson as a grunting henchman. This was a serious upgrade in intellect and charisma, but Nolan still wanted a character who was a physical match for Batman – indeed, one capable of breaking his back (as he had done in the *Knightfall* series of comics).

He is played by *Inception's* Tom Hardy (part of the growing number of established Nolan players), bulked up by 200lb, wrapped in a sheepskin jacket designed to echo both Dickens' revolutionaries and a WWII military aesthetic, and beneath a face mask shaped like the jaws of a wild animal, through which he valiantly tries to direct a performance. 'Bane is someone ravaged by pain from a trauma suffered long ago,' explained Nolan. 'And the mask dispenses a type of anaesthetic that keeps his pain just below the threshold so he can function.'[7] The lack of available expression hampers Hardy's range – as did an initially dense sound edit that left audiences complaining they couldn't understand a word he said. So much so, Nolan had to remix it.

He's a presence, no doubt about that. And with the crackling voice – once we could make it out – of Ian McKellen playing Professor Moriarty over a walkie-talkie. Nolan called the accent 'colonial'[8]: could it have been the kind of thing he would have heard day in day out at boarding school? In fact, it became something of a contest among critics to try and get a fix on Hardy's vocal athletics. 'Sean Connery on Appletinis,'[9] hooted *Movieline*. 'Darth Vader with an Irish accent,'[10] offered *Easy Reader News* (and the bronchial rasping is surely Nolan's homage to Vader). 'Vincent Price talking through a window fan,'[11] smirked the *Village Voice*.

▼ A more dapper-looking Hardy at the premiere – one of a growing number of actors whom Nolan frequently returns to.

▲ The look for Hardy's Bane mixed Second World War fighter pilot and guerrilla with a science-fiction face mask that makes him almost part-machine.

THE DARK KNIGHT RISES 111

Hardy went on record as saying he based it on an Irish bare-knuckle boxer named Bartley Gorman. 'He's the king of the gypsies,' he explained, 'and he's a boxer, a bare-knuckle boxer, an Irish traveller, a gypsy.'[12] Albeit a gypsy king who is overseeing the assembly of a nuclear bomb with which to lay waste to Gotham and complete the League of Shadows' destiny. If the Joker was Gotham's id, then Bane is its Super-ego. In other words, he talks like a Bond villain.

He is also a mirror of Batman, without the civility of the Wayne-alter ego to rely on – another orphan trained into supremacy by the League of Shadows. Notice how hero's and villain's face coverings are opposites: Batman's cowl covers everything but his nose and mouth, while Bane's steampunk inhaler covers only his nose and mouth. Each is to an extent defined by their voice. All of Nolan's villains cause Batman to question his own calling. They show a path he might have taken. All of the villains represent part of his personality – though Nolan would contend that the Joker is a law unto himself.

In the same way that Batman's cause is an obsession, said Nolan, 'Bane is fanatical, he is convinced by what he is doing.'[13] He is a general, Robespierre crossed with Schwarzenegger. Nolan likened him to Kurtz from *Apocalypse Now* (and is there a tincture of Brando in that voice?) – a man with a mission. 'Which, again, takes us back to the Homeric epic villains where the whole idea was to raze the thing to the ground, then salt the fields and just completely annihilate,'[14] added Jonah.

For the energy of a city at war with itself, Nolan bid his team look at Gillo Pontecorvo's acclaimed 1966 docudrama about the Algerian uprising against their French occupiers, *The Battle of Algiers*. They also watched David Lean's *Doctor Zhivago* for how that romantic classic portrays a Moscow transformed by revolution, with empty streets, crowded interiors, and the bite of the Russian winter. Nolan was again drawing upon the history of film to vivify the comic-book landscape. Fritz Lang's faithful *Metropolis* provided him with the relationship between 'architecture and theme.'[15] The idea of social strata made literal with the poor relegated to the sewers. Bane's uprising will spew out of the sewers that run beneath the city, the embodiment of its corruption, which has a certain Dickensian and Langian flavour to it.

▼ The poster for Fritz Lang's *Metropolis* – a direct influence on *The Dark Knight Rises*, and a guiding spirit across all of Christopher Nolan's films.

▲ Nolan studied David Lean's epic *Doctor Zhivago* to see how he created scenes of the Russian Revolution.

▶ Bigger is better – Nolan inspects the frame through one of his beloved IMAX cameras. Over half the film was shot using this huge format.

112 CHRISTOPHER NOLAN

THE DARK KNIGHT RISES 113

▶ Though never named as such in the film, there was no missing the fact that Anne Hathaway's jewel thief was an updated version of Catwoman.

Midway through the film, the hero will literally be broken by this foe – the supermano-a-supermano showdowns do have the ungainliness of wrestling – and locked away in a far-off prison, back in the League's almost medieval world. Known as The Pit, its exteriors were filmed in the wilderness of Jaipur when the seven-month shoot began on 6 May 2011. The depths of the prison were created as a set in the vast confines of the Cardington hangars. Conceived by Jonah, it's an extraordinary construction, open to the sky like the bottom of a well: there is nothing preventing escape except the almost impossible climb up above the Escher-like stairways. 'The secret is not to use a safety rope,' noticed Kim Newman in *Sight & Sound*, 'but to rely on strength of character.'[16] Wayne's arduous climb serves as a metaphor for the rebirth of Batman. With Nolan's inverted tendencies, this is a fall-and-rise story.

Jonah had to convince his brother about Catwoman. Nolan struggled to shake the image of Eartha Kitt vamping it up in the sixties television show, and worried the character might defy the poise of their world. 'It was about who would this person be in real life,'[17] he insisted, and Jonah mapped out Selina Kyle (she is only ever dubbed 'the Cat'[18]) as a drifter figure

▲ Street fighters – Bane (Tom Hardy) and Batman (Christian Bale) duke it out in snowy Gotham in broad daylight.

with a criminal record, determined to get her hands on the 'clean slate'[19] technology, which will forever clear her name. She wants her freedom from the Orwellian grip of Gotham.

While the casting was hotly debated (would it be Natalie Portman or Keira Knightley or Lady Gaga?), for Nolan it was always about 'the authenticity'[20] that Anne Hathaway would bring, inside and out. He liked that she had an instinct for showmanship, which the character needed, what he called 'a dancelike quality'[21] in the cat-burglar's movement. That said, she still endured a gruelling training program for months to perfect her high-kicking style, and proves a worthy foil-cum-love interest for Batman-cum-Bruce. Kyle will both betray and offer salvation for Batman (and thus betray her own deviant soul), and the standout Hathaway brings a verve and humour to challenge all the gothic seriousness. Marginally better adjusted, she is the third film's equivalent of the Joker.

THE DARK KNIGHT RISES

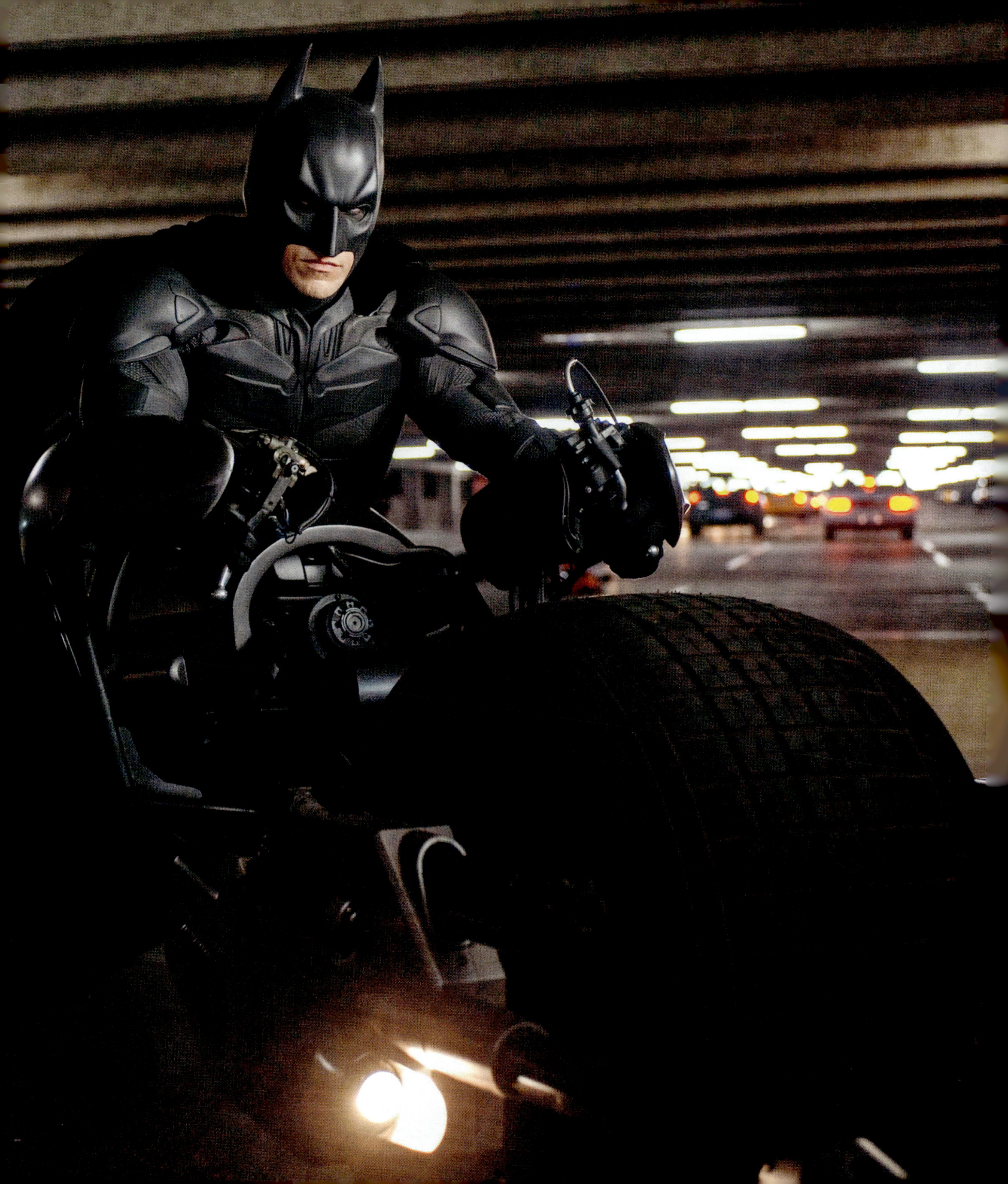

▲ In search of scale for his battleground, Christopher Nolan also shot a lot of Gotham in Pittsburgh, a location that provided a suitably chilly climate.

◀ Gary Oldman is finally promoted to Commissioner Gordon, but is still fighting the good fight at street level.

▲ Joseph Gordon-Levitt as the rookie cop who aids Batman's cause and will prove to have a significant identity.

◀ A promotional image of Christian Bale astride the Batpod, ready to slide between traffic on the chaotic streets of Gotham – with Chicago once again providing a road system for the action.

THE DARK KNIGHT RISES

> " *Time and memory, those Nolan fascinations, all play their part. The ghosts of dead parents, dead loves, and dead villains fill the cold air of the winter-gripped city.* "

There is another villain hiding in plain sight. Forming a love triangle with the flighty Selina. Having disrupted Cobb's imagination in *Inception*, Marion Cotillard plays seductive business woman Miranda Tate who is secretly Talia al Ghul – more dual identities – daughter of Liam Neeson's Ra's al Ghul from *Batman Begins*. As Newman also pointed out in *Sight & Sound*, she has 'exactly the same motivation' as Batman: 'making the city pay for the death of the father.'[22] Time and memory, those Nolan fascinations, all play their part. The ghosts of dead parents, dead loves, and dead villains fill the cold air of the winter-gripped city. To add to the stew and round up the mythology... Cillian Murphy's Scarecrow completes a cameo in each film, presiding over a kangaroo court to try the fate of Gotham's rich, where Bane sits like Dickens' Madame Defarge.

If the film is the story of expansion, it is also one of detonation. For a cerebral man, Nolan sure loves to blow the joint. With Batman in exile, Bane takes over the city, blowing up a football field and a succession of bridges in a rare but majestic CGI-generated shot, leaving the island cut off from the outside world. Holding the fort as best they can until the Dark Knight returns are Commissioner Gordon (Gary Oldman) and an idealistic rookie cop named John Blake (Joseph Gordon-Levitt), another who hides a dual identity. In a rare example of Nolan being playful, we learn his legal name is Robin.

Once more Nolan draws our attention to the timing of his story. The second half quickens into a countdown, and back into a Bond-like mode, with

▲ Partners in crime-fighting – the identity of Joseph Gordon-Levitt's Blake will begin to connect the dots between the debonair Bruce Wayne and Batman.

◀ Femmes fatales – Wayne (Bale) will find himself caught between two mysterious women. Firstly, the slippery Selina Kyle (Anne Hathaway)...

Bane's bomb rigged to blow. 'You tell a story over a long time-span and then accelerate it at the end, so time is very elastic in the film,'[23] explained Nolan. The clock starts ticking as it will through *Dunkirk*, for which the latter half of *The Dark Knight Rises* feels like a trial run. He had read that it was Lang who had realized that you countdown to an explosion. If you counted upwards there was no limit. You need the sense of an ending approaching. Various strands of story and character and location and momentum are intertwined with Hans Zimmer's cascading music. Action films, Nolan insisted, are a 'piece of music.'[24] You need to flow in and out of crescendos.

The epic gives way to a war film, the pell-mell of battle in the streets. 'It is a complete shattering of the structures of society,'[25] said Nolan. Morgan Freeman's fantastic Mr Lucius Fox provides Batman with a bespoke combo of helicopter and Harrier Jump Jet, like a flying lobster, which he christens simply The Bat.

Even the social anxieties reflected by *The Dark Knight Rises* have grown in scope, with capitalism itself under scrutiny. The film was written during the financial collapse of 2008, and parallels can be drawn between Bane's assault on the Gotham stock market and the New York Occupy Wall Street movement, which was active when they were shooting in New York. 'We literally had to schedule around them,'[26] said Nolan. It was important that Wayne lose everything in order to triumph. But Nolan insisted his Batman films were not 'political acts.'[27] Rebellion and social control are both cast in a problematic light, and Nolan was accused of conservatism.

▲ ...and secondly, the beguiling businesswoman Miranda Tate (Marion Cotillard), here pictured with Lucius Fox (Morgan Freeman).

THE DARK KNIGHT RISES 119

▶ Christopher Nolan patrols the wintry Pittsburgh set of *The Dark Knight Rises*, with the new militarized Tumbler revealing the film's secret guise as a war movie.

▼ A farewell to arms – Nolan was determined to bring his Batman saga to a fitting conclusion, without any plans to return.

▶ While getting a more mixed reaction than its predecessor, *The Dark Knight Rises* was still a billion-dollar hit, completing a hugely influential trilogy.

Released on 20 July 2012, his final Batman film was met with equal parts rapture and diffidence. Nolan wasn't untouchable. There was an undercurrent of backlash (Batlash?) 'Nolan has become hooked on the grandiose, at times even the biblical,'[28] said the *New Statesman*. *The Dark Knight Rises*, scolded *The New Yorker*, 'is murky, interminable, confused, and dropsical with self-importance.'[29] There was no let-up at the box office as it opened with $160 million, before going on to crack the billion mark, but there was, unfairly, a pervading sense that this was a lesser film than its predecessors.

The trilogy ends with Wayne and Kyle alive and well in Paris, with a clean slate, much like the director. Does it signify anything that this resembles a shot straight out of *Inception*? Another dream? Meanwhile, Robin follows the path to the Batcave, just as Nolan had dreamed it, and we are left to wonder if he's being primed to take over. A parting gift from Nolan to Warner to match the playing card he had left behind in *Batman Begins*. But he shrugged it off. The studio was entitled to do what it wants, but as far as he was concerned it was a thematic gesture, 'which is that Batman is a symbol. He can be anybody, and that was very important to us.'[30] That theory didn't sit well with fans – didn't he *need* to be a billionaire playboy who did a lot of push-ups? Or his young protégé? They wanted to believe Bale might return.

'I think what we endeavoured to do was not the complete story of Batman but our complete story of this character,'[31] reflected Jonah, while his brother was as good as his word – he has never returned to Gotham or superheroes. Nolan produced the attempt to lend DC's other stalwart, Superman in *Man of Steel*, a similar verisimilitude, with director Zack Snyder and English actor Henry Cavill in the lead role. But leaping tall buildings and taking flight didn't bend well to the realism of his universe (neither did Snyder's combination of slick and frenetic). Nolan would retreat as the DC universe, and superhero movies in general, became clogged up with mythology and a glowering overabundance of CGI. Compared with the cultural dominance of the genre in its wake, the *Dark Knight* trilogy is the exceptional that proves the rule.

THE FIFTH DIMENSION

Interstellar (2014)

For his eighth trick, he took to the stars, through wormholes and into new dimensions, creating a science fiction epic that paid tribute to both Spielberg and Kubrick

Over the summer of 1977, Christopher Nolan saw *Star Wars* seven times. He was back in Chicago, where George Lucas' science fiction phenomenon opened six months before it did in the UK, which was another kind of time travel. Every birthday outing with every local friend returned him to the embrace of *Star Wars*, until he knew it by heart. But more than the thrilling mythology of cosmic knights and swaggering space pirates, he began to obsess about how it was made. He bought every magazine, read every 'making-of' story, learning about special effects, the cunning of filmmakers, and felt a calling begin to stir. 'It gave me the sense that movies can take you on a journey,'[1] he recalled. And that somewhere behind it all there was a storyteller.

Then back in London not long afterwards, his father took him to see *2001: A Space Odyssey* on the big screen, Stanley Kubrick's high-minded encounter with aliens. So slow and enigmatic, it was nothing like *Star Wars*, but its immensity spoke to him on a 'primal'[2] level – he wanted to know what it all meant, but he also understood it was about the *experience*. You could become lost in a film. The scale of it all, he said, 'suggested the biggest potential of movies.'[3]

There was a third significant science-fiction experience. Though the memory is less specific, he can recall being filled with the wonder and optimism of Steven Spielberg's *Close Encounters of the Third Kind*, the story of an ordinary man plucked from his family to travel into the stars.

Between these three very different films, Nolan became filled with the possibilities of science fiction (the sway of *Blade Runner* came a little later). Unlike so many of his peers, who see only confinement, he likes the classifications of genre. He leans into genre, embraces it, bouncing his ideas off the walls. But he also crosses boundaries. All his films are infiltrated by an aura of science fiction: even the 'realistic' trio of *Memento*, *Insomnia*, and *Dunkirk* are constructed with an experimental verve. So the chance to step boldly into the genre was something he had been waiting for since he began to experiment with a Super 8 camera.

▲ Voyage of discovery – a new world is discovered on the edge of a black hole, depicted in CGI with a realism that made even astrophysicists marvel.

INTERSTELLAR

Interstellar had been Spielberg's Starchild. Around the millennium, having developed a taste for sophisticated science fiction with *A.I. Artificial Intelligence* and *Minority Report*, he had turned to the latest discoveries in astrophysics to fuel a film around the mysterious properties of black holes. In fact, the origins lie even further back in time, when Carl Sagan (renowned astronomer and author of the novel *Contact*) set producer Lynda Obst up on a blind date with theoretical astrophysicist, Nobel laureate and Caltech superstar Kip Thorne. This didn't lead to romance, but it did inspire an eight-page treatment for a film based on the most outlandish concepts in real-world science. Singularity movies, if you will, like *The Black Hole* or *Event Horizon*, treated the premise as the springboard for supernatural nonsense.

In 2007, Spielberg brought in Jonah Nolan to help him conceive of a story and write the script. Jonah went deep, studying relativity with Thorne at Caltech, getting his head around Albert Einstein's theories and the confounding nature of spacetime. With the brothers having what Jonah described as a 'symbiotic'[4] relationship, discussing material, indeed regularly discussing quantum physics, Christopher kept abreast of the project's progress over the following four years. Then, in one of those solar flares that strike the Hollywood universe, Spielberg moved his output deal to Disney, and his big-brained sci-fi film was left stranded at Paramount without a director. So Jonah simply enquired whether his brother might be interested in the chance to fuse the scope and verisimilitude of Kubrick with the emotion of Spielberg and his own cinematic cunning. You might call it destiny. Nolan officially signed on in 2012, with Spielberg remaining as executive producer.

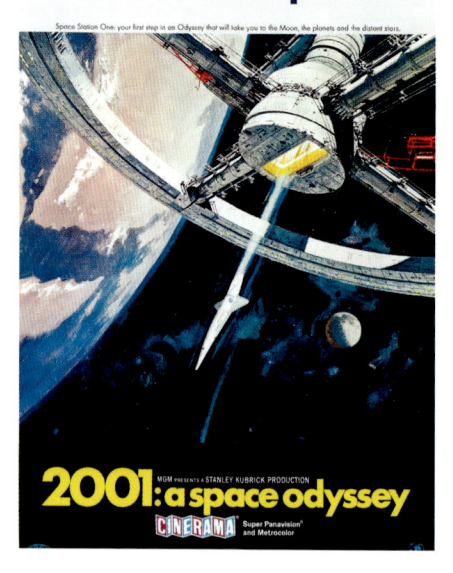

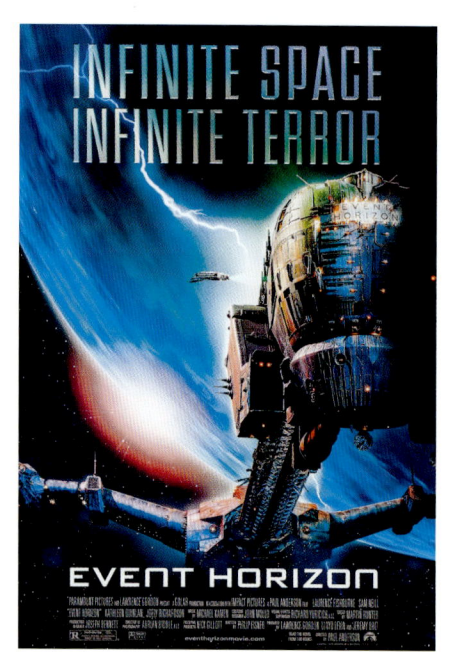

Such was Nolan's market value that a highly lucrative deal was struck, whereby Nolan's regular studio Warner Brothers handed over the rights to a *Friday the 13th* remake and a future *South Park* movie in return for the foreign distribution rights to a $165 million cosmic odyssey.

'I really felt that there was an extraordinary opportunity there to tell a very intimate story of human connection and relationships and contrast it with the cosmic scale of the overall events,'[5] he said. Put it another way, he foresaw a science fiction movie that could combine the teachings of Einstein and Frank Capra. It was to be a film about saving humanity and the trials of fatherhood.

It was at this time that Nolan met up with Hans Zimmer, now his court composer. He asked him to write a piece of music around the relationship between a father and a child, nothing more, and gave him a day to do it. Zimmer returned with four minutes for piano and strings. Rather than listen to a recording, the director came

▲ To infinity and beyond – there is a history of space exploration in the movies – from the definitive *2001: A Space Odyssey* to the highly speculative *Event Horizon*.

▶ Family saga – Christopher Nolan was determined to marry the vastness of space with the intimacy of a family story. From the left: son Tom (Timothée Chalamet), grandfather Donald (John Lithgow), father Cooper (Matthew McConaughey), and daughter Murphy (Mackenzie Foy).

124 CHRISTOPHER NOLAN

in person to Zimmer's Santa Monica studio, and took a seat on a couch right behind him at the piano. 'So I play it without looking at him,' said Zimmer. Four minutes later the composer swivels round to face his director.

'So, what do you think?' he asks.

Nolan is leaning back with that faraway look in his eyes. 'Hmm, suppose I better make the movie.'

'What is the movie?'[6] presses Zimmer.

And Nolan explains his plan for a science fiction tale on the grandest scale about intergalactic exodus and the frontiers of science and philosophy. But for all the special effects and the vastness of space, this fragile piece of music would be the heart of the film. 'I wanted to challenge him to write the music without knowing the genre,'[7] explained Nolan, and he would use that piece as his true north through the challenge of what was to come. He was inverting the filmmaking process – starting with the score.

Nolan slimmed down his brother's storytelling flourishes, making their epic more rational, more personal. Gone were Jonah's fractal aliens, a space station positioned beyond time and space, and a machine that could redirect gravity. What stayed is the near-future tale of a dying Earth, and the voyage taken by a reluctant astronaut through a wormhole that has appeared beside Saturn with the promise of habitable planets on the other side.

'When you call a film *Interstellar*,' he said with a smile, 'you are making a pretty big promise to the audience to get out and explore, I guess, what it means to be human.'[8] It was a strange phenomenon: the farther out he ventured into the universe, the more sincere his filmmaking became. 'It's a very simple story in a lot of ways,' he reflected. 'It is about a father and his relationship with his children and his destiny to leave his children behind.'[9]

The six-month shoot began on 6 August 2013 in Alberta, Canada, south of where they had shot the snowy exteriors of *Inception*. For his fragmenting Earth of 2067, Nolan wanted to evoke the desolate prairie-land of John Steinbeck, using Ken Burns' 2012 documentary series *The Dust Bowl* as guide. What he called 'an all-American iconography.'[10] It is an

◀ Subtle dystopia – Christopher Nolan wanted to depict mankind's bleak future in realistic terms, including the return of the Midwestern dust bowl.

▼ Essentially, *Interstellar* is a father-daughter story between Murphy (Mackenzie Foy) and hero Cooper (Matthew McConaughey), inspired by Nolan's relationship with his own daughter.

understated Norman Rockwell-styled apocalypse, with vast skies and rolling landscapes. Time is already distorting – the future looks like the past. They planted five hundred acres of corn ready to be burned, and whipped up a synthetic dust storm with giant turbines blowing cardboard fragments. The rusty cloud blooms over that symbol of Americana, the baseball game. Meanwhile, the film's political subtext has sharpened in relevance, as we learn that in this depleted America scientific knowledge is disparaged and the Moon landings decried as fakes. Conspiracy is the new religion, and NASA has been outlawed. Jonah was channelling a frustration toward America's lost potential: 'I grew up [in the era of] Apollo space travel, we were promised jetpacks and fucking teleportation and instead we got fucking Facebook and Instagram.'[11]

We view impending ecological doom through the prism of a family. Widower Cooper (Matthew McConaughey) is a former NASA pilot turned farmer, with two children, fifteen-year-old Tom (a young Timothée Chalamet) and twelve-year-old Murphy (Mackenzie Foy). Within the time warp of the film, they will grow into Casey Affleck and Jessica Chastain. Murphy will finally be played by Ellen Burstyn.

126   CHRISTOPHER NOLAN

▶ Unusually, Interstellar is a blockbuster with a scientist – Cooper (Matthew McConaughey, left) – as its hero.

More immediately, strange patterns in the dust direct Cooper to a secret NASA bunker, where he agrees to lead a fourth mission through the wormhole in the good ship *Endurance*.

Nolan liked the everyman quality in McConaughey. He was movie-star handsome, but his aw-shucks Texan drawl and emotional availability made him likeable. He exuded decency, despite having recently revived a flagging career in the dark transformations of *True Detective* and *Dallas Buyers Club*. A hard-edged take on the genre wasn't unknown to him. He had appeared in Robert Zemeckis' adaptation of Sagan's *Contact*, with its ambiguous alien presence, wormholes, and father-daughter bonds a clear forerunner for *Interstellar* (it was also produced by Obst).

Consciously or not, *Interstellar* completed a trilogy of films with *Insomnia* and *Inception* connected by phonetically similar titles and by the relationship between extraordinary environments and troubled heroes. Not entirely selfless, Cooper has the same yearning for adventure that steals away Richard Dreyfuss in *Close Encounters of the Third Kind*, but he is trying to save humanity. Cooper might be a new breed, but in true Nolan fashion he will be wracked by the guilt.

INTERSTELLAR 127

The *Endurance* manifest is filled out with Dr Amelia Brand (Anne Hathaway making the leap from Catwoman to overly earnest scientist), Doyle (Wes Bentley), and Romilly (David Gyasi), with Sir Michael Caine at mission control as Professor John Brand, Amelia's father (transposing Cooper's dilemma, she is a daughter leaving behind her father).

We get a genuine countdown, crosscut with Cooper's heart-rending farewell to Murphy, giving her his wristwatch to remember him by. It's a common misconception that Nolan makes chilly films. That he's more Kubrick than Spielberg. They can be literally cold and tonally dark (with that film noir thing), but passions course beneath the clockwork. The magicians of *The Prestige* are driven by emotional storms; *Memento* is a tragedy. But he was charting unknown waters. This was a personal epic, a tearjerker. Nolan was now the father of four and knew the heartache of leaving his children behind to go off and make a film, something he channelled directly into Cooper's departure. The young Murphy was based on his eldest, Flora; the working title of *Interstellar* was *Flora's Letter*.

Chastain recalled meeting Flora when she visited the set. 'All of the clues fell into place. You had to be a little bit of a detective, and when I figured it out, I was incredibly moved: *Interstellar* is a letter to his daughter.'[12]

'Chris is a lot of things we've been taught contradict each other,' said Hathaway. 'He's a workaholic, but he's a present, loving father. He's a serious filmmaker, but he loves stupid comedy. He's an exemplary human being, but he is a human being.'[13]

Cooper and Nolan are not so far apart: family men, scientists and guilt-laden adventurers.

Leaving behind the golden, earthly hues of Spielbergian Earth, the film travels toward alien Nolan landscapes: glacial distances like half-remembered dreams, an ash-and-pewter palate, seas like a sheet of marble. The mission will visit two planets on the far side of the wormhole, in the vicinity of the black hole named *Gargantua*. One presents a vast ocean, the other a frozen wasteland. These were the images of Earthbound explorers: ocean and ice, Christopher Columbus and Ernest Shackleton. Dutch-Swedish cinematographer Hoyte van Hoytema turned for stimulation to the moody science fiction textures of Russian director Andrei Tarkovsky (*Solaris, Mirror, Stalker*), while Nolan screened Philip Kaufman's stirring depiction of the early days of the NASA space programme *The Right Stuff* for his crew.

The crew of the *Endurance* will be met with natural and human

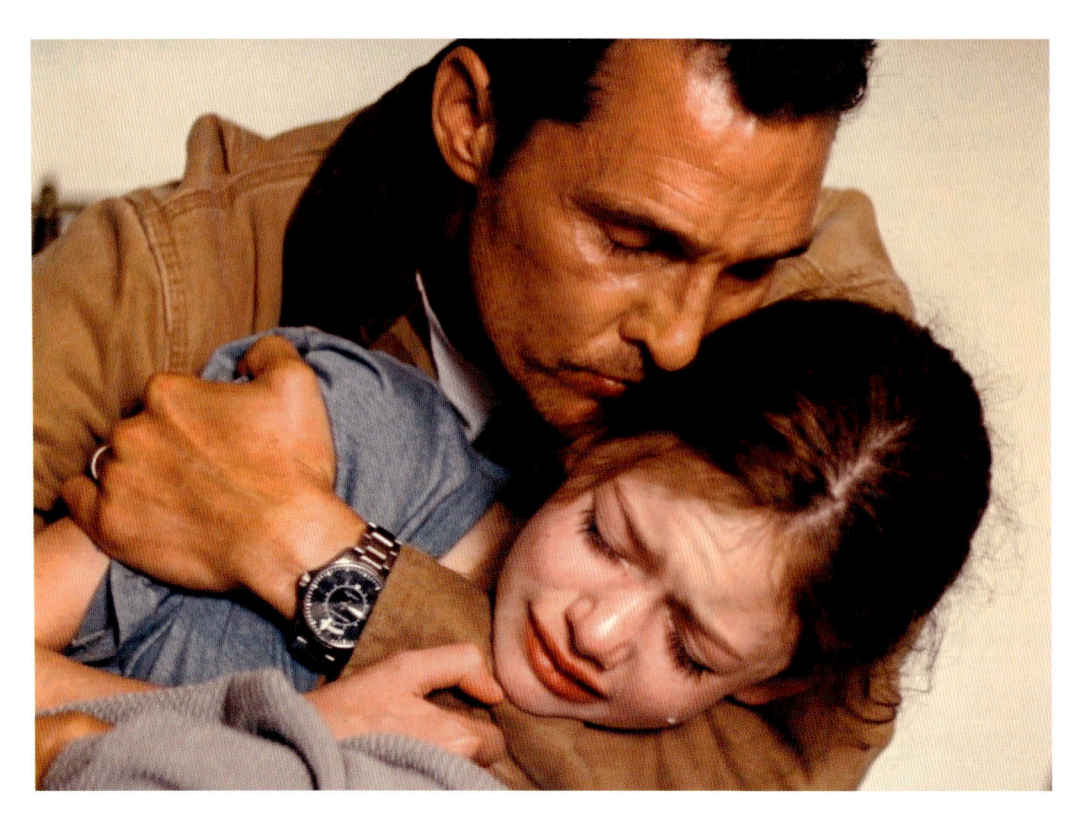

◀ Cooper (Matthew McConaughey) makes his devastating farewell to his daughter Murphy (Mackenzie Foy). Despite being Christopher Nolan's most overtly emotional film, *Interstellar* is never sentimental.

disaster. On the oceanic planet, a tidal wave (echoing the dust cloud) will engulf the landing party. *Interstellar* presents Nolan's fascination with the subjectivity of time on a symphonic level, and the closer you are to a black hole, the more severe the dilation of time becomes. When they finally make it back to the orbiting *Endurance*, where Gyasi awaits them, twenty-three years have elapsed. The dilation of time in *Interstellar* is the equivalent of the dream levels in *Inception*, and will inform *Dunkirk* to come. The parallels with the filmmaking process are even more redolent. Nolan was following the example set by his idol Kubrick, who turned time into music in his masterpiece *2001: A Space Odyssey*, where you can leap thousands of years in a single cut from spinning bone to spinning spaceship, before slowing to excruciating detail to show a scientist arriving on the Moon.

▲ Astronauts Cooper (McConaughey), Brand (Anne Hathaway), and Romilly (David Gyasi). Like his hero Stanley Kubrick with *2001: A Space Odyssey*, Nolan was determined to depict deep space travel as something contemporary.

◀ Hathaway's Brand watches in horror as disaster looms in the shape of a giant tidal wave.

INTERSTELLAR 129

◀ A second frozen planet (shot on the Icelandic glaciers) offers no hope for mankind.

▼ A promotional image of the exploration team discovering an oceanic world. From the left: Brand (Anne Hathaway), Cooper (Matthew McConaughey), and Doyle (Wes Bentley).

It was a film of departures – in setting, in storyline, in its bold use of sentiment – but it was also a film of returns. Nolan and his team went back to Vatnajökull National Park in Iceland to shoot the frozen planet, where they discover Matt Damon's abandoned scientist Dr Mann, a Ben Gunn figure, driven to the edge by a lack of human contact. It turns out he has faked his report on this bleak place, and his madness will lead the mission into greater turmoil.

As with the *Dark Knight* films, the design philosophy was function over form. There should be nothing futuristic, decreed Nolan. Everything, he promised, 'was based on contemporary reality.'[14] They used NASA as a benchmark – the International Space Station, the shuttle programme, all those intricate docking procedures – so that everything came with a tactile sense of purpose. Switches had to earn their place on a console. The *Endurance* is constructed as a wheel made of twelve interlocked pods like the points on a clock, with a landing craft dock in the centre. To evoke interplanetary space travel they built a full-sized version of their lander craft, the *Ranger*, on a soundstage at Sony Pictures Studios in Culver City, which could pitch and yaw on hydraulic rams, with Nolan often handling the remote control. It was more simulator than set. 'I wanted actors to look out the window, and see what they would really see there,'[15] he said. Instead of the statutory green screens, Nolan's team mounted eighty-foot-tall wraparound screens, onto which they projected specially made footage of moving star fields.

Nolan was keen to include a pair of robots as part of the ship's crew, but they were forbidden from being anthropomorphized like C-3PO. He wanted a Kubrickian variation on artificial life: a set of shapeshifting rectilinear metal blocks, HAL reconfigured as a giant sliding-block puzzle as polished as kitchenware. TARS and CASE were created as effectively full-scale puppets piloted on set by the actor Bill Irwin (who also provides the voice of TARS, with Josh Stewart voicing CASE). Nolan's instructions were clear: Irwin needed to give life to something designed with the functionality of a tripod. 'The character comes out of the way he performs it,'[16] said the director, and there is a strange body language to its sliding configurations. It also has a setting for humour. 'A giant sarcastic robot,'[17] sighs Cooper, as he deals with an AI assistant.

> ❝ *Leaving behind the golden, earthly hues of Spielbergian Earth, the film travels toward alien Nolan landscapes: glacial distances like half-remembered dreams... seas like a sheet of marble.* ❞

▲ The grown-up Murphy (Jessica Chastain) following in her father's footsteps as a scientist.

▶ The *Endurance* spacecraft was based on NASA concepts for deep space travel – with its twelve interlocking pods symbolically resembling the hours on a clock.

With Thorne on the film as an executive producer and scientific sounding board, the leaps into infinity were based on the possibilities of real physics. 'Which are beyond what you could dream up as a screenwriter,'[18] laughed Nolan. So he simply asked what a black hole would look like.

Interstellar features the most intense use of CGI in any Nolan film. Which was inevitable. But this was CGI with a difference. Thorne generated equations that would guide the designs the way physics governs the real universe. If light around a wormhole didn't move in a straight line, how could that be described mathematically? Thorne would send his equations to the effects team along with pages of explanation. They were more like research papers, cutting-edge science, which were then transformed into computer-simulated models.

For *Gargantua*, the black hole into which Cooper will fall beyond the event horizon, they needed to incorporate gravitational lensing: the distortion and magnification of light by a gravitational field. Individual frames took one hundred hours to render; mind-boggling levels of computation were involved, with a corona of encircling detritus, known as accretion disks, there to emphasize the sphere looking like a golden halo. When Thorne saw the results, he was amazed. These weren't simply ground-breaking special effects, these were scientific revelations.

Rescued from oblivion by the mysterious, unseen beings (future humans, conjectured some; alien gods, said others; God himself, hollered yet more), Cooper is sealed inside a tesseract, a hyper-geometric holding cell within the black hole, through which he will strain to communicate across time and space. With its proliferation of planes and angles, this was the most advanced of Nolan's Escher-inspired creations: a prison like those that entrap Bruce Wayne, and a box of tricks like those used by the magicians in *The Prestige*, only in five dimensions, which include a vantage point from behind the back of the bookshelves in Murphy's room.

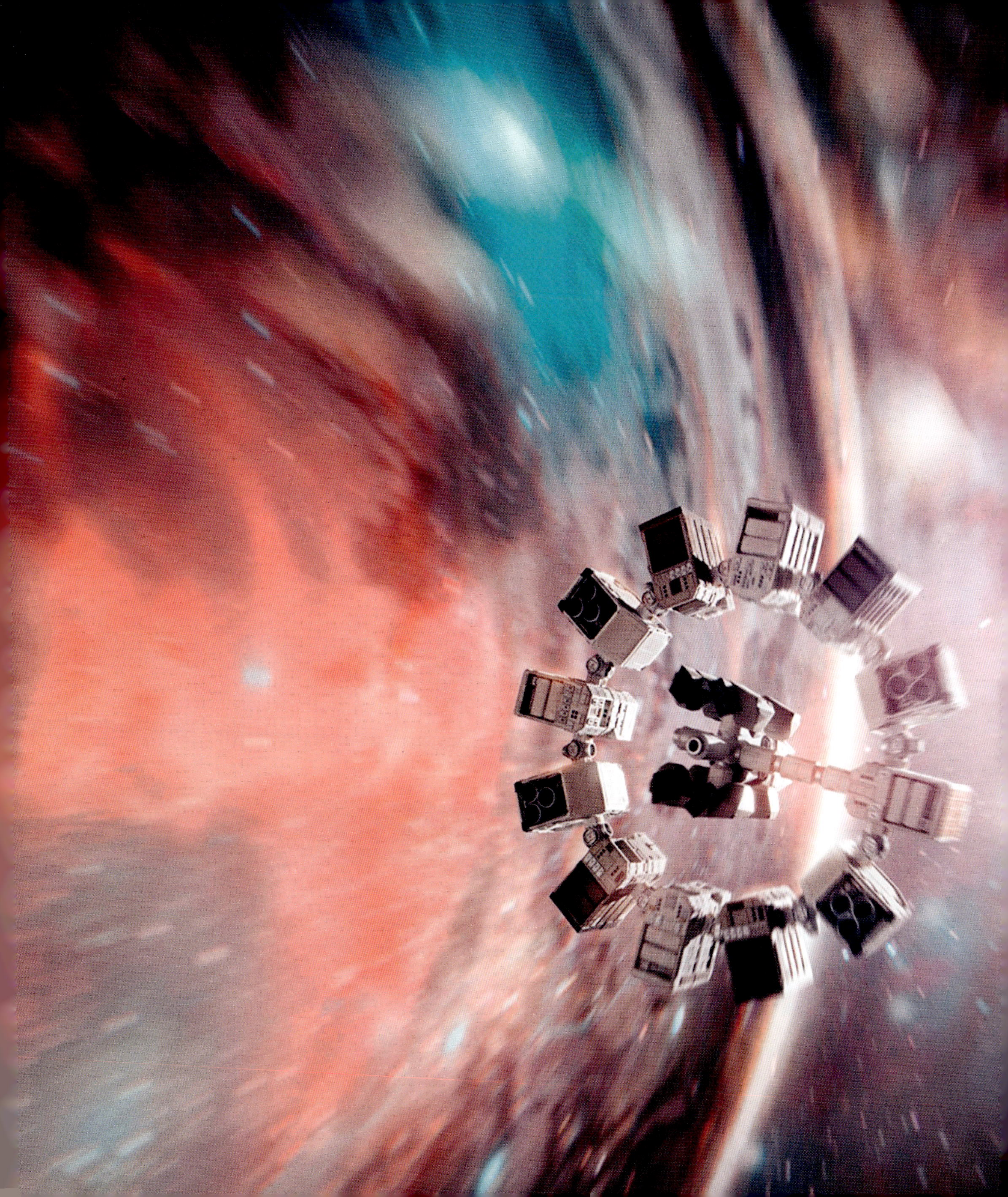

▲ Cooper (Matthew McConaughey) adrift in the tesseract, the five-dimensional construct that will allow him to communicate across time and space, and baffle audiences everywhere.

The equivalent of Kubrick's sensory overload in the Stargate of *2001: A Space Odyssey* and the neoclassical hotel room that lay beyond, things come full circle, with time bending back on itself... and the ghost in Murphy's room, stirring up the dust, proves to be Cooper himself. 'You could read it as a ghost story,' said Nolan. 'The notion of the parent as a ghost of the child's future.'[19] As she grows older, and becomes Chastain's scientist, Cooper will feed the data from the black hole, enabling her to complete the gravitational device needed for mass exodus.

There were some complaints that this was all a little convenient – the director's hand slipping in from offstage. The absentee aliens were, Nolan insisted, a direct analogy to Kubrick's silent masters of the monolith in *2001: A Space Odyssey*. For all its mind-blowing maths, the tesseract returns us to the central, binding theme – parenthood. We swing back to Spielberg, and even Lucas' galaxy-binding Force. For Nolan it was about emotional connections, a father reaching out to his daughter across time and space, and from behind her bookshelves. 'Love is the one thing we're capable of perceiving that transcends dimensions of time and space,'[20] insists Brand, suggesting that love is as much a universal force as gravity.

▲▲ The *Endurance* emerges near the giant singularity *Gargantua* – an accurate onscreen visualization of astrophysicists' hypotheses about how a black hole might appear close up.

▲ In a classic Nolan move, a tesseract-bound Cooper (McConaughey) loops back to the beginning of the movie to witness his young self with Murphy (Mackenzie Foy).

INTERSTELLAR 135

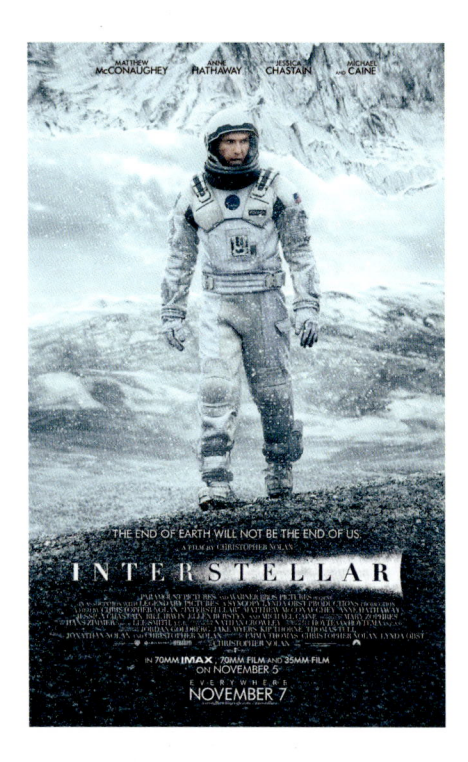

▲ Another huge hit for Christopher Nolan, *Interstellar* was further proof that there was an appetite for serious-minded blockbusters.

◣ Nolan and McConaughey on the set of the landing craft *The Ranger*, built at full scale to enable the actors (and director) to feel as close to space travel as possible.

Critics were perplexed by this sudden turn toward the sentimental. This was the first and so far only occasion where one of Nolan's films might not be classified as a variation on film noir. Intellectually, *Interstellar* was already a lot to take onboard – singularities and dilations and tesseracts, oh my. But mixed with such a rich shot of humanism, the result was almost overwhelming. During postproduction there were forty-five scoring sessions with Zimmer, including a church-organ lamentation. The film ran to two hours and forty-nine minutes. It was immense.

'Fans of Nolan's finest works… will long for more narrative rigour as raw science, rich sentimentality and rank silliness battle for the heart and soul of this very personal project,'[21] sighed Mark Kermode in the *Observer*. 'It's an almost convincing simulation of a great mainstream movie made by an entity from another dimension,'[22] smirked Andrew O'Hehir in *Salon*.

Nolan countered that this was truly who he was – an optimist (only in his looking-glass universe could a dystopia inspire his most upbeat work). 'I worry about things, but at the same time I have a lot of faith in people coming together to solve problems.'[23] Wasn't this what he encountered every day on a movie set? With a worldwide box office tally of $700 million, one thing was clear: audiences were still willing participants in his grand schemes, whether they truly understood them or not. Besides, Nolan, the master puzzle maker, the invisible alien overlord, insisted that solving the film intellectually didn't matter. It was just an 'entertainment,'[24] he iterated again and again on talk shows. It was about the *experience*.

Scientific Fiction

How Christopher Nolan anchors his storytelling with real science

◀ Thermodynamic range – the Protagonist (John David Washington), going forwards, battles with the same character, played by the same actor, going backwards, in *Tenet*.

Amnesia (*Memento*): the basis for Nolan's film noir is the very real condition of anterograde amnesia – the inability to form new memories after damage to the hippocampus. While full retrograde amnesia (no memory at all) is a common if exaggerated trope in movies from *Spellbound* to *The Bourne Identity*, anterograde amnesia is unusual (romcom *50 First Dates* has Drew Barrymore repeatedly forgetting she has fallen in love). Inspired by neuropsychological studies, *Memento* gained special praise for its accuracy: 'The fragmented, almost mosaic quality to the sequence of scenes in the film also cleverly reflects the "perpetual present" nature of the syndrome,'[1] claimed clinical neuropsychologist Sallie Baxendale in the *British Medical Journal*.

Insomnia (*Insomnia*): another familiar movie trope – typically as a function of mental dissolution in the likes of *Taxi Driver* and *Fight Club* – is again elevated by the rigours of the Nolan process. What Nolan is particularly fascinated by is the *effect* of insomnia. How a flagging brain distorts perception. In short, how our eyes deceive us, something that will echo throughout his films. He read the work of German physician Hermann von Helmholtz, whose *Treatise on Psychological Optics* proposed that our eyes were not sufficient to truly perceive the world. Perception is merely an attempt to assemble what is happening.

Electricity (*The Prestige*): among its illusions, *The Prestige* is also a film about material progress. In other words, science. Yet, in Nolan's ironic games, this is revealed as a form of magic with which it is possible to defy nature, and personified in David Bowie's Nikola Tesla, who in reality developed a system for electrical supply. Interestingly, the contrast between the film's two versions of The Transported Man trick – one electrically charged, the other sleight of hand – reflects Nolan's ambivalence toward so-called technological progress in filmmaking. The suspect magic of CGI.

Subconscious (*Inception*): Nolan's elaborate heist movie is not so much about the human subconscious as set inside it. But key to the overall structure of his action film is the Freudian idea of dream interpretation. Nolan is concerned with *how* we dream. In his article, *The Neuroscience of Inception*, published in *Wired* magazine, Jonah Lehrer pointed out that scientists had found 'that when adults were watching a film their brains showed a peculiar pattern of activity.'[2] One that was very similar to brain activity when sleeping.

Singularity (*Interstellar*): The most overt marriage of pure science and storytelling came with Nolan's space odyssey. The script originated with a concept of using wormholes to traverse the universe and the time-distorting effects of black holes (singularities), but with the aid of astrophysicist Kip Thorne, Nolan would expand his enquiry into multi-dimensional constructs. Vitally, the film never violates established physical laws. In fact, Thorne wrote an accompanying book, *The Science of Interstellar*, to back up the film with equations.

Anxiety (*Dunkirk*): Nolan's concentrated war movie is as much a study in the transference of fear from screen to audience as it is a depiction of surviving against terrible odds. Through the combination of image, music, and sound, we are *literally* made tense. Nolan creates a subconscious cinematic process, as if he is putting us within the bounds of the film.

Entropy (*Tenet*): While not as strictly true to the laws of physics as *Interstellar*, with the aid of Thorne, Nolan devised a hypothetical reversal of the second law of thermodynamics. In simple terms, this states that entropy always increases – which gives us the flow of time. Order is destined to become chaos. You can't unscramble eggs. Strictly speaking, this is a matter of probability. In other words, it is extremely unlikely that you could *never* unscramble eggs, but not impossible. QED: time could be reversed. It is therefore also highly improbable but not impossible to unscramble *Tenet*.

137

ON THE BEACH

Dunkirk (2017)

For his tenth trick, he set about turning a Second World War legend, the miraculous rescue of British troops from a French beach, into the ultimate escape movie

The origin story became a standard on the *Dunkirk* publicity trail. How, twenty-five years before, in the mid-nineties, Christopher Nolan and then future wife and producer Emma Thomas sailed across the English Channel toward the French coast. It was May, the same month Operation Dynamo was launched. They were in their twenties, just kids, and inexperienced sailors. There was a friend onboard who knew something about sailboats, but an intrepid adventure gave way to a nightmare voyage. The spring weather was uncooperative, turning cold and rough not long after they left port. Nolan estimated that it took them nineteen uncomfortable hours, fighting the treacherous currents to stay on course. It was after dark when they finally arrived in Dunkirk. 'I was so fucking glad to be there,'[1] he said, offering a rare crack in his usual sangfroid.

The name of that seaside town on the northernmost tip of France resonates across history – textbook stuff about the flotilla of British vessels, from fishing boats to cruisers, plucking the 1940 British Expeditionary Force from the sands of Dunkirk at the eleventh hour. In the process, a military disaster was rewritten as a victory of courage and ingenuity, optimism rekindled in the face of defeat, inculcating a surge of national pride that would eventually help win the war. They called it the Dunkirk Spirit.

'Dunkirk is a story that British people were raised on – it's in our bones,' recalled Nolan. 'It's a defeat… and yet a defeat in which something marvellous happens.'[2] Examine the numbers and it was almost biblical. 338,000 were rescued from the 18km stretch of beach under the direst of circumstances: shallow berths, squabbling elements, German bombing, invisible U-boats, and a defensive perimeter dwindling by the hour. It was about communal heroism. The instinct for courage.

Nolan knew his history well enough; it was drummed into idling boarding school boys by rote. But his arduous experience in making that short trip brought a new level of respect for the reality of the evacuation. What it must have been like for the terrified soldiers stranded at the end of the world, bombs cascading onto the beach, the few naval ships crammed to the gills with the wounded, uncertainty peeling into desperation among the men. What it must have been like for the ordinary men at the helms of those boats venturing into a war zone. 'We have a job to do,'[3] declares Mark Rylance's unwavering Mr Dawson at the helm of

▶ The soldier's story – dubbed 'Tommy', Fionn Whitehead arrives on the beach, but his nightmare is only just beginning.

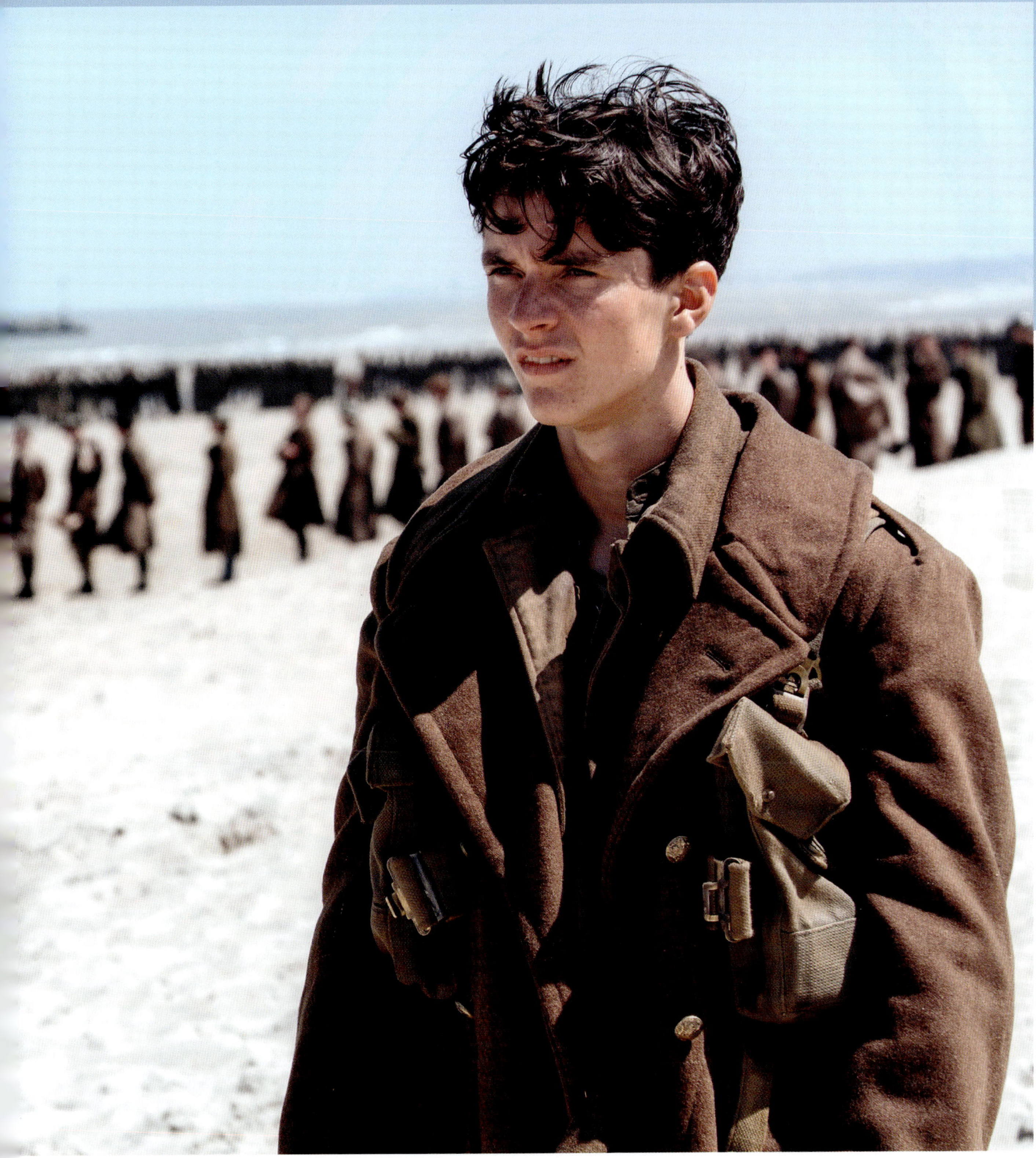

a boat no bigger than the one in which Nolan had set forth. What it must have been like for the fighter pilots engaging the enemy, trying to buy them time.

'That was the seed of wanting to eventually tell the story,'[4] Nolan recognized – not that he was conscious of it at the time.

Ideas grow from their inception. While whole years drifted by, consumed with heavyweight projects, a Dunkirk movie took shape in his imagination. Plans occasionally stirred by a visit to Churchill's War Rooms off the Mall in London, or the gift of Joshua Levine's book *Forgotten Voices of Dunkirk* from Thomas, now his wife, which spoke so readily about the contrasting realities of the situation. No one experienced those events the same way. Levine would be hired as an advisor on the film.

'I wanted to do something that frightened me a lot,'[5] admitted Nolan, and taking on history cast in bronze was a daunting prospect. This was 'sacred ground.'[6] Through Levine, he sought out the few remaining veterans, now in their nineties. They brought the salt-tang of memory. There were men who strode out into the waves – whether to try and swim home, or because they had simply given up, it was impossible to tell. Either way, their bodies washed back up onto shore as the tide changed. And Nolan doesn't shrink from such heart-rending images.

Visually, he homed in on descriptions of the moles, the concrete breakwaters on either side of the harbour that stretched out into the sea like slender fingers. The eastern one was almost a mile long, topped with

▼ In the footsteps of history: a real-life image from Operation Dynamo in 1940, showing a Royal Navy vessel docking back on British shores with its cargo of relieved Tommies.

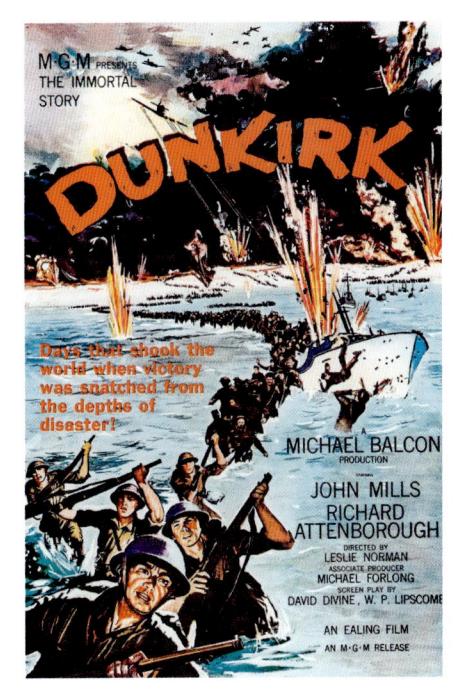

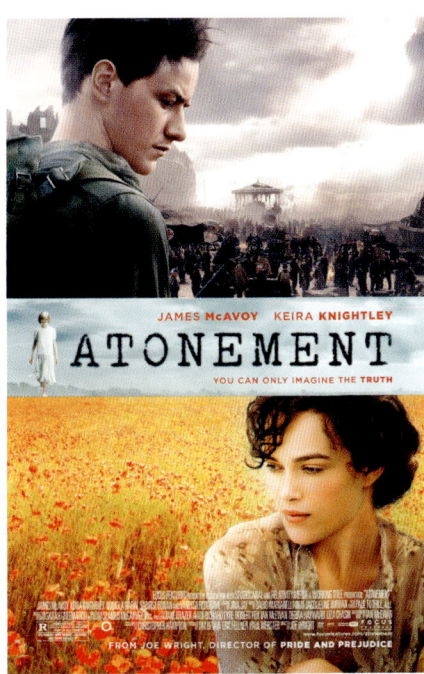

◀ There are surprisingly few films that have tackled Dunkirk. But among the few are Leslie Norman's stalwart *Dunkirk* from 1958 – and Joe Wright's famed tracking shot from 2007's *Atonement*.

a wooden promontory. It was another devastating image, and oh-so-British: men queuing along these walkways, hoping for brief passage crammed on a boat, a single face turned to the sky as an enemy Stuka begins another descent, its siren howling on the wheel struts. Then they duck in successive waves, steadying their helmets, a ripple of fear moving through the crowd. This road to nowhere was a symbol of the life-or-death urgency that lay beneath jaunty folklore.

What surprised and encouraged Nolan, as it always did, was that modern cinema had never told this story. There was a 1958 classic, *Dunkirk*, sturdy and stiff-upper-lipped, as directed by Leslie Norman and starring such stalwarts as John Mills and Richard Attenborough. Pure myth. In recent terms, there was really only the striking, surreal twelve-minute tracking shot following James McAvoy along the beach in Joe Wright's *Atonement*.

'What I'm really looking for is passion – you need to love what you are doing,' said Nolan. 'It is tough to be passionate about something that has already been done.'[7]

He often thought about how he watched films, analyzing his response to the story. He had this internal Geiger counter for slack logic. 'If the rules are internally consistent,' he reflected, 'the audience will believe.'[8]

Back in Chicago in the early eighties, when he first saw *Raiders of the Lost Ark*, he had willingly given himself up to Spielberg's thrilling world. He was never the same again. But he had still fixated on a particular moment – the scene when Indy is spotted swimming to the Nazi U-boat and heading down the hatch seconds before it submerged. For regular kids, it was another slice of heroic nonsense among the hero's many escapades. But Nolan kept thinking how hard that would be to swim the distance between boat and sub, pulling yourself up out of the water in soaking clothes. Movies find it so hard to convey breathlessness, he thought. With *Dunkirk*, he wanted to deal with how physically draining it was to get onto a boat.

Over breakfast, the usual venue for discussions of future projects, Nolan mentioned to Thomas that he was ready to tell the Dunkirk story in his inimitable style. To *Nolanize* history, which meant another experiment in form. Thomas joked that reading any of her husband's unusual scripts for the first time was a nerve-wracking experience, taken 'with a large glass of red wine'[9] at her side.

Early on, Nolan had wondered aloud if he could make the film without the use of a script at all – improvise the whole damn thing. Foreseeing logistical chaos and a budget disappearing into the brine, Thomas managed to talk him down from there. The *Dunkirk* script still came in at an emaciated seventy-six pages, half of what you might expect for a $100 million production. 'I refer to it as the intimate epic,'[10] he said. His ambition was to immerse the audience in what he called 'aggressively human-scale storytelling, visually.'[11]

DUNKIRK 141

> *" ... It was almost biblical, 338,000 were rescued from the 18km stretch of beach under the direst of circumstances.... It was about communal heroism. The instinct for courage. "*

▶ The view from the air – Jack Lowden pilots one of three Spitfires hoping to strike against the Luftwaffe.

▼ The view from the ground – promotional art of Fionn Whitehead, whose only drive is to get off the beach.

In typically abstruse fashion, there would be no generals in rooms pushing miniature ships around on maps, but the subjective immediacy of what he called his 'land, sea, and air approach.'[12] Recalling how *Inception* dances between dreams like notes on a stave, this was a conventional story told in the most unconventional way. The film breaks down into three perspectives on the same event, each embodying a different element. On land, focusing on one soldier, dubbed Tommy (Fionn Whitehead), among the thousands anxiously trying to find a way off the beach. On sea, with the small civilian crew of a cruiser, *Moonstone* (named after the Wilkie Collins mystery novel), skippered by Rylance's Mr Dawson, who have bravely joined the motley armada across the Channel. While in the air, we follow the efforts of Farrier (regular Tom Hardy), the pilot of a Spitfire deftly intercepting the furies of the Luftwaffe. But there would be no backstory, no exposition: Nolan would create empathy for his characters in the moment. The final element, fire, would arise at the point where the stories converge with the oil slick of a sinking destroyer ignited by the falling angel of a downed German fighter.

With familiar Nolan cunning, each of the trilogy of experiences would play to a different time signature. Here were the temporal gambits of *Memento* and *Inception*, applied to the grand traditions of the war movie. In real terms, the land story covers a day, the journey by sea three hours, and the aerial combat no more than ten minutes. The director's intention was to put us on that windswept beach, on the water, and inside the cockpit of a Spitfire. 'I wanted the audience to feel like they are there,'[13] he said.

Kubrick once told French critic Michel Ciment that 'a film is – or should be – more like music than like fiction. It should be a progression of moods and feelings. The theme, what's behind the emotion, the meaning, all that comes later.'[14]

No filmmaker has taken the master's wisdom to heart like Nolan. There is a musical device known as the Shepard tone, which you can hear in the scores for *The Prestige* and *The Dark Knight*. Put simply, three ascending scales are braided together to create the impression of a single rising pitch that keeps on building. With *Dunkirk* he was going to do that with narrative. Three strands of rising anxiety entwined to create an almost unbearable pitch of tension. Not for a single second can we relax. The terror seeps out of the screen and into our rigid limbs.

When Nolan came to pitch *Dunkirk* to an expectant Warner Brothers, he referenced propulsive, borderline science fiction thrillers like *Gravity* and *Mad Max: Fury Road*, as well as the 'Dunkirk moments'[15] in films such as *Independence Day*. Forget the formality of history, he told them, and imagine an entire film running on the currents of a white-knuckle third act. They knew to trust his ideas, even if he was venturing from the avant-garde cool of house style. There would be no skyscrapers, no steel-grey suits, but the film would soar. His only previous period story, *The Prestige*, had the novelty of rival magicians and the unravelling of ornate tricks. Now, for the first time in his career, there would be an objective reality beyond the confines of the movie.

'It's always been the case that a filmmaker who wanted to work in the studio system has to find a way to work around it,'[16] he laughed, as ever the countercurrent to Hollywood thinking. Nolan was intent on giving people something they *didn't know* they wanted.

The contrast with his previous film *Interstellar* is striking. This wasn't only a matter of genres. According to cultural critic Darren Mooney, the two films reveal Nolan's split nationality: the future-gazing *Interstellar* was a purely American story about a mission to save mankind; whereas the historical *Dunkirk* was a very British myth 'in which the mere act of survival becomes a substitute for victory.'[17]

Tommy's desperation to find a way off the beach, a mission that at times borders almost on slapstick, like one of Buster Keaton's existential comedies, is a primal current. Survival is its own form of courage. As he repeatedly becomes trapped in the bowels of flooding ships – including a startling

▶ Fionn Whitehead's desperate Tommy fulfils the film's central thesis – that survival itself is a form of courage.

forty-five-degree roll with the camera fixed to the metal wall – the film almost jumps track into the realms of *Inception's* nightmares. If you strip away the historical context, you are left with the urges of a disaster movie.

But Nolan sought a twofold response. As well as a visceral reaction, we still had to understand what an incredible story this was. In the nearest thing to convention, the beach scenes cut back to that stalwart Kenneth Branagh as evacuation chief Commander Bolton, impressing upon us that desperation shook the entire chain of command. But grit held firm.

The grip of the thriller would be married to the glow of the epic. They were mixing the same 70mm format as *Lawrence of Arabia* with vast IMAX frames, where the size of the image was perfect for taking in the detail of a cockpit or dank hold. It was a format that swallowed the viewer whole.

During *Dunkirk's* long, studious preparation in late 2015 and into 2016, Nolan screened films for his department heads and key cast – a taste of what he intended. Here was a curious mix: David Lean's flawed and flowery *Ryan's Daughter* (for the immediacy of the elements), Hitchcock's *Foreign Correspondent* (for the plane crashing into the ocean), *Speed*, *Unstoppable*, *Chariots of Fire*, and silent classics like *Intolerance* and *Sunrise*. '*Dunkirk* needed that silence, that simplicity,'[18] he noted of the latter two, but they were films of great showmanship as well. Lastly, he screened Henri-Georges Clouzot's *The Wages of Fear*, arguably the greatest exercise in movie tension there has ever been, wherein dissolute truck drivers transport nitroglycerine across treacherous mountain roads. A film whose gripping effectiveness is found in its concentration on detail, right down to the grinding shift of gears.

▲ Running on empty – Whitehead races to the shore. When Christopher Nolan pitched the film to the studio, he likened it to action thrillers like *Speed* and *Unstoppable*.

▲ Standing tall – while Christopher Nolan is determined to place us into the immediacy of history, Kenneth Branagh as Commander Bolton provides a sense of the bigger picture.

He also took advice from Spielberg, who had brought a new verisimilitude to the depiction of the Second World War with *Saving Private Ryan*, which Nolan surveyed from a pristine 35mm print, before deciding 'it had the wrong kind of intensity'[19] for *Dunkirk*. While we see the silhouettes of enemy fighters and bombers – the dread Stukas, Messerschmitt and Heinkel bombers - not once do we spy an enemy soldier. In a sense, he was operating closer to *Jaws*, with the water lapping at the camera.

Production began among the waves of history on 14 May 2016, on location in Dunkirk, where, weeks before shooting, Nolan and production designer Nathan Crowley had walked the 18km stretch of beach, film and history unfurling in their minds. They rebuilt the moles to their original specifications – the foundations still beneath the water. Determined to resist the synthetic hordes of CGI, Nolan held to traditional methods. It was his defining contradiction – the analogue futurist who foreswore digital flexibility. *Dunkirk* needed to be real to cast, crew, and audience.

He took advice from production designer Alan Tomkins, a veteran of Bond and *Batman Begins*, who had worked on *A Bridge Too Far*, Richard Attenborough's 1977 epic about the

◀ By any means necessary – the soldiers brave the freezing surf of Dunkirk beach to get the wounded to a ship.

▼ British soldiers come under aerial attack on the mole, whose mile-long promontory provided an access point for boats, but also left the men horribly exposed.

failed Arnhem offensive (Operation Market Garden), which to Nolan's eye really held up. Tomkins explained how in the background they had painted the outline of soldiers on glass edged in foil, which would glint in the sunlight giving the illusion of movement. Nolan would use aluminium. They had cardboard cut-outs not only of soldiers, but entire ships.

'What computer graphics are missing is serendipity,' he said. 'It's animation basically. There are no accidents.'[20] You need to tease the eye with trickery – the anomaly makes it real.

As does the weather, which turned as swiftly as it had on his foolish Channel crossing, lashing them with storms, tearing up scenery, and churning up a soapy froth onto the beach. But Nolan kept shooting until it was all but unsafe. The rawness of the elements fixed everyone's attention – this is what the soldiers had dealt with. At times, they could barely stand. 'Just keep going,'[21] was his mantra. Get it into the camera. Besides, bad weather looks good on film. For all his technical prowess, his control, Nolan responded to his surroundings. 'The reality of being there, of being in nature, frankly, it frees you up as a filmmaker just to use your eyes, use your ears, absorb it, and try to capture what speaks to you.'[22]

They moved onto Urk in the Netherlands for four weeks, from where they shot scenes of *Moonstone* on the open sea and Jack Lowden's sinking Spitfire, as he strains to free himself from the cockpit. Entrapment is a running theme. Cast and crew had ridden lifeboats to Belgium and back in order to get their sea legs, and Rylance was often actually steering the boat in scenes done with minimal crew, a bomber flying overhead for real. Nolan wanted to put the actors 'into a closeness with reality.'[23] He shed his usual formality for a wetsuit, and stood in the surf, with the cameras mounted on platforms in the water.

DUNKIRK

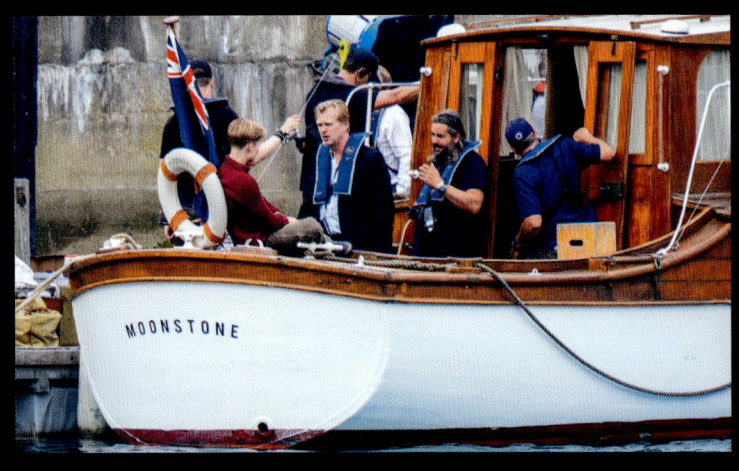

◄ Christopher Nolan (third from the left) mounts a shot on *Moonstone*, the small cruiser making the treacherous Channel crossing.

▼ Elemental filmmaking – the conditions on Dunkirk beach made things very real. From the left: Nolan, Harry Styles, Aneurin Barnard, and Fionn Whitehead.

▶ The analogue approach – to keep things in camera, Nolan chose to use cut-outs instead of digital effects.

▼ The struggle is everything – cinematographer Hoyte van Hoytema and Nolan (not in uniform) line up a shot of Whitehead diving for cover.

'Between the ships, rebuilding the moles, flying Spitfires, pulling real cockpits into old Russian planes, flying Spitfires into the sea for real, it was tough,' recalled Crowley. 'It was physically tough. This is the most physical film I think we've ever done.'[24]

They reached for the sky out of Lee-on-Solent airfield in Hampshire. Working Spitfires were borrowed from American billionaires and repainted to exact specifications with genuine serial numbers. The practical effects team also used different scale models, including full-scale Spitfires they could catapult into the sea. Banking through enamel blue skies, the aerial sequences were dangerously exhilarating, and Nolan knew he had to rein them in lest it become too magical. Such 'eye candy'[25] had the potential to release tension rather than heighten it. Nolan wanted to 'teach an audience how difficult it was to dogfight.'[26]

The keen-eared will know that it is the director's lucky star, Sir Michael Caine, we hear over the comms from home base: 'Keep them peeled. They'll come out of the sun.'[27]

Heroism in its most traditional form is found in Hardy's Farrier, continuing his sorties against enemy planes even as his fuel runs out of reach of a return home. It's a tribute being paid to family stories of Nolan's grandfather, who had died flying bomber missions with the Royal Air Force. During shooting, the crew held their breath and then cheered the sight of the plane, its engine silenced, gliding to a perfect landing on the great ribbon of beach. And then the powerful image of Hardy's stoic pilot, setting his faithful Spitfire alight and watching it burn like a Viking funeral.

As he had on previous films, Nolan hired Hans Zimmer as equal-parts composer, sound effects editor, and special effect. Film as music, music as

◀ Tom Hardy returns for his third Christopher Nolan film as heroic Spitfire pilot Farrier.

▶ Mark Rylance as Mr. Dawson, the skipper of *Moonstone*. The three central characters each represent a different generation: Rylance's veteran, Hardy's seasoned pilot, and Whitehead's new recruit.

▼ Two timelines intersect as the Spitfires pass over *Moonstone* – the film will reach a crescendo when all three stories converge.

film. During *Inception* the great growls of the score, the Devil's whale song, had worked to throw our senses into turmoil. With *Dunkirk*, Nolan wanted the relentless urging of a ticking clock, and Zimmer would layer the score with a recording of the director's own stopwatch to give the film a pulse.

'If there are Method actors, I suppose I'm a Method composer,' reflected Zimmer. 'I went to the beach [at Dunkirk]. This sounds insane, but I was in the neighbourhood, and I went knowing they were shooting there on the greyest, most foul day. I picked up a handful of sand and put it in a jar and took it with me.'[28]

His score, tormenting notes into untold frequencies, is like a fourth braid entwined into the structure. Then finally, as the boats appear, and Branagh sheds a tear for England, Elgar's stirring *Nimrod*, from the *Engima Variations*, is heard, its familiar notes distended but uplifting. It's as near as we have come to Nolan being sentimental. 'I didn't really say this to Hans, but it played at my father's funeral a few years ago. I just find it unbearably moving.'[29]

Reviews bordered on the ecstatic, once critics had got their breath back. 'Every element of Nolan's prior films has been honed to near-perfection here,'[30] cried Karen Han of *SlashFilm*.

DUNKIRK 151

▲ *Dunkirk* was another triumph over preconditioned Hollywood thinking – a Second World War epic that was received like a blockbuster.

Christopher Orr of *The Atlantic* didn't hold back. 'It is classic in its themes – honour, duty, the horror of war – yet simultaneously Nolan's most radical experiment since *Memento*. And for all these reasons, it is a masterpiece.'[31]

There were dissenters, those who saw only the tightly wound clockwork, but if not quite a masterpiece, *Dunkirk* is the most assured expression of Nolan's widescreen aesthetic. It marries the pressure-cooker concentration of his early films with the boldness of a post-*Dark Knight* titan. And it is a reminder of how emotional his storytelling can be. He gets readily discussed in technical terms, and puzzled over like a mystic, but there is a surge of euphoria like the rush of a drug as the narratives converge and salvation comes for many, if not all. At its core, it is a film about not dying. The relief is overwhelming.

By now we were ready for Nolan's mastery of time: repeated runs at the same incident, points where the timelines cross, with the trio of Spitfires shooting over *Moonstone*, and shell-shocked Cillian Murphy glimpsed before his trauma, a man of quiet command. Yet time is inexorably running out. We are headed toward the crossing of the streams: *Moonstone* plucking poor Tommy from the water, Farrier shooting down the last German plane. It felt like the first time we had exhaled in hours. Or clocked onto the fact we had seen Harry Styles in the supporting cast – rumour had it that Nolan had no idea he was a member of One Direction when he auditioned.

Still, awaiting the film's release, the director was a nervous wreck. 'You want to get it out there in the largest possible way,'[32] he said. But this was a Second World War story – would it translate to anyone under forty? More confident, Thomas said it was 'the sum of everything we've learned in prior movies.'[33]

Its success would surpass even Nolan's deepest hopes. Crucially, *Dunkirk* played as both historical drama and blockbuster. A total of $527 million worldwide (including his biggest-ever haul in the UK, where it spoke across generations) reinforced his Midas Touch, the brainbox brand. Oscar nominations followed, eight of them, including Best Picture, Best Director, and Best Cinematography, though *Dunkirk* would lose out to Guillermo del Toro's romantic monster movie *The Shape of Water*. Even through the prism of the Second World War, Nolan was still adjudged as too ascetic and complex.

Which didn't stop certain parties in his (semi-) home co-opting the film on behalf of a nationalistic fervour, known as Brexit, of which he wanted no part. The whole point of his film, he assured reporters, was to expose the desperate realism beneath the symbolism of the Dunkirk Spirit.

'Dunkirk has always been a Rorschach test for people, but I think the confusion we see today between patriotism and nationalism is extremely tricky. I don't believe that we want any political faction to own patriotism, or to own Dunkirk.'[34]

Survival can be a complicated business.

▲ Producer Emma Thomas and Nolan displaying his 2018 Nomination Medallion for Outstanding Directorial Achievement in Feature Film from the Directors Guild of America.

DUNKIRK 153

APOCALYPTIC THINKING

Tenet (2020) & *Oppenheimer* (2023)

For his eleventh trick, he made a spy thriller in which time could flow in both directions, but had he finally asked too much of his diligent viewer? For his twelfth, he will tell the true story of the father of the atomic bomb, a scientist who harnessed the power to destroy worlds

When *Tenet* opened it was like time had stopped. The world was held in the grip of a global pandemic, society locked down. Offices, bars, restaurants, shops, airports, studios, and cinemas were left dark and empty. Life felt like a Christopher Nolan plot, apocalyptic and mystifying. Temporarily, as it turned out, the summer of 2020 offered respite. Time briefly resumed, a window in which Warner Brothers could, at the third time of asking, release Nolan's latest film – a messiah thriller to save cinema or one to bedevil us as never before. Depending on your take, and *Tenet* remains sharply divisive, this was a film in tune with the grim tenor of the times… or another exhausting challenge to be overcome.

In simple terms, *Tenet* is outrageously complicated. A spy movie that leans back and forth in time, grand and forbidding, the very concept of a film stretched to its limits. A puzzle box without a lock, almost suffocating in its obscurity. Individual scenes were fabricated with a sophistry so brilliant it would take hundreds of viewings to decipher what was going on. We had to take it on trust that Nolan was in control. And we did. But even the critical reception had two directions of flow – for and against. Masterpiece or indulgence run amok.

'*Tenet* finds the filmmaker unable to get out of his own way,'[1] stewed *Film Frenzy*. 'Think of it as *Mission: Indecipherable*,'[2] sniggered *The New Yorker*. In the pro camp, going with the flow, was Peter Bradshaw in the *Guardian*, who saw genius in its temporal dance. '… *Tenet* is preposterous in the tradition of Boorman's *Point Blank*, or even Antonioni's *Zabriskie Point*, a deadpan *jeu d'esprit*, a cerebral cadenza, a deadpan flourish of crazy implausibility – but supercharged with steroidal energy and imagination.'[3] Was it an arthouse blockbuster?

By Nolan standards, the box office was muted. A total of $363 million worldwide, against a budget of $200 million, marked his first commercial hiccup (taking into account the extensive marketing involved). That does need to be framed against a potential audience spooked about going back into a cinema at all, and Warner Brothers' questionable insistence on simultaneously releasing their slate on the HBO streaming channel in the USA.

▶ When the mask fits – John David Washington stars as *Tenet*'s unnamed protagonist wearing the breathing gear that indicates he is moving against the flow of time.

TENET & OPPENHEIMER   155

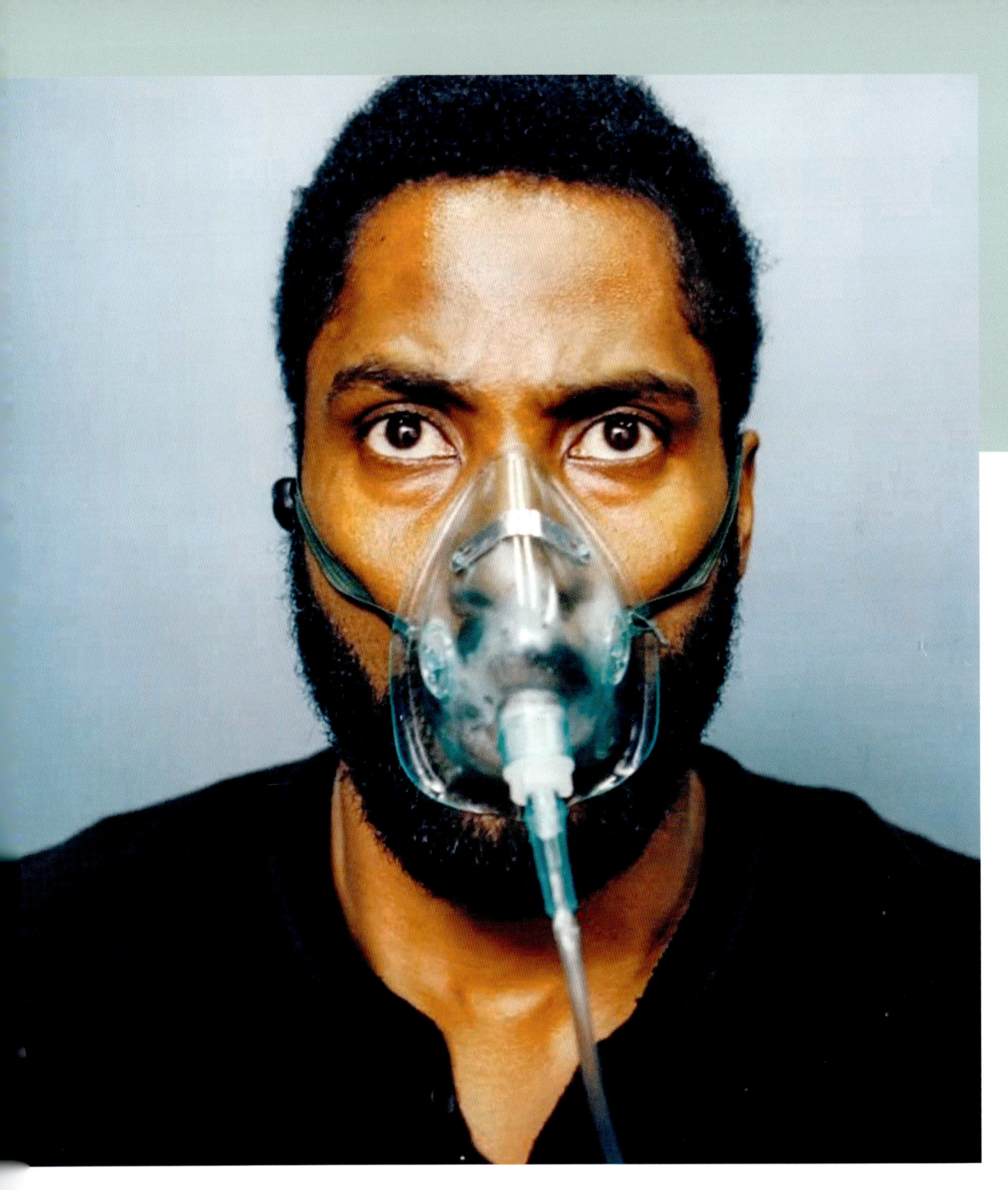

◀ The Sator Square, the Latin art piece discovered in the ruins of Pompeii that inspired *Tenet*'s palindromic title. All five words are used in the film.

▼ Defying gravity – Christopher Nolan inverts his own iconography by having his heroes bungee *up* a building.

Nolan was incensed. 'Some of our industry's biggest filmmakers and most important movie stars went to bed the night before thinking they were working for the greatest movie studio and woke up to find out they were working for the worst streaming service.'[4]

But that was then… And this is now. All Nolan films have an afterlife. They haunt us like dreams, stories incepted into our unconscious. Nolan has often spoken of his 'dimensional thinking'[5] – that each film has a life beyond what is on the screen. Maybe what we needed with *Tenet* was time.

It began as a concept. No more than an image – bullets springing back out of a wall and into the barrel of a gun, as they do at the beginning of *Memento*. Remember Nolan's discovery of the editing deck beneath the Bloomsbury Theatre, running film back and forth, reel to reel. There's an earlier memory still: aged sixteen, staying with a family in Paris, bettering his French, and discovering that the father was editing a documentary. Nolan watched him running the film as he dubbed a voice-over, the footage remaining pin-sharp whichever direction it flowed.

The potential of a story able literally to turn back and forth in time – not via structural conventions such as flashbacks, but as a fictional

156   CHRISTOPHER NOLAN

> *" It had to be a complete experience, but the entire chronology is like a living Escher drawing constantly taking hairpin turns to confront earlier scenes head on. "*

reality – finally took form in 2014. The point, he said, where the 'ideas were in balance.'[6] There were folders full of notes, reams of hand-drawn diagrams, the arrow of time veering across graphs. This was when he decided to wrap a science fiction impulse within the cool veneer of a spy movie. 'It would be a clandestine thing, which fits nicely with the theme of retroactive danger,'[7] he said, imagining a cold war between past and future.

The title, for once, came early. 'The palindrome was the jumping-off point,'[8] said Nolan. He was making a film that would read the same backwards and forwards, derived from the Sator Square, a Latin artefact found in the ruins of Pompeii, whose five words always read the same however you rotate it. All five – 'SATOR', AREPO', 'TENET', 'OPERA', and 'ROTAS' – are used in the film. What's more, a tenet, by definition, is a principle or doctrine held to be true, especially by a group or profession. So this was a film about the notion of belief. 'We are imprisoned in our view of the passage of time,' he explained. 'Objective reality is a leap of faith.'[9]

Cut to 2018, when Nolan joined the artist-photographer Tacita Dean at a conference in Mumbai on the future of film. He was struck by something she said about how the camera was the 'first machine in history'[10] to literally *see* time. That opened up a visual perception of how his new film would work. 'You have to experience it to properly understand it,' he said. 'It speaks to the essence of cinema.'[11] As he had on the *Dark Knight* films, Nolan brought in production designer Nathan Crowley with the script not yet done. He hadn't cracked the last act, finding himself blocked for months, and the process of visualizing the world of *Tenet* untied the knot.

We had to see time.

'This film more than any of the others will be much easier – and frankly more fun – to watch than to read,'[12] insisted producer Emma Thomas upon finishing the script. Jonah Nolan decreed that it was the culmination of everything his brother had done to date – a Nolan film about Nolan films. In other words, the best way to navigate the maze of *Tenet* is by the auspices of Nolan's back catalogue. 'It's like *Inception* but complicated,'[13] joked Nilo Otero, his first assistant director, having read the script and swallowed hard.

Even more than his layer cake of dreams, you can feel the tug of *Memento* in the Möbius-strip inscrutability of *Tenet*. Backstory lies in the future, and even then is more alluded to than expository.

As Nolan repeatedly insisted when he ran the gamut of talk shows, as scrupulously polite as ever, *Tenet* was not a time-travel movie. We are always following 'the same timeline,'[14] he implored to the rictus grins of his pristine hosts. That of the protagonist, known only as the Protagonist (John David Washington), which happens to flow both ways. He never makes any leap in time, he only changes direction. The key concept is the theoretical inversion of entropy (the second law of thermodynamics, to be exact, wherein energy always heads toward chaos not order – in the anti-Nolanwise direction), which would amount to a reversal of time compared to anything that wasn't reversed (i.e. the rest of the world). The smashed jar is restored. The bullet goes back into the gun. There is also a hint at the possibility of multiple realities opening up with each inversion...

Wait, wait. We need to start again. What is going on in movie terms? Well, we follow the exploits of the Protagonist, possibly an undercover CIA agent, working to foil a terrorist attack on a Ukrainian opera house. However, the whole explosive occasion turns out to be a cover for recruiting him to the secret organization known as Tenet, which is attempting to foil an apocalyptic attack from the future. Aided by a dapper British agent who calls himself Neil (Robert Pattinson), who has a Masters in physics and an uncanny knowledge of the aforementioned temporal mechanics,

▶ The scene of the time crime – Neil (Robert Pattinson) and The Protagonist (John David Washington) inspect the aftermath of a shoot-out still to come.

▼ Extra-special forces – the Protagonist (Washington) and Neil (Pattinson) make for a new generation of spy, crossing the border not between East and West but past and future.

158 CHRISTOPHER NOLAN

the Protagonist will follow the trail of inverted materials to the deeply unpleasant Russian arms dealer Sator (Kenneth Branagh), using his estranged wife, the willowy English beauty Kat (Elizabeth Debicki), as a way in.

Along the way, the forces of good and evil, present and future, will make use of a series of 'turnstiles'[15] – revolving steel doorways like giant clockwork cogs through which a person is inverted to pass back through recent scenes *the other way*. At two points, the Protagonist fights his inverted and non-inverted selves. Letting the audience, as Nolan put it, 'in on the joke'[16] was vitally important. It had to be a complete experience, but the entire chronology is like a living Escher drawing constantly taking hairpin turns to confront earlier scenes head-on. The same car chase is enacted twice by hurtling back down the same highway, fallen buildings rebound into existence, explosions funnel into nothingness. 'Does your head hurt yet?'[17] enquires Neil of the Protagonist with a smile. Not half.

Warner greenlit the production without blinking, encouraged that this mind-bending thriller bore the hallmarks of another *Inception* – dreams were switched out for time and heists for espionage, but the suits remained chic and the action propulsive.

If *Tenet* is the culmination of everything he had made so far, it was also a culmination of all his influences: Stanley Kubrick, Ridley Scott, Jorge Luis Borges, the labyrinthine mysteries of film noir. With it being Nolan's first entry into the spy genre, the allusions to James Bond were automatic: gadgets, exotic locations, speechifying baddies, and Sir Michael Caine giving off wafts of M within the bastions of an English gentlemen's club. But the mood is closer to John le Carré's realist fiction, where the plot lingers out of reach (cinematographer Hoyte van Hoytema had worked on the 2011 adaptation of *Tinker Tailor Soldier Spy*). 'Fritz Lang is probably the most important filmmaker to what my idea of film is,'[18] said Nolan, and the Austrian auteur had all but invented the espionage genre with his 1928 silent epic *Spies*, involving an international spy ring deploying technological threats, a world entrapped in geometrical imagery.

There was geopolitical inspiration too, real-world things that had piqued Nolan's interest and been filed away for future use. He had read about Freeports, airport hinterlands where billionaires stash valuables in ultra-secure warehouses, away from the beady eye of the taxman. A fake heist at Oslo Airport (shot at Los Angeles International Airport), with a full-scale 747 (a carcass rescued from an aeroplane graveyard in Victorville, California) crashing into a warehouse, spilling gold bars onto the tarmac like the dollar bills in Kubrick's *The Killing*, will unveil the first turnstile. And he researched the secret cities scattered across the old Soviet Union, abandoned sites of nuclear testing, imagining Stalsk-12 as an irradiated moonscape of rubble and ruin, where Sator had lived among the detritus, digging up a delivery from the future.

Nolan wanted to invert the idea of casting too – to reverse the flow of expectations. When it came to the Protagonist, rather than look to the A-list, as he had with Leonardo DiCaprio and Matthew McConaughey, he was drawn to the relatively unknown Washington (son of Denzel), who had shone in Spike Lee's comedy-thriller *BlacKkKlansman*. Nolan had been invited to see the film personally by Lee while in Cannes. He was there in the company of a freshly minted fiftieth anniversary print of *2001: A Space Odyssey*, which he introduced – further proof of his largesse toward cinema history and his debt to Kubrick.

'It just caught my eye, the degree of charisma he had,'[19] he recalled. Washington managed the trick of being cool and sexy and enigmatic, and yet uncynical. The Protagonist is the most straightforwardly heroic and emotionally open central character Nolan has ever created. Washington, who had once aspired to being a professional football player, was staggered by the physicality required. Even with training from a former Navy SEAL, it was relentless. Six days into shooting, he collapsed from exhaustion, the reality of a Nolan production readily apparent.

You could say the Protagonist is almost a vigilante, working extra-legally, and often hidden beneath a mask. We are told his mission transcends national interest. Which makes him reminiscent of Batman, but not so much in possession of dual identities as having none at all. He is a blank slate. He doesn't even get a name, let alone a backstory (largely because his background is in front of him), much like the Man with No Name from Sergio Leone's *Dollars Trilogy*, a mythic figure thrust into the immediacy of a plot. There was also a nod here to *The Prisoner*, the sixties British spy series (delivered with a tincture of sci-fi) in which Patrick McGoohan's existentially troubled hero was only ever known by a number. The hero of *Spies* is referred to as No. 326.

The Protagonist must pass through the story in a state of unblissful ignorance, learning as he goes, resolute to the point of fanaticism that he is on the side of good. There is, said Nolan, 'something really compelling about jumping into a story and being told to concentrate on the here and now.'[20] We assemble what we can as the Protagonist does, learning on the run.

With a blond forelock, cut-glass accent, and air of exceeding competence, Neil was modelled on a certain breed of fine-tuned British attachés, embassy veterans who rarely saw home soil. Thomas's father had been such a career diplomat, and she recognized the type instantly. Having shaken off the shallow stardom conferred by the *Twilight* movies, Pattinson had an appetite for off-the-grid indies and unusual takes on genre. Nolan saw a compelling presence in *High Life*, *The Lighthouse*, and the heist-thriller *Good Time*. They met and chatted for three hours in his office, and Pattinson left having no idea what the film was, but still got the part.

More than the Protagonist, it is the buoyant, purposeful Neil who most resembles Nolan, with a more louche disposition (he is like a decent rendition of Cobb in *Following*). We rely on Pattinson to lighten the mood, and as the film proceeds the camaraderie (and impending tragedy) between the heroes becomes central. It is the start and end of a 'beautiful friendship,'[21] says Neil, quoting *Casablanca*.

Nolan had admired Branagh as the classical villain Iago in the 1995 movie version of *Othello*, and also liked the idea of inverting the nobility the actor had brought to *Dunkirk*. Sator was to be soulless, an absolute brute, though he never gains the febrile terror of the Joker.

The shoot was enough to tax even Nolan's ability to think in three dimensions, though he claimed the 'frustration'[22] excited him. It had to be as precise as surgery. One piece out of place and the edifice would tumble. He employed a pre-viz technician (in charge of the computer-animated visualizations of scenes that had been made in advance) to stand on set and check everything for multi-dimensional continuity.

They shot for six months from 22 May 2019, beginning deliberately on soundstages in Burbank with the hand-to-hand combat between Washington and his inverted/non-inverted selves in the Oslo Freeport set. That was a

◀ Inverted casting – Kenneth Branagh flows against type as the film's vile antagonist Sator.

▶ Elizabeth Debicki as Kat, Sator's estranged wife, who will play a pivotal role in events – but not as the expected romantic lead.

▲ In another reversal of convention, it is the friendship that develops between Neil (Robert Pattinson) and the Protagonist (John David Washington) that forms the emotional core of the film.

steep but necessary five-day learning curve, figuring out a fight where the combatants' moves are, as Nolan put it, 'palindromically correct.'[23] Friendly physicist Kip Thorne advised on the science: air would flow differently for an inverted character, so they needed respirators; and a duplicate hero would always come out of the turnstile in the opposite direction. That sequence taught them how to think differently as the production took in Estonia, Italy, England, Denmark and India, before looping back to California.

Beyond some inverted bungee jumping on the bustling streets of Mumbai and a sojourn off the Neapolitan coast, with its racing catamarans and lavish yachts, *Tenet* doesn't resemble a Bond movie at all. We open into a jolt of action with the terrorist siege in a Ukrainian opera house (the film's overture!) Filmed at Linnahall in Tallinn, Estonia, a Soviet leftover resembling a grounded UFO, the sequence is a song to concrete. Notice too that as the Protagonist is tortured (by his own side – it's inverted torture) in what looks like a railway depot, the trains either side of him are symbolically moving in different directions.

There is a glowering brutalism to the entire film. It's grey to the point of monochrome, as if a future dystopia

TENET & OPPENHEIMER

◀ A car chase like no other – the central action sequence becomes symbolic of the film's concept of time, with cars hurtling in two directions.

has bled backwards into the present. It makes Gotham look like Paris. When the Protagonist hides out, preparing himself for the mission to come, like Bruce Wayne he seeks isolation, living inside a wind turbine in the Baltic.

The most audacious twist comes halfway through, sending the Protagonist back through that car chase in order to save Kat, shot with an inverted bullet. Naturally this involved an eighteen-wheel articulated truck, a ten-wheel military wrecker, and a hook-and-ladder fire truck built specially for the occasion. Did we miss that this is the most action-packed of all Nolan's films, including the *Dark Knight* trilogy? They shot for three weeks over a 3 km stretch of multi-lane highway in Estonia, fathoming stunts beat by beat, swerve by swerve, forwards and backwards, where heat becomes cold, oil drips up from the ground, and tyres spin in the opposite direction.

For the finale, where the forces of Tenet are arrayed against Sator's plan to unleash the Algorithm on mankind, they were back in Southern California, filming the sprawling, baffling battle scene of Stalsk-12, which involved a temporal pincer movement. The urban gives way to the desert, and a frenzy of inversions as soldiers fight in both directions, designated into red and blue troop divisions – a colour coding that had run throughout: red for forwards, blue backwards. The title gains another layer of meaning as the two units start ten minutes apart. It was the chance to throw crazy, inverted ideas at the screen – many of them impossible to take in – and it was all achieved on location at an abandoned mine in the Coachella Valley. Fiona Dourif, playing the leader of the blue team, wryly described the spectacle as 'backwards paintball.'[24] There was one abiding rule throughout the dizzying ninety-six days of production – no piece of footage could ever flow backwards.

'Don't try to understand it. Feel it,'[25] Clémence Poésy's unamused scientist Barbara (Q Branch with added particle physics) informs a bemused Protagonist early on. Effect comes before cause – think in the opposite direction. This is also a sly instruction on Nolan's behalf to the audience. Resist the urge to figure things out. Make a leap of faith. Something he claims for every single thing he has made. He wants to elicit an emotional response over an intellectual one. In *Memento*, it is Leonard's primal need for vengeance that drives the film, as it is the Protagonist's urge to save the world. The film was made for the cinema, he insisted, not to be freeze-framed on DVD (or streaming).

But that was never going to sate the Nolanologists, certain they had been set the ultimate challenge. The ongoing dilemma posed by the Nolan Method is brought to a point of crisis in *Tenet*. How do we go with the flow when the film pulls at us like gravity to decipher its riddles?

So we must go back and explain the plot again. Or try to. This time widening the shot for the big picture. In the near future a female scientist invents an algorithm to invert entropy, reversing time's arrow. But it has catastrophic potential. Like J. Robert Oppenheimer and the atomic bomb, she despairs at what she has given to the world. Constructing the algorithm in physical form and then breaking it into pieces, she scatters it back in time, before killing herself so the knowledge will be lost. *Even further* into the future, in a world confronting environmental collapse (political themes shimmer in the distance like heat waves: scientific hubris, nuclear damnation, environmental catastrophe), unseen villains instruct Sator to reclaim the lost parts of the algorithm and destroy mankind in the present. Which opens up a lot of conjecture over the Grandfather Paradox, which even Nolan scampers past.

◀ Star John David Washington is determined to remain at the heart of the action at *all times*.

◀ One of *Tenet*'s many objectives was its exploration of how the basic conventions of action scenes are dependent on our concept of time. The idea of a U-turn takes on a whole new meaning…

▼ … as does the classic 'coolly-walking-away-from-an-explosion' shot. In this case, an unruffled and inverted Sator (Kenneth Branagh).

TENET & OPPENHEIMER

▲ Despite the almost monochromatic urban settings, Christopher Nolan plays instructive games with colour. Red signals those going forward in time, blue those moving backwards.

◀ Bullet time – Sator (Kenneth Branagh) shoots Kat (Elizabeth Debicki), leaving her with an inverted wound.

Meanwhile, somewhere in the future, the secret organization Tenet commence their plan to save the present. Neil, we come to understand, has been sent from the future to assist the Protagonist by the Protagonist (one theory has it that he is the grown-up version of Kat and Sator's son Maximilien). From the red tag on his backpack, we know him to be the mysterious soldier helping the Protagonist in the opera house. Furthermore, the Protagonist not only recruited Neil, he effectively recruits *himself*. He is controlling everything – the mastermind behind his own story. You could say, the Protagonist is also the director.

During the wrap party for *Tenet*, Pattinson presented Nolan with a gift: an anthology of speeches given by Oppenheimer following the Second World War, in which he expressed his growing doubts about atomic power. 'It's eerie reading,' said Nolan, 'because they're wrangling with this thing they've unleashed. How's that going to be controlled?'[26]

That collection was part of a chain reaction already underway. On 8 October 2021, Nolan announced he would write and direct an adaptation of the Pulitzer-winning biography *American Prometheus: The Triumph and Tragedy of J. Robert Oppenheimer* by Kai Bird and Martin J. Sherwin. Called simply *Oppenheimer*, it is a biopic that will surely cut right to the heart of the Faustian bargain made with man's mastery of the atom. 'Now I am become death, the destroyer of worlds,'[27] Oppenheimer was reputed to have uttered – witnessing the first fruits of his project, a mushroom cloud billowing from the sand, as he quoted the sacred Hindu text the *Bhagavad Gita*. Nolan reflected that he grew up in the post-nuclear age. The shadow of annihilation has hung over all our lives since that day in May 1944.

▲ Christopher Nolan (left) brings a whole new meaning to the idea of directing as sculpting with time.

◀ Released during the Pandemic, *Tenet* became the first film of Nolan's career to be a relative failure at the box office. But it continues to draw fans back to its chronological riddles.

TENET & OPPENHEIMER

▲▲ Inverting physics – the Protagonist (John David Washington) learns that the second law of thermodynamics no longer applies. Therefore the bullet goes back into the gun.

▲ An unamused Barbara (Clémence Poésy, *Tenet's* spin on 007's Q) reveals a collection of inverted material – and outlines the potential for apocalypse.

▲ Thinking differently – the Protagonist (Washington), and the audience, are taught to conceive of time as a two-way street. The slab of concrete is moving from the future to the past.

TENET & OPPENHEIMER   167

▲ The real Dr. J. Robert Oppenheimer, known as the father of the atomic bomb, and subject of Christopher Nolan's twelfth film.

◤ Uncanny – star Cillian Murphy as Oppenheimer, bearing a more than striking resemblance to the actual scientist.

▶ The epicentre of history – the real Oppenheimer (fourth from the left) inspects the remains of the first atomic test site, with Lt. Gen. Leslie Groves (centre – to be played by Matt Damon in the film).

168   CHRISTOPHER NOLAN

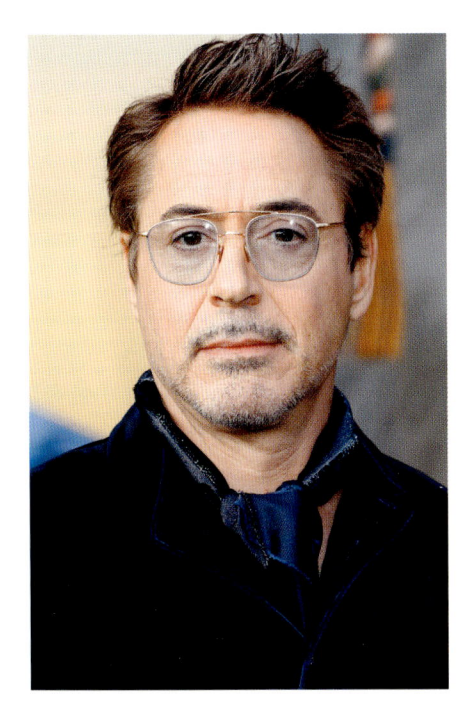

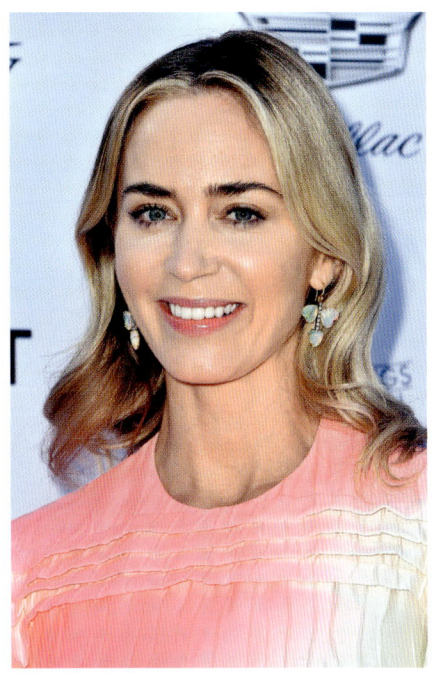

Brilliant, outspoken, highly strung, with a mystical, Sanskrit-reading bent that contradicted his scientific purity, Oppenheimer is a strange and elusive target. Biographer Tom Shone draws parallels with Nolan. Both are slender, well spoken, aristocratic, and remote. They are equally technicians and shamans. Oppenheimer had influenced the apocalyptic thinking in *Tenet*. There is a direct reference. 'You're familiar with the Manhattan Project?'[28] *Tenet* elder Priya Singh (Dimple Kapadia) asks the Protagonist. That was the codename for the covert development of the atomic bomb among the arid ranges of Los Alamos in New Mexico during the Second World War, the consequences of which, political, scientific, and human, figuratively thrust the world onto a new timeline. On 6 and 9 August 1945, bombs were dropped on the Japanese cities of Hiroshima and Nagasaki, as a result of which up to 266,000 perished. The great theoretical physicist felt he 'had blood on his hands.'[29]

It is both a departure and a story entirely in keeping with Nolan's work. The sins of science is a theme carried over from *Interstellar* and *Tenet*; we met Tesla, the father of electricity, in *The Prestige*; and after *Dunkirk*, this is a second epic set during the Second World War. At the time of writing, production was due to begin in early 2022, for a release date of 21 July 2023. The cast line-up was impressive, with Cillian Murphy finally taking centre stage in his sixth Nolan film as Oppenheimer. He has that twitchy, calculating, inscrutable quality. Emily Blunt plays his wife, Katherine Oppenheimer; Robert Downey Jr. is Lewis Strauss, President Truman's man on the new Atomic Energy Commission; Matt Damon is Lt. Gen. Leslie Groves, in command at Los Alamos; Florence Pugh is Jean Tatlock, the Communist Party member who had an affair with Oppenheimer, drawing him under a shadow of suspicion; Benny Safdie is rival Hungarian physicist Edward Teller; with Rami Malek and Josh Hartnett in smaller roles.

▶▶ *Oppenheimer*'s stellar cast: Robert Downey Jr. plays Lewis Strauss, head of the New Atomic Commission...

▶ ...Emily Blunt portrays Katherine Oppenheimer, the scientist's long-suffering wife...

▲ ... and Matt Damon is Lt. Gen. Leslie Groves, who was in command of the Manhattan Project at Los Alamos.

TENET & OPPENHEIMER   169

▲ Always the smartest man on set – Nolan and cinematographer Hoyte van Hoytema during the making of *Tenet*.

Nolan's twelfth film is also the opportunity to make good on his lost Howard Hughes project. We can expect a biopic like no other, with van Hoytema's austere visuals and Nolan's structural trickery enfolding atomic physics, Second World War politics, the devastation in Japan, marriage, love, genius, and Oppenheimer's fall from grace amid the Cold War paranoias he helped foster.

Significantly, after the debacle with HBO, the director severed his ties with Warner, and the rights to *Oppenheimer* were the subject of a Hollywood-wide bidding war, with Universal, MGM, Sony, Paramount, and rather ironically Apple and Netflix all eager for the new Nolan, even a $100 million biopic of an enigmatic scientist. In the face of the superhero conformity – the radiation he helped leak into the world – his brand stands strong. Universal won, enticing the director with the promise of a one-hundred-day theatrical window.

And so we take leave of Nolan in mid-flow, history at his fingertips, sat in his library built in the style of Frank Lloyd Wright within the grounds of his Los Angeles home (a British refinement to an American estate), its shelves filled with classics, detective novels, pulp fiction, books on art, architecture, history, science, and film, and no doubt the odd fifth dimension.

Endings, as Nolan will tell you, are vital. They shape our view of the whole story, in this case that of Christopher Nolan CBE, in his fifth decade. He remains Hollywood's modern promethean, a filmmaker of thrilling contradictions: architect and artist, scientist and romantic, traditionalist and avant-garde radical – within whose work control rages with chaos, logic wrestles with belief, function confronts form, and reality vies with dream. We often speak of him as a new Kubrick, but he charts currents as unclassifiable as David Lynch and as thrilling as James Cameron. Truthfully, there is no one like him.

No director has taken us closer to the action, yet his films inhabit hyperreal worlds, sensory cascades of image, music and sound effect, mind-boggling departures from linear storytelling. 'Everything in front of him is always under the microscope,'[30] said Jonah. Make that an electron microscope. Great cinema, Nolan once said, should tell us that there is more to the world than meets the eye. 'I make films that are huge endorsements of that idea,'[31] he confirmed. They are nuclear powered B-movies, explorations into the fabric of reality, and puzzle boxes to which only he has the key.

Don't try and understand it. Just feel it.

▲ Modern Promethean – Nolan at the Cannes Film Festival. No other director has challenged the orthodoxy of Hollywood with such success.

SOURCES

INTRODUCTION
1. Inception: *The Shooting Script*, Christopher Nolan, Insight Editions, 2010
2. *Writer's Bloc Presents: Christopher Nolan*, Tom Shone and Kenneth Branagh, Eventbrite, 2 December 2020

THE HYBRID KID
1. *Christopher Nolan on* Following, VICE via YouTube, 24 August 2014
2. Ibid
3. *I was there at the Inception of Christopher Nolan's film career*, Matthew Tempest, *Guardian*, 24 February 2011
4. *The Nolan Variations: The Movies, Mysteries and Marvels of Christopher Nolan*, Tom Shone, Faber & Faber, 2020
5. Ibid
6. Ibid
7. Ibid
8. Ibid
9. *Christopher Nolan on Dreams, Architecture, and Ambiguity*, Robert Capps, *Wired*, 29 November 2010
10. *The Nolan Variations: The Movies, Mysteries and Marvels of Christopher Nolan*, Tom Shone, Faber & Faber, 2020
11. *The World of Raymond Chandler: In His Own Words*, Raymond Chandler and Barry Day (editor), Vintage Books, 2014
12. *The Nolan Variations: The Movies, Mysteries and Marvels of Christopher Nolan*, Tom Shone, Faber & Faber, 2020
13. Ibid
14. *I was there at the Inception of Christopher Nolan's film career*, Matthew Tempest, *Guardian*, 24 February 2011
15. *Christopher Nolan: A Critical Study of the Films*, Darren Mooney, McFarland and Company, 2018
16. *The Nolan Variations: The Movies, Mysteries and Marvels of Christopher Nolan*, Tom Shone, Faber & Faber, 2020
17. *Christopher Nolan interview*, Kenneth Turan, Slamdance Film Festival via YouTube, 7 October 2013
18. *Christopher Nolan interview*, Scott Tobias, AV Club, 5 June 2002
19. *Christopher Nolan on* Following, VICE via YouTube, 24 August 2014
20. *Christopher Nolan on Directing*, BAFTA Guru via YouTube, 18 January 2018
21. Ibid
22. *Creepy* Following *Does More with Less*, Mick LaSalle, SFGATE, 2 July 1999
23. *Christopher Nolan interview*, Kenneth Turan, Slamdance Film Festival via YouTube, 7 October 2013
24. Following *Blu-ray notes*, Scott Foundas, The Criterion Collection, 1999

SIDEBAR: MICRO NOLAN
1. *The Nolan Variations: The Movies, Mysteries and Marvels of Christopher Nolan*, Tom Shone, Faber & Faber, 2020
2. *Jeremy Theobald interview*, Dan Jolin, Empire, June 2009

THROUGH THE LOOKING GLASS
1. *Memento Mori*, Jonathan Nolan, Esquire, 29 January 2007 (reissue)
2. *The Nolan Variations: The Movies, Mysteries and Marvels of Christopher Nolan*, Tom Shone, Faber & Faber, 2020
3. Ibid
4. Chinatown and The Last Detail: *Two Screenplays*, Robert Towne, Grove Press, 1997
5. *The Nolan Variations: The Movies, Mysteries and Marvels of Christopher Nolan*, Tom Shone, Faber & Faber, 2020
6. Live *Memento* Q&A: Christopher Nolan and Guillermo del Toro, *via Movieline*, 10 February 2011
7. *The Nolan Variations: The Movies, Mysteries and Marvels of Christopher Nolan*, Tom Shone, Faber & Faber, 2020
8. Ibid
9. *Indie Angst*, Scott Timberg, *New Times Los Angeles*, 15-21 March 2001
10. *The Traditionalist*, Jeffrey Ressner, *DGA Quarterly*, Spring 2012
11. *Christopher Nolan interview*, IFC, Memento DVD, Pathé, 2000
12. Ibid
13. *Something to Remember*, Ed Kelleher, *Film Journal International*, March 2001
14. Memento *production notes*, Newmarket Capital Group, 2000
15. *Something to Remember*, Ed Kelleher, *Film Journal International*, March 2001
16. Ibid
17. *Fuhgeddaboudit!*, Jay A. Fernandez, *Time Out New York*, 15 March 2001
18. Memento & Following, Christopher Nolan, Faber & Faber, September 2001
19. Ibid
20. *Christopher Nolan Interview*, IFC, Memento DVD, Pathé, 2000
21. *Indie Angst*, Scott Timberg, *New Times Los Angeles*, 15-21 March 2001
22. *Backward Reel the Grisly Memories*, A.O. Scott, *New York Times*, 16 March 2001
23. *Memento review*, Lisa Nesselson, *Variety*, 14 September 2000
24. Memento: *You Won't Forget It*, Desson Howe, *Washington Post*, 30 March 2001
25. *How Did I Get Here?*, Anthony Lane, *The New Yorker*, 11 March 2001
26. Live *Memento* Q&A: Christopher Nolan and Guillermo del Toro, *via Movieline*, 10 February 2011
27. Memento's *puzzle structure hides big twists and bigger profundities*, Scott Tobias, AV Club, 11 August 2012
28. Live *Memento* Q&A: Christopher Nolan and Guillermo del Toro, *via Movieline*, 10 February 2011
29. *The Nolan Variations: The Movies, Mysteries and Marvels of Christopher Nolan*, Tom Shone, Faber & Faber, 2020
30. *Christopher Nolan on Interstellar Critics, Making Original Films and Shunning Cell-phones and Email*, Scott Feinberg, *Hollywood Reporter*, 3 January 2015
31. *Christopher Nolan talks about* Insomnia *and other future projects*, Dean Kish, *Showbiz Monkeys*, 7 May 2002
32. Insomnia *DVD*, Warner Bros. Home Entertainment, 2002
33. Insomnia *review*, Philip French, *Observer*, 31 August 2002
34. Insomnia: *a dream cast, murder and madness*, Moira Macdonald, *Seattle Times*, 24 May 2002
35. *Christopher Nolan interview*, Mike Eisenberg, screenrant.com, 4 June 2010
36. *Hard Day's Night*, David Edelstein, *Slate*, 24 May 2002
37. Insomnia *review*, Peter Bradshaw, *Guardian*, 30 August 2002
38. Insomnia *DVD*, Warner Bros. Home Entertainment, 2002

THE INTIMIDATION GAME
1. *Michael Caine Reveals How Christopher Nolan Convinced Him To Play Alfred*, Tim Lammers, Looper.com, 25 August 2021
2. Ibid
3. *Indie Angst*, Scott Timberg, New Times Los Angeles, 15-21 March 2001
4. *Christopher Nolan: the man who rebooted the blockbuster*, Tom Shone, *Guardian*, 4 November 2014
5. *David Ayer on why he won't be making a director's cut of* Suicide Squad, Matt Prigge, *Metro USA*, 5 August 2016
6. *Christopher Nolan*, Geoff Andrew, *Guardian*, 27 August 2002
7. *Christopher Nolan on Directing*, BAFTA Guru via YouTube, 18 January 2018
8. *Christopher Nolan on Batman Begins*, Scott Holleran, Box Office Mojo, 2005

9. *Christopher Nolan on Directing*, BAFTA Guru via YouTube, 18 January 2018
10. *The Dark Knight Trilogy: The Complete Screenplays*, Christopher Nolan, Jonathan Nolan & David S. Goyer, Faber & Faber, 2012
11. *Batman Begins: How Christopher Nolan Rebuilt Batman*, Owen Williams, *Empire*, July 2012
12. *Christopher Nolan*, Geoff Andrew, *Guardian*, 27 August 2002
13. *Batman Begins: How Christopher Nolan Rebuilt Batman*, Owen Williams, *Empire*, July 2012
14. *Christopher Nolan interview*, Stephen Smith, *BBC Newsnight* via YouTube, 16 October 2015
15. *The Nolan Variations: The Movies, Mysteries and Marvels of Christopher Nolan*, Tom Shone, Faber & Faber, 2020
16. Ibid
17. *Batman Begins: How Christopher Nolan Rebuilt Batman*, Owen Williams, *Empire*, July 2012
18. Ibid
19. *Christopher Nolan on Batman Begins*, Scott Holleran, *Box Office Mojo*, 2005
20. *Batman Begins: How Christopher Nolan Rebuilt Batman*, Owen Williams, *Empire*, July 2012
21. *Christopher Nolan on Directing*, BAFTA Guru via YouTube, 18 January 2018
22. *Dream Thieves*, David Heuring, *American Cinematographer*, July 2010
23. *The Nolan Variations: The Movies, Mysteries and Marvels of Christopher Nolan*, Tom Shone, Faber & Faber, 2020
24. Ibid
25. Batman Begins *review*, Ben Walters, *Time Out*, 16 June 2005
26. *How Did Bruce Wayne Become Batman?*, David Ansen, *Newsweek*, 19 June 2005
27. Batman Begins *review*, Kenneth Turan, *Los Angeles Times*, 14 June 2005
28. *Batman Director Christopher Nolan Reveals Why* The Dark Knight *Almost Never Happened*, Olivia Ovenden, *Esquire*, 14 May 2018
29. *Christopher Nolan on* Batman Begins, Scott Holleran, *Box Office Mojo*, 2005

SIDEBAR: PSYCHIC SCENERY

1. *Christopher Nolan commentary*, Memento *DVD*, Pathé, 2000
2. *The Nolan Variations: The Movies, Mysteries and Marvels of Christopher Nolan*, Tom Shone, Faber & Faber, 2020
3. *The Secrets of Tenet: Inside Christopher Nolan's Quantum Cold War*, James Mottram, Titan Books, 2020

THE TRANSPORTED MEN

1. *The Nolan Variations: The Movies, Mysteries and Marvels of Christopher Nolan*, Tom Shone, Faber & Faber, 2020
2. *Nothing Up Their Sleeves: Christopher & Jonathan Nolan on the Art of Magic, Murder and* The Prestige, Den Shewman, *Creative Screenwriting*, September/October 2006
3. Memento *director turns to magic as Batman stalls*, unattributed, *Guardian*, 17 April 2003
4. *Christopher Nolan interview*, Tribute.ca, uploaded 28 May 2013
5. *Behind the Magic with* Prestige *Cast*, unattributed, *Access*, 24 October 2006
6. *The Prestige – Screenplay*, Jonathan Nolan and Christopher Nolan, Faber & Faber, 2006
7. Ibid
8. *Ten Years Later, Why We're Still Obsessed with* The Prestige, Colin Biggs, *Screen Crush*, 20 October 2016
9. *You Won't Believe Your Eyes*, Dan Jolin, *Empire*, 29 September 2006
10. Ibid
11. Ibid
12. The Prestige *Blu-ray*, Warner Bros. Home Entertainment, 2017
13. *You Won't Believe Your Eyes*, Dan Jolin, *Empire*, 29 September 2006
14. Ibid
15. *The Nolan Variations: The Movies, Mysteries and Marvels of Christopher Nolan*, Tom Shone, Faber & Faber, 2020
16. Ibid
17. *The Prestige – Screenplay*, Jonathan Nolan and Christopher Nolan, Faber & Faber, 2006
18. *You Won't Believe Your Eyes*, Dan Jolin, *Empire*, 29 September 2006
19. *The Prestige – Screenplay*, Jonathan Nolan and Christopher Nolan, Faber & Faber, 2006
20. Ibid
21. *Christopher Nolan interview*, Mark Kermode, *Culture Show* via YouTube, uploaded 4 August 2012
22. *The Prestige – Screenplay*, Jonathan Nolan and Christopher Nolan, Faber & Faber, 2006
23. Ibid
24. The Prestige *review*, Walter Chaw, *Film Freak Central*, 25 October 2006
25. *Christopher Nolan: A Critical Study of the Films*, Darren Mooney, McFarland and Company, 2018

WHY SO SERIOUS?

1. *A Life in Pictures: Christopher Nolan*, Edith Bowman, BAFTA, 2017
2. *Christopher Nolan: The Movies, The Memories – Jonathan Nolan on The Dark Knight*, Dan Jolin, *Empire*, July 2010
3. *The Making of Heath Ledger's Joker*, Dan Jolin, *Empire*, December 2009
4. *The Dark Knight Trilogy: The Complete Screenplays*, Christopher Nolan, Jonah Nolan & David S. Goyer, Faber & Faber, 2012
5. *Batman's Burden: A Director Confronts Darkness and Death*, David M. Halbfinger, *New York Times*, 9 March 2008
6. *Christopher Nolan Interview – The Dark Knight*, Steve Weintraub, *Collider.com*, 20 July 2008
7. *Dark Knight Review: Nolan Talks Sequel Inflation*, Anne Thompson, *Variety*, 6 July 2008
8. *The Dark Knight Trilogy: The Complete Screenplays*, Christopher Nolan, Jonah Nolan & David S. Goyer, Faber & Faber, 2012
9. *The Making of Heath Ledger's Joker*, Dan Jolin, *Empire*, December 2009
10. *The Nolan Variations: The Movies, Mysteries and Marvels of Christopher Nolan*, Tom Shone, Faber & Faber, 2020
11. Ibid
12. *Christopher Nolan Says Heath Ledger Initially Didn't Want to be in Superhero or Batman Movies: 6 Things Learned from the FSLC Talk*, unattributed, *IndieWire*, 29 November 2012
13. *Christopher Nolan Reflects on his Batman Trilogy, Heath Ledger & More*, Katie Calautti, *cbr.com*, 3 December 2012
14. *A Look Inside Heath Ledger's sinister 'Joker journal' for* The Dark Knight, Christopher Hooton, *Independent*, 10 August 2015
15. Ibid
16. *The Dark Knight Trilogy: The Complete Screenplays*, Christopher Nolan, Jonah Nolan & David S. Goyer, Faber & Faber, 2012
17. *Batman's Burden: A Director Confronts Darkness and Death*, David M. Halbfinger, *New York Times*, 9 March 2008
18. *Christopher Nolan Interview – The Dark Knight*, Steve Weintraub, *Collider.com*, 20 July 2008
19. *Dark Knight Review: Nolan Talks Sequel Inflation*, Anne Thompson, *Variety*, 6 July 2008
20. *The Nolan Variations: The Movies, Mysteries and Marvels of Christopher Nolan*, Tom Shone, Faber & Faber, 2020
21. *Dark Knight a stunning film*, Tom Charity, CNN, 18 July 2008
22. *Dark Knight Review: Nolan Talks Sequel Inflation*, Anne Thompson, *Variety*, 6 July 2008
23. *Batman's Burden: A Director Confronts Darkness and Death*, David M. Halbfinger, *New York Times*, 9 March 2008
24. *The Dark Knight Trilogy: The Complete Screenplays*, Christopher Nolan, Jonah Nolan & David S. Goyer, Faber & Faber, 2012
25. *Hans Zimmer and James Newton Howard on Composing the Score to* The Dark Knight, David Chen, *SlashFilm*, 8 January 2009
26. *Dark Knight Review: Nolan Talks Sequel Inflation*, Anne Thompson, *Variety*, 6 July 2008
27. *Batman's Burden: A Director Confronts Darkness and Death*, David M. Halbfinger, *New York Times*, 9 March 2008
28. Dark Knight: *Ledger Terrific*, Mike LaSalle, *SFGATE*, 17 July 2008
29. *Heath Ledger Peers Into The Abyss in* The Dark Knight, Scott Foundas, *Village Voice*, 16 July 2008
30. The Dark Knight r*eview*, Keith Phipps, *AV Club*, 17 July 2008
31. *The Nolan Variations: The Movies, Mysteries and Marvels of Christopher Nolan*, Tom Shone, Faber & Faber, 2020
32. *Joker's Wild*, unattributed, *Wizard Universe*, 8 February 2008
33. *No joke, Batman*, Roger Ebert, *Chicago Sun-Times*, 16 July 2008
34. *The Dark Knight Trilogy: The Complete Screenplays*, Christopher Nolan, Jonah Nolan & David S. Goyer, Faber & Faber, 2012

HEAD SPINNING

1. *The Nolan Variations: The Movies, Mysteries and Marvels of Christopher Nolan*, Tom Shone, Faber & Faber, 2020
2. Ibid
3. *A Man and His Dream: Christopher Nolan and Inception*, Dave Itzkoff, *New York Times*, 30 June 2010
4. *Christopher Nolan interview: Can* Inception *director save the summer?*, Scott Foundas, *SF Weekly*, 14 July 2010
5. Crime of the Century, Dan Jolin, *Empire*, July 2010
6. *A Man and His Dream: Christopher Nolan and Inception*, Dave Itzkoff, *New York Times*, 30 June 2010
7. Crime of the Century, Dan Jolin, *Empire*, July 2010
8. Ibid
9. *A Man and His Dream: Christopher Nolan and Inception*, Dave Itzkoff, *New York Times*, 30 June 2010
10. Crime of the Century, Dan Jolin, *Empire*, July 2010
11. Ibid
12. *The Man Behind the Dreamscape*, Dave Itzkoff, *New York Times*, 30 June 2010
13. *Christopher Nolan interview: Can* Inception *director save the summer?*, Scott Foundas, *SF Weekly*, 14 July 2010
14. Ibid
15. *The Influences of* Inception, Dave Itzkoff, *New York Times*, 30 June 2010
16. Inception: *The Shooting Script*, Christopher Nolan, Insight Editions, 2010
17. *This Time the Dream's on Me*, A.O. Scott, *New York Times*, 15 July 2010
18. Crime of the Century, Dan Jolin, *Empire*, July 2010
19. *A Man and His Dream: Christopher Nolan and Inception*, Dave Itzkoff, *New York Times*, 30 June 2010
20. *Dream Thieves*, David Heuring, *American Cinematographer*, July 2010
21. Ibid
22. *Christopher Nolan interview: Can* Inception *director save the summer?*, Scott Foundas, *SF Weekly*, 14 July 2010
23. *Dream Thieves*, David Heuring, *American Cinematographer*, July 2010
24. Ibid
25. *Christopher Nolan interview: Can* Inception *director save the summer?*, Scott Foundas, *SF Weekly*, 14 July 2010
26. Crime of the Century, Dan Jolin, *Empire*, July 2010
27. Ibid
28. *Christopher Nolan interview: Can* Inception *director save the summer?*, Scott Foundas, *SF Weekly*, 14 July 2010
29. Inception *review*, Philip French, *Observer*, 18 July 2010
30. *Dream Factory*, David Denby, *The New Yorker*, 19 July 2010
31. *Christopher Nolan interview: Can* Inception *director save the summer?*, Scott Foundas, *SF Weekly*, 14 July 2010
32. Inception: *The Shooting Script*, Christopher Nolan, Insight Editions, 2010
33. *The Nolan Variations: The Movies, Mysteries and Marvels of Christopher Nolan*, Tom Shone, Faber & Faber, 2020

THE BIG GOODBYE

1. *The Dark Knight Trilogy: The Complete Screenplays*, Christopher Nolan, Jonah Nolan & David S. Goyer, Faber & Faber, 2012
2. *The Nolan Variations: The Movies, Mysteries and Marvels of Christopher Nolan*, Tom Shone, Faber & Faber, 2020
3. The Dark Knight Rises *Extensive Behind the Scenes Featurette*, Movieclips via YouTube 8 July 2012
4. *The Nolan Variations: The Movies, Mysteries and Marvels of Christopher Nolan*, Tom Shone, Faber & Faber, 2020
5. *Christopher Nolan interview*, Elvis Mitchell, *KCRW The Treatment*, uploaded 13 September 2015
6. Ibid
7. *The Real Reason Bane Wears a Mask in Batman*, Jonah Schuhart, Looper.com, 30 April 2021
8. *The Nolan Variations: The Movies, Mysteries and Marvels of Christopher Nolan*, Tom Shone, Faber & Faber, 2020
9. *Ambitious, Thrilling* Dark Knight Rises *Undermined By Hollow Vision*, Michelle Orange, *Movieline*, 19 July 2012
10. *Who Does Bane from* The Dark Knight Rises *Sound Like?*, Matt Singer, *Indiewire*, 25 July 2012
11. Ibid
12. *Tom Hardy Explains the Inspiration for His Bane Voice*, Jennifer Vineyard, *Vulture*, 17 July 2012
13. *Christopher Nolan interview*, Elvis Mitchell, *KCRW The Treatment*, uploaded 13 September 2015
14. *The Dark Knight Trilogy: The Complete Screenplays*, Christopher Nolan, Jonah Nolan & David S. Goyer, Faber & Faber, 2012
15. *The Nolan Variations: The Movies, Mysteries and Marvels of Christopher Nolan*, Tom Shone, Faber & Faber, 2020
16. *Film review:* The Dark Knight Rises, Kim Newman, *Sight & Sound*, 28 April 2014
17. The Dark Knight Rises *Extensive Behind the Scenes Featurette*, Movieclips via YouTube 8 July 2012
18. *The Dark Knight Trilogy: The Complete Screenplays*, Christopher Nolan, Jonah Nolan & David S. Goyer, Faber & Faber, 2012
19. Ibid
20. The Dark Knight Rises *Extensive Behind the Scenes Featurette*, Movieclips via YouTube 8 July 2012
21. Ibid
22. *Film review:* The Dark Knight Rises, Kim Newman, *Sight & Sound*, 28 April 2014
23. *Christopher Nolan interview*, Elvis Mitchell, *KCRW The Treatment*, uploaded 13 September 2015
24. Ibid
25. Ibid
26. *The Nolan Variations: The Movies, Mysteries and Marvels of Christopher Nolan*, Tom Shone, Faber & Faber, 2020
27. Ibid
28. The Dark Knight Rises *review*, Ryan Gilbey, *New Statesman*, July 2012
29. *Batman's Bane*, Anthony Lane, *The New Yorker*, 23 July 2012
30. The Dark Knight Rises, Scott Foundas, *Film Comment*, Winter 2012/2013
31. *Jonah Nolan Finally Explains Robin's Role In* The Dark Knight Rises, Kirsten Acuna, *Business Insider*, 17 October 2012

THE FIFTH DIMENSION

1. *Christopher Nolan interview*, CBS This Morning via YouTube, 16 December 2014
2. *The Nolan Variations: The Movies, Mysteries and Marvels of Christopher Nolan*, Tom Shone, Faber & Faber, 2020
3. *Christopher Nolan interview*, CBS This Morning via YouTube, 16 December 2014
4. *Inside* Interstellar, *Christopher Nolan's emotional space odyssey*, Jeff Jensen, *Entertainment Weekly*, 16 October 2014
5. *Christopher Nolan on* Interstellar *Critics, Making Original Films and Shunning Cell-phones and Email*, Scott Feinberg, *Hollywood Reporter*, 3 January 2015
6. Hans Zimmer interview
7. *The Nolan Variations: The Movies, Mysteries and Marvels of Christopher Nolan*, Tom Shone, Faber & Faber, 2020
8. *Christopher Nolan interview*, CBS This Morning via YouTube, 16 December 2014
9. Ibid
10. *Christopher Nolan Uncut: on* Interstellar, *Ben Affleck's Batman, and the Future of Mankind*, Marlow Stern, *The Daily Beast*, 10 November 2014
11. Ibid
12. *Inside* Interstellar, *Christopher Nolan's emotional space odyssey*, Jeff Jensen, *Entertainment Weekly*, 16 October 2014
13. Ibid
14. *Christopher Nolan Interview – Interstellar*, James Kleinmann, *HeyUGuys* via YouTube, 5 November 2014
15. Ibid
16. Ibid
17. Interstellar: *The Complete Screenplay*, Christopher Nolan & Jonathan Nolan, Faber & Faber, 2014
18. *Christopher Nolan on* Interstellar *Critics, Making Original Films and Shunning Cell-phones and Email*, Scott Feinberg, *Hollywood Reporter*, 3 January 2015

19. *The Nolan Variations: The Movies, Mysteries and Marvels of Christopher Nolan*, Tom Shone, Faber & Faber, 2020
20. *Interstellar: The Complete Screenplay*, Christopher Nolan & Jonathan Nolan, Faber & Faber, 2014
21. *Interstellar review – if it's spectacle you want, this delivers*, Mark Kermode, *Observer*, 9 November 2014
22. *Interstellar: Christopher Nolan's grand space opera tries to outdo 2001*, Andrew O'Hehir, *Salon*, 5 November 2014
23. *Christopher Nolan Uncut: on Interstellar, Ben Affleck's Batman, and the Future of Mankind*, Marlow Stern, *The Daily Beast*, 10 November 2014
24. *Christopher Nolan interview*, CBS This Morning via YouTube, 16 December 2014

SIDEBAR: SCIENTIFIC FICTION

1. *Memories aren't made of this: amnesia at the movies*, Sallie Baxendale, *British Medical Journal*, 18 December 2004
2. *The Neuroscience of Inception*, Jonah Lehrer, *Wired*, 26 July, 2010

ON THE BEACH

1. *The Nolan Variations: The Movies, Mysteries and Marvels of Christopher Nolan*, Tom Shone, Faber & Faber, 2020
2. *Christopher Nolan Wants You to Silence Your Phones*, Adam Grant, *Esquire*, 19 July 2017
3. *Dunkirk: The Complete Screenplay*, Christopher Nolan, Faber & Faber, 21 July 2017
4. *The Nolan Variations: The Movies, Mysteries and Marvels of Christopher Nolan*, Tom Shone, Faber & Faber, 2020
5. *Christopher Nolan's Latest Time-Bending Feat? Dunkirk*, Cara Buckley, *New York Times*, 12 July 2017
6. *Christopher Nolan on Dunkirk, Consulting Steven Spielberg, and Taking His Kids to Phantom Thread*, Christina Radish, *Collider*, 8 February 2018
7. *Christopher Nolan Wants You to Silence Your Phones*, Adam Grant, *Esquire*, 19 July 2017
8. *The Nolan Variations: The Movies, Mysteries and Marvels of Christopher Nolan*, Tom Shone, Faber & Faber, 2020
9. *For Christopher Nolan's Producer And Partner Emma Thomas, Maintaining A Winning Streak Is Essential*, Joe Utichi, *Deadline*, 23 February 2018
10. *Christopher Nolan explains the biggest challenges in making his latest movie Dunkirk into an 'intimate epic'*, Jason Guerrasio, *Business Insider*, 11 July 2017
11. Ibid
12. Ibid
13. Ibid
14. *Kubrick: The Definitive Edition*, Michel Ciment, Faber & Faber, 2003
15. *Christopher Nolan interview: 'To me, Dunkirk is about European unity*, Robbie Collin, *Telegraph*, 23 December 2017
16. Ibid
17. *Christopher Nolan: A Critical Study of the Films*, Darren Mooney, McFarland and Company, 2018
18. *The Nolan Variations: The Movies, Mysteries and Marvels of Christopher Nolan*, Tom Shone, Faber & Faber, 2020
19. Ibid
20. *Christopher Nolan interview: 'To me, Dunkirk is about European unity*, Robbie Collin, *Telegraph*, 23 December 2017
21. *The Nolan Variations: The Movies, Mysteries and Marvels of Christopher Nolan*, Tom Shone, Faber & Faber, 2020
22. *Tick-Tock: Christopher Nolan on the rhythm of Dunkirk*, Jake Coyle, *ZayZay.com*, 14 July 2017
23. *Dunkirk – Christopher Nolan Interview*, David Griffiths, *Buzz Australia*, August 2017
24. *Dunkirk Production Designer Nathan Crowley On 'Rawness, Simplicity & Brutalism' of World War II Epic*, Matt Grobar, *Deadline*, 28 November 2017
25. *The Nolan Variations: The Movies, Mysteries and Marvels of Christopher Nolan*, Tom Shone, Faber & Faber, 2020
26. Ibid
27. *Dunkirk: The Complete Screenplay*, Christopher Nolan, Faber & Faber, 21 July 2017
28. *Ticking Watch. Boat Engine. Slowness. The Secrets of the Dunkirk Score*, Melena Ryzik, *New York Times*, 26 July 2017
29. Ibid
30. *Dunkirk Review: Christopher Nolan has Made Another Great Film*, Karen Han, *SlashFilm*, 21 July 2017
31. *Christopher Nolan's Dunkirk is a Masterpiece*, Christopher Orr, *The Atlantic*, 21 July 2017
32. *Christopher Nolan's Latest Time-Bending Feat? Dunkirk*, Cara Buckley, *New York Times*, 12 July 2017
33. Ibid
34. *Christopher Nolan interview: 'To me, Dunkirk is about European unity*, Robbie Collin, *Telegraph*, 23 December 2017

APOCALYPTIC THINKING

1. *View from the Couch: The Curse of Frankenstein, Mister Roberts, Tenet, etc.*, Matt Brunson, *Film Frenzy*, 18 December 2020
2. *Tenet is Dazzling, Deft, and Devoid of Feeling*, Anthony Lane, *The New Yorker*, 3 September 2020
3. *Tenet review – supremely ambitious race against time makes for superb cinema*, Peter Bradshaw, *Guardian*, 25 August 2020
4. *Christopher Nolan Slams His Tenet Studio Warner Bros Over HBO Max Windows Plan*, Anthony D'Alessandro, *Deadline*, 7 December 2020
5. *The Nolan Variations: The Movies, Mysteries and Marvels of Christopher Nolan*, Tom Shone, Faber & Faber, 2020
6. *Christopher Nolan on Tenet – The Full Interview*, Geoff Keighley, Cortex Videos via YouTube, 21 December 2020
7. *The Secrets of Tenet: Inside Christopher Nolan's Quantum Cold War*, James Motram, Titan Books, 2020
8. *Christopher Nolan on Tenet – The Full Interview*, Geoff Keighley, Cortex Videos via YouTube, 21 December 2020
9. Ibid
10. *The Nolan Variations: The Movies, Mysteries and Marvels of Christopher Nolan*, Tom Shone, Faber & Faber, 2020
11. Ibid
12. *The Secrets of Tenet: Inside Christopher Nolan's Quantum Cold War*, James Motram, Titan Books, 2020
13. Ibid
14. *Christopher Nolan on Tenet – The Full Interview*, Geoff Keighley, Cortex Videos via YouTube, 21 December 2020
15. *Tenet: The Complete Screenplay*, Christopher Nolan, Faber & Faber, 2020
16. *Writer's Bloc Presents: Christopher Nolan*, Tom Shone and Kenneth Branagh, Eventbrite, 2 December 2020
17. *Tenet: The Complete Screenplay*, Christopher Nolan, Faber & Faber, 2020
18. *The Nolan Variations: The Movies, Mysteries and Marvels of Christopher Nolan*, Tom Shone, Faber & Faber, 2020
19. *The Secrets of Tenet: Inside Christopher Nolan's Quantum Cold War*, James Motram, Titan Books, 2020
20. *Christopher Nolan on Tenet – The Full Interview*, Geoff Keighley, Cortex Videos via YouTube, 21 December 2020
21. *Tenet: The Complete Screenplay*, Christopher Nolan, Faber & Faber, 2020
22. *The Nolan Variations: The Movies, Mysteries and Marvels of Christopher Nolan*, Tom Shone, Faber & Faber, 2020
23. *The Secrets of Tenet: Inside Christopher Nolan's Quantum Cold War*, James Motram, Titan Books, 2020
24. Ibid
25. *Tenet: The Complete Screenplay*, Christopher Nolan, Faber & Faber, 2020
26. *The Nolan Variations: The Movies, Mysteries and Marvels of Christopher Nolan*, Tom Shone, Faber & Faber, 2020
27. *American Prometheus: The Triumph and Tragedy of J. Robert Oppenheimer*, Kai Bird & Martin J. Sherwin, Atlantic Books, 2009
28. *Tenet: The Complete Screenplay*, Christopher Nolan, Faber & Faber, 2020
29. Ibid
30. *Christopher Nolan: the man who rebooted the blockbuster*, Tom Shone, *Guardian*, 4 November 2014
31. Ibid

ACKNOWLEDGEMENTS

To alight upon Christopher Nolan as a subject in this series was both a delight and a daunting challenge for a writer. But in daring the maze of his imagination, I have come to appreciate what a formidable and endlessly fascinating filmmaker he truly is. This has been a book of angles and equations, of deciphering riddles, of thinking differently, but at heart it is a book about the power of filmmaking as a medium. My respect for Nolan has been redoubled, and my mind stretched like never before. Therefore, my thanks go foremost to Nolan: long may he continue to test our cinematic mettle. Closer to home, but no less inspiring, my eternal thanks go to the team at Quarto: my editor Jessica Axe, for her genuine excitement and calm authority; copy editor Nick Freeth, who has been stretched like never before and not found wanting (even by Tenet); and the brilliant, patient Sue Pressley at Stonecastle Graphics, who doesn't simply design the books, she fully embraces the subject. For much-needed advice, my gratitude also goes to experienced Nolanologist and friend Dan Jolin.

PICTURE CREDITS

AA Film Archive / Alamy Stock Photo 121; Abaca Press / Alamy Stock Photo 169c; AF archive / Alamy Stock Photo 13r, 31l, 53a, 67, 82a, 112r, 135a; Album / Alamy Stock Photo 39a, 39b, 40ar, 41, 86b, 93, 127a, 132, 165a; Allstar Picture Library Ltd. / Alamy Stock Photo 8l, 74l; ANNE-CHRISTINE POUJOULAT / AFP via Getty Images 7; Barbara Alper / Getty Images 11, 14–15l; BFA / Alamy Stock Photo 16c, 45r, 74r, 81r, 90l, 124al, 124r, 136l, 165b; Bjanka Kadic / Alamy Stock Photo 17; Collection Christophel / Alamy Stock Photo 51, 52, 82b, 86a, 110, 116, 152; dpa picture alliance / Alamy Stock Photo 169l; Entertainment Pictures / Alamy Stock Photo 60l; Everett Collection Inc / Alamy Stock Photo 8r, 13l, 15r, 18a, 20–21r, 22, 23l, 23r, 26–27, 34, 36r, 45l, 111r, 114–115l, 117br, 118, 168al; Graham Hunt / Alamy Stock Photo 148a; Guido Paradisi / Alamy Stock Photo 156a; INTERFOTO / Alamy Stock Photo 12, 140; LANDMARK MEDIA / Alamy Stock Photo 137, 156–157l, 158, 159, 162, 163a, 163c, 166al, 166bl, 166–167r; Michael Buckner / Getty Images 24r; Moviestore Collection Ltd / Alamy Stock Photo 4–5, 16r, 18b, 49, 58–59, 65b, 66a, 66b, 78, 85, 90r, 94, 100, 102a, 104; Paul Smith / Alamy Stock Photo 169r; Photo 12 / Alamy Stock Photo 19, 31r, 32–33; Pictorial Press Ltd / Alamy Stock Photo 30, 101a, 141r; PictureLux / The Hollywood Archive / Alamy Stock Photo 9, 161b, 163b; RBM Vintage Images / Alamy Stock Photo 168b; REUTERS / Alamy Stock Photo 87, 91; ROBYN BECK/AFP / Getty Images 153; Shawshots / Alamy Stock Photo 112l; SilverScreen / Alamy Stock Photo 16l; Stephane Cardinale / Corbis via Getty Images 171; Sylvain Lefevre / Getty Images 149a; TCD/Prod.DB / Alamy Stock Photo 20l, 24l, 25, 28–29, 35a, 35b, 36l, 37, 38, 40al, 40b, 42–43, 44, 46a, 46b, 47, 48a, 48b, 50, 53b, 54l, 54–55r, 56, 58, 60–61r, 62, 63, 65a, 68a, 68b, 69a, 69b, 70, 71, 72–73, 75, 76, 77, 79, 80–81l, 83, 84, 89, 92, 95a, 95b, 96–97, 98–99, 101b, 102b, 103b, 105a, 105b, 107, 108, 109, 113, 115r, 117a, 117bl, 119a, 119b, 120a, 120b, 122–123, 125, 126a, 126–127b, 128, 129a, 129b, 130a, 130–131r, 133, 134–135l, 135b, 136r, 139, 141l, 142–143l, 143a, 144b, 144–145ar, 146, 147a, 147b, 148b, 149b, 150a, 150–151b, 151a, 155, 160, 161a, 164a, 164b, 170; Universal Pictures 168ar; WENN Rights Ltd / Alamy Stock Photo 103a, 111l.